WORKBOOK TO ACCOMPANY

INTERMEDIATE ALGEBRA

A STRAIGHTFORWARD APPROACH
FOR COLLEGE STUDENTS

WORKBOOK TO ACCOMPANY

INTERMEDIATE ALGEBRA
A STRAIGHTFORWARD APPROACH
FOR COLLEGE STUDENTS

MARTIN M. ZUCKERMAN
city college of the
city university of new york

W · W · NORTON & COMPANY · INC · NEW YORK

First Edition

ISBN 0 393 09159 7

1 2 3 4 5 6 7 8 9 0

CONTENTS

---

* Indicates optional topic.

PREFACE

This WORKBOOK is intended to supplement INTERMEDIATE ALGEBRA:
A STRAIGHTFORWARD APPROACH FOR COLLEGE STUDENTS. It is written
for students who are having difficulty understanding some of the
material in the text, as well as for students in self-study
programs. The WORKBOOK also provides the student with review
material. Further illustration of techniques presented in the
text is given in the form of KEY TOPICS. Each KEY TOPIC is
accompanied by additional problems for the student to work (KEY
EXERCISES).

The format of the WORKBOOK is extremely simple. On each left-hand
page examples are worked out illustrating KEY TOPICS. On the
corresponding right-hand page several KEY EXERCISES are given for
each KEY TOPIC. For instance, the student should first read KEY
TOPIC A on the left and then work through the KEY EXERCISES under
A to the right. The student can then proceed to KEY TOPIC B on
the left, followed by KEY EXERCISES B on the right, and so on.

Answers to all of the KEY EXERCISES are provided at the back of
the WORKBOOK.

WORKBOOK TO ACCOMPANY

INTERMEDIATE ALGEBRA

A STRAIGHTFORWARD APPROACH
FOR COLLEGE STUDENTS

CHAPTER 1

ARITHMETIC REVIEW

▶ 1.1   The Real Line (text page 1)

KEY TOPICS

A.   Plot the following numbers on the real line L:

(a) 4   (b) -3   (c) $\frac{3}{2}$ (d) π (e) $\frac{-5}{4}$

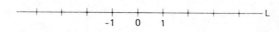

Figure 1.1

SOLUTION.

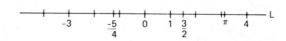

B.   (a)   4 < 7 because   4 lies to the left of   7 on L.

(b) -2 < 1 because -2 lies to the left of 1.

(c) -6 < -3 because -6 lies to the left of -3.

KEY EXERCISES

A.

1. Plot the following numbers on the real line L in Figure 1.2 .

    (a) 3   (b) -2   (c) $\frac{3}{4}$ (d) $\frac{-3}{4}$ (e) -π

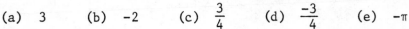

Figure 1.2

2. Each of the points P, Q, R, S, T, U in Figure 1.3 represents one of the following numbers. Indicate which number is represented by each point.

    $\frac{5}{2}$, $\frac{-3}{2}$,   1.9 ,   2.1 ,   -1.9,   -2.1

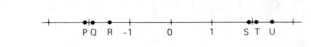

Figure 1.3

B.   Fill in "<" or ">".

3. 2   6   4. -2   -6   5. $\frac{1}{4}$ $\frac{1}{2}$

6. $\frac{-1}{4}$ $\frac{-1}{2}$ 7. 0   -1   8. 3   π

Fill in "left" or "right".

9. On L, 3 lies to the _____ of 10.

10. On L, 20 lies to the _____ of 10.

11. On L, -2 lies to the _____ of 2.

12. On L, -5 lies to the _____ of -6.

1 RIGHT

► 1.2   Absolute Value (text page 9)

KEY TOPICS

A.   Determine the inverse of:

      (a) 6   (b) -3   (c) 0   (d) $\left|\dfrac{-1}{2}\right|$

SOLUTION.

      (a) -6   (b) 3   (c) 0   (d) $-\dfrac{1}{2}$

B.   Determine the indicated absolute values:

      (a) $|15|$ (b) $|-9|$ (c) $\left|\dfrac{-3}{4}\right|$ (d) $|0|$

SOLUTION.

      (a) 15   (b) 9   (c) $\dfrac{3}{4}$ (d) 0

C.   Fill in "<", ">", or "=".

      (a) $|-4|$ $|4|$ (b) $\left|\dfrac{-1}{2}\right|$ $\dfrac{-1}{2}$

      (c) .3 $|-.3|$ (d) 1 $-|1|$

SOLUTION.

      (a) $|-4| = |4|$ (Both equal 4.)

      (b) $\left|\dfrac{-1}{2}\right| > \dfrac{-1}{2}$ $\left(\left|\dfrac{-1}{2}\right| = \dfrac{1}{2}\right)$

      (c)   .3 $= |-.3|$

      (d)   1 $> -|1|$ (because $-|1| = -1$ and $1 > -1$)

13. On L, -3 lies to the _____ of 2.

14. On L, $\frac{1}{10}$ lies to the _____ of $\frac{1}{5}$.

KEY EXERCISES

A. Determine the inverse of each number.

1. 20 _____   2. .34 _____   3. $-\frac{1}{3}$ _____

4. π _____   5. -0 _____   6. $|-1.6|$ _____

B. Determine the indicated absolute values.

7. $|-12|$ _____   8. $|0|$ _____

9. $\left|\frac{-7}{5}\right|$ _____   10. $|.05|$ _____

C. Fill in "<", ">", or "=".

11. 12 $|12|$ 12. 3 $|-2|$ 13. $|2|$ $|-3|$

14. $|-2|$ $|-3|$ 15. $|-3|$ $-(-3)$ 16. $|-3|$ $\frac{1}{3}$

D.   Which negative number is 4 units from the origin?

SOLUTION.

    -4 is 4 units from the origin.

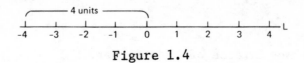

Figure 1.4

▶ 1.3   Addition and Subtraction of Two Numbers (text page 12)

KEY TOPICS

A.   Add: 208 + 312

SOLUTION.

$$
\begin{array}{r}
208 \\
312 \\
\hline
520
\end{array}
$$

B.   Add: 38 + (-57)

SOLUTION.

    Subtract:
$$
\begin{array}{r}
57 \\
38 \\
\hline
19
\end{array}
$$

    The larger absolute value, 57, corresponds to the negative
    number, -57. Therefore

$$38 + (-57) = -19$$

C.   Subtract the bottom number from the top one.

$$
\begin{array}{r}
-1420 \\
743 \\
\hline
\end{array}
$$

D.

17. Which numbers are 2 units from the origin? _____

18. Which positive number is $\frac{1}{2}$ unit from the origin? _____

19. Which negative number is 1.4 units from the origin? _____

KEY EXERCISES

A.   Add, as indicated.

1.   481 + 187 _____

2.   (−2093) + (−5058) _____

3.   (−136 271) + (−252 690) _____

4.   208 652
    692 107

5.   − 834
   −1260

B.   Add, as indicated.

6.   294 + (−183) _____   7.   (−29) + 14 _____

8.   205 + (−177) _____   9.   386   10. −3001
                        −249   2872

C.   Subtract the bottom number from the top one.

11. 408   12. 267   13. −149   14. 262   15. −1470
    204   358   −126   −184   1693

SOLUTION.

      Change 743 to −743, and add: −1420
                                              − 743
                                            −2163

D.   Subtract −49 from 94.

SOLUTION.

      94 − (−49) = 94 + 49   94
                                          49
                                     143

▶ 1.4   Addition and Subtraction of Three or More Numbers
        (text page 19)

KEY TOPICS

A.   −172
             −196
             − 68
             −105
             −541

B.   Find the value of: 36
                                −26
                                −19
                                 8
                                63

SOLUTION.

      Rearrange the numbers, and add the positive and negative
numbers separately.

            36   −26
             8   −19
           63   −45
          107

                    Add: 107
                           − 45
                            62

      The resulting sum is 62.

D.

16. Add −27 and −44. _____

17. Subtract 52 from 83. _____

18. Subtract −29 from 63. _____

KEY EXERCISES

A. Find the value of each sum.

1.	22	2.	−36	3.	208	4.	−107	5.	680
	12		−27		492		−94		263
	13		−48		96		−28		104
	18		−92		389		−106		835
	91		−61						725

B. Find the value of each sum.

6.	43	7.	282	8.	636
	−28		143		−792
	−39		−96		−894
	−72		−72		−104
	101				−260
					1228

9. 20 + 14 + (−8) + (−16) + (−12) _____

10. (−31) + 17 + 92 + (−55) + (−13) _____

C.   Subtract as indicated.

$$(6 - 4) - (10 - 8) - 7 - 4$$

SOLUTION.

$$(6 - 4) - (10 - 8) - 7 - 4 =$$
$$\underbrace{}_{2} - \underbrace{}_{2} - 7 - 4 = -11$$

D.   Find the value of

$$20 + 9 - [3 - (8 - 5)].$$

SOLUTION.

Work from the inner parentheses outward.

$$20 + 9 - [3 - (8 - 5)] = 20 + 9 - [3 - 3]$$
$$= 20 + 9 - 0$$
$$= 29$$

E.   Subtract the sum of 13 and 8 from the sum of 29 and –10.

SOLUTION.

$$13 + 8 = 21$$

$$29 + (-10) = 19$$

Subtract 21 from 19: $\begin{array}{r} 19 \\ -21 \\ \hline -2 \end{array}$

▶ 1.5   Multiplication and Division (text page 23)

KEY TOPICS

A.   Multiply: $(-4)(-7)(-3)$

SOLUTION.

There is an odd number of negative factors. The product is negative.

$$(-4)(-7)(-3) = -84$$

5 LEFT

C.   Subtract as indicated.

11. 12 – 8 – 2 _____   12. 9 – 4 – (3 – 2) _____

13. (12 – 6) – (4 – 3) _____

14. 3 – (4 – 7) – (6 – 9) _____

D.   Find each value.

15. [16 – (13 – 8)] – 10 _____

16. 33 – [(6 – 5) – (5 – 8)] _____

17. 9 + [17 – (31 – 14) – 7 – (8 – 5)] _____

18. 36 – (27 – [18 – (9 – 4)]) _____

E.

19. Subtract 10 from the sum of 27 and 15. _____

20. Subtract the sum of 8 and 13 from the sum of 10 and 19. _____

21. Subtract the sum of 102 and 207 from 1000. _____

22. Subtract 10 minus –8 from –12 minus –7. _____

KEY EXERCISES

A.   Multiply:

1. 22 (–7) _____   2. (–22) (–7) _____

3. 6 (–3) (–4) _____   4. (–2) (–4) (–5) _____

5. (–8) (–2) (–3) (–1) _____

B.   Multiply: 124
                   632

SOLUTION.

                    124
                    632
                    248
                    372
                    744
                    78368

C.   (a) $\dfrac{-96}{-12} = 8$ (b) $\dfrac{-96}{12} = -8$

Note that in (a), the quotient, 8, is positive because the
dividend, -96, and divisor, -8, have the same sign. In (b),
the quotient is negative because dividend and divisor have
different signs.

D.   Divide: $13\overline{)1820}$

SOLUTION.

                    140
            $13\overline{)1820}$
                    13
                    52
                    52
                     0

E.   Find the value of:

$$\frac{(-2)(-3)}{(7)(5)}$$

SOLUTION. $\dfrac{(-2)(-3)}{(7)(5)} = \dfrac{6}{35}$

▶ 1.6   Combining Operations (text page 31)

KEY TOPICS

A. $17 + 2 \cdot 4 = 17 + 8 = 25$

B.   Multiply:

6.   −207   7.   23   8.   3062   9.   1438
        −188   12   40   2829

C.   Divide or indicate that division is not defined.

10. $\frac{-24}{6}$ _____   11. $\frac{-24}{-8}$ _____

12. $\frac{36}{-9}$ _____   13. $\frac{0}{6}$ _____   14. $\frac{6}{0}$ _____

D.   Divide:

15. $22\overline{)110}$ 16. $37\overline{)148}$ 17. $19\overline{)1140}$ 18. $16\overline{)256\ 000}$

E.   Find the value of each.

19. $\frac{2(-5)}{-10}$ _____   20. $\frac{(-3)\ (-2)\ (-4)}{24}$ _____

21. $\frac{(-1)\ 3}{(-2)\ (-5)}$ _____   22. $\frac{(-7)\ (-2)}{(-1)\ (-3)}$ _____

KEY EXERCISES

A.

1. 6 + 4 · 3 _____   2. (6 + 4)3 _____

3. 6(4 + 3) _____   4. 8[5 + (2 − 4)] _____

5. (−2 + 5) (3 + 8) _____

B. $9 + \dfrac{8}{4} = 9 + 2 = 11$

C. $\dfrac{(-2)(4-3)+8}{3} = \dfrac{(-2)(1)+8}{3} = \dfrac{6}{3} = 2$

D. Multiply the sum of 2, 3, and 5 by 4.

SOLUTION.

$$2 + 3 + 5 = 10$$
$$10 \cdot 4 = 40$$

▶ 1.7   Positive Integral Exponents (text page 34)

KEY TOPICS

A. (a) $6^2 = 6 \cdot 6 = 36$ (b) $(-7)^2 = (-7)(-7) = 49$

B. (a) $2^3 = 2 \cdot 2 \cdot 2 = 8$ (b) $2^6 = 2 \cdot 2 \cdot 2 \cdot 2 \cdot 2 \cdot 2 = 64$

B.

6. $4 + \dfrac{10}{2}$ _____

7. $\dfrac{4 + 10}{2}$ _____

8. $\dfrac{8 + 7}{5}$ _____

9. $\dfrac{20}{2 + 3}$ _____

10. $\dfrac{6 - 18}{3 - 6}$ _____

C.

11. $\dfrac{-3 + 6(-1)}{2 - 20}$ _____

12. $\dfrac{3(-1) + 8 \cdot 3}{(3 - 6)\ 7}$ _____

13. $\dfrac{18 + 3 - 1}{2(-2)}$ _____

14. $\dfrac{-12 + 3}{-3} + 3 - 12$ _____

15. $\dfrac{40 - 18 + 3}{5} - \dfrac{3 \cdot 8}{-1 - 2}$ _____

D.

16. Multiply the sum of 8 and 5 by 7. _____

17. Add 2 to the product of 5 and 3. _____

18. Subtract 4 from the product of 2 and -3. _____

19. Divide the product of 8 and 4 by the sum of 3 and 5. _____

KEY EXERCISES

A.

1. 5^2 _____

2. $(-4)^2$ _____

3. $(-3)^2$ _____

4. 10^2 _____

5. 20^2 _____

B.

6. 3^3 _____

7. $(-2)^4$ _____

C. (a) $(3 + 5)^2 = 8^2 = 64$ (b) $3 + 5^2 = 3 + 25 = 28$

(c) $(3 \cdot 5)^2 = 15^2 = 225$ (d) $3 \cdot 5^2 = 3 \cdot 25 = 75$

D. Add the cube of 2 and the square of −3.

SOLUTION.

$$2^3 = 8 \qquad\qquad\qquad (-3)^2 = 9$$

$$8 + 9 = 17$$

8. 5^3 _____   9. 2^5 _____

10. 10^4 _____

C.

11. $(2 + 1)^2$ _____   12. $2 + 1^2$ _____

13. $2^2 + 1^2$ _____   14. $(3 \cdot 2)^2$ _____

15. $3 \cdot 2^2$ _____   16. $3^2 \cdot 2^2$ _____

D.

17. Add the square of 2 and the cube of 2. _____

18. Subtract the cube of 2 from the square of 5. _____

19. Divide the cube of 4 by the square of 2. _____

CHAPTER 2

POLYNOMIALS

▶ 2.1   Terms and Polynomials (text page 41)

KEY TOPICS

A.   Which of the following expressions are terms?

   (a)   3xy   (b) $\frac{x}{2}$ (c)   x + 1

SOLUTION.

   Expressions (a) and (b) are terms. In (a), 3x is the product
   of the constant 3 and the variables x and y. In (b), $\frac{x}{2}$ is
   the product of the constant $\frac{1}{2}$ and the variable x. Expression
   (c) involves the <u>sum</u> of a variable, x, and a constant, 1, and
   is not itself a term.

B.   Determine the coefficient of each term.

   (a)   20x   (b) $\frac{x^3}{3}$ (c) $\frac{x^2}{3} \cdot 4yz$

SOLUTION.

         (a)   20   (b) $\frac{1}{3}$ (c) $\frac{4}{3}$

C.   Rewrite each term so that its coefficient appears first.
      Also, simplify this coefficient.

   (a)   4x(3y)   (b) $2x^2 \cdot \frac{y}{2} \cdot 3z$

SOLUTION.

   (a)   4x(3y) = 12xy   (b) $2x^2 \cdot \frac{y}{2} \cdot 3z = 3x^2yz$

KEY EXERCISES

A. Which of the following expressions are terms?

1. x _____

2. xy _____

3. $2xyz^2$ _____

4. y + 5 _____

5. $\frac{y}{4}$ _____

6. $\frac{4}{y}$ _____

B. Determine the coefficient of each term.

7. 7xyz _____

8. $\frac{5x}{3}$ _____

9. (2x) (3y) _____

10. 3x · (-2y)z _____

11. 3x · 0y _____

C. Rewrite each term so that its coefficient appears first. Also, simplify this coefficient.

12. 3x · 5y _____

13. $\frac{x^2}{2}$ · 4y _____

14. $3x^2 \cdot \frac{y}{5}$ _____

15. (2x) (5y) t _____

9 RIGHT

D.   Which of the following expressions are polynomials?

(a) $\dfrac{x^3 y}{2}$ (b) $3x^2 + 2xy$ (c) $\dfrac{2}{x}$

SOLUTION.

Expressions (a) and (b) are polynomials. (a) is a term; (b) is a sum of terms. Expression (c) involves dividing by a variable. This is not a polynomial.

▶ 2.2   Numerical Evaluation (text page 46)

KEY TOPICS

A.   Evaluate $x^2 - 2x + 1$ when $x = 3$.

SOLUTION.

Substitute 3 for each occurrence of x.

$$3^2 - 2 \cdot 3 + 1 = 9 - 6 + 1 = 4$$

B.   Evaluate $t^2 + 5$ when

(a) t = 0,   (b) t = -2.

SOLUTION.

(a) $0^2 + 5 = 5$ (b) $(-2)^2 + 5 = 4 + 5 = 9$

C.   Evaluate $x^2 - 2xy + 3y$ when $x = 5$ and $y = -1$.

SOLUTION.

Substitute 5 for each occurrence of x and -1 for each occurrence of y:

$$5^2 - 2(5)(-1) + 3(-1) = 25 + 10 - 3$$

$$= 32$$

10 LEFT

D.   Which of the following expressions are polynomials?

16. x^2yz^2 _____   17. $2x - 5y$ _____

18. $\dfrac{x + 1}{2}$ _____   19. $\dfrac{1}{x}$ _____

20. $\dfrac{x + y + 3z^2}{5}$ _____

KEY EXERCISES

A.   Evaluate each polynomial for the specified value of the
      variable.

1. $2x + 1$ [x = 1] _____

2. $3x^2 - 2x$ [x = 2] _____

3. $y^3 - y + 1$ [y = -1] _____

4. $x^4 - 3$ [x = 2] _____

5. $z^3 - z^2 + 5z - 2$ [z = 3] _____

B.

6.   Evaluate $x^2 + 3$ when (a) x = 0   (b) x = 4. _____

7.   Evaluate $2y - 3$ when (a) y = 1   (b) y = -1. _____

8.   Evaluate $t^3 + t^2 - t$ when (a) t = 2   (b) t = -2. _____

9.   Evaluate $x^2 + 4x + 2$ when (a) x = 1   (b) x = 10. _____

C.   Evaluate each polynomial for the specified values of the
      variables.

10. $2x - y$ [x = 2, y = 1] _____

11. $x^2 - y^2$ [x = 1, y = -1] _____

12. $3x + 5y$ [x = 5, y = 3] _____

10 RIGHT

▶ 2.3   Addition and Subtraction (text page 50)

KEY TOPICS

A.   (a)   5xyz and **–3xzy** are similar. The two terms differ only
            in their numerical coefficients and in the order of
            their variables.

      (b) x^2y and xy are not similar because the two terms differ
            in the exponent of x.

B.   (a)   7x + 2x – 5x = 4x

      (b) $2x^2 + 5x + 3y + x^2 - x + y = (2x^2 + x^2) + (5x - x) + (3y + y)$

                                    $= 3x^2 + 4x + 4y$

      Note that similar terms are grouped together.

C.   Add: $\begin{array}{r} 5a - 3b + c - d \\ 2b + c \\ \underline{3a \qquad - c + d} \\ 8a - b + c \end{array}$

D.   Subtract the bottom polynomial from the top one.

                          $\begin{array}{r} 2x - 5y \\ \underline{-3x + 2y} \end{array}$

13. $2t^2 - st + 3s$ [s = 3, t = 2] _____

14. $x^2yz - 4xyz^2$ [x = 1, y = 2, z = 3] _____

KEY EXERCISES

A.   Indicate which pairs of terms are similar.

1.   4x and −x _____   2.   3xyz and 2yz _____

3.   6 and −2 _____   4. x^2z and xz^2 _____

5. $4x^3yz^2$ and $-2yz^2x^3$ _____

B.   Simplify:

6.   10a + 5a _____

7.   8xy − 3xy + xy _____

8.   3m + 4n − 2m + 6n _____

9.   x + y − z + 2x − 3y − 4z _____

10.   a + b + 2c − 3 + 2c − 3b + 1 _____

C.   Add:

11.   2x + 3y
    5x − y
    7x + 8y

12.   4r + 2s − t
    6r + s
        3s − t

13.   w + x − y + z
        2x   − z
    3w   + y
    2w   + 2y − 5z

14. $x^2 - y^2 + 2x - y$
    $2y^2 \quad\quad + y$
    $3x^2 \quad\quad + x$
    $x^2 \quad\quad - 2x + 3y$

D.   Subtract the bottom polynomial from the top one.

15.   2a + 4b
     a + 2b

16.   3x + 5y
    2x − 2y

SOLUTION.

Change the signs of the terms of the bottom polynomial, and add. Thus first change $-3x + 2y$ to $3x - 2y$:

$$\begin{array}{r} 2x - 5y \\ \underline{3x - 2y} \\ 5x - 7y \end{array}$$

E. Simplify the polynomial:

$$3x - [2x + 4y - (x - y) - (3y - 2x)]$$

SOLUTION.

$$
\begin{aligned}
3x - [2x + 4y - (x - y) - (3y - 2x)] &= 3x - [2x + 4y - x + y - 3y + 2x] \\
&= 3x - 2x - 4y + x - y + 3y - 2x \\
&= (3x - 2x + x - 2x) + (-4y - y + 3y) \\
&= -2y
\end{aligned}
$$

▶ 2.4 Multiplication (text page 56)

KEY TOPICS

A. Multiply x^3 by x^2.

SOLUTION.

Write down the base and add the exponents.

$$x^3 \cdot x^2 = x^{3+2} = x^5$$

B. Determine $(2x^2 y)(-3x^4 y^2)$.

SOLUTION.

Group all numerical coefficients at the beginning. Group powers of the same variable together.

$$(2x^2 y)(-3x^4 y^2) = 2(-3)(x^2 \cdot x^4)(y \cdot y^2) = -6x^6 y^3$$

17. $x + y - z$
      $\underline{2x - y + z}$

18. $5r + s - 2t - u$
      $\underline{-r + s - 2t + 2u}$

E.   Simplify each polynomial.

19. $2a + 3b - c - (2a - b + c)$ _____

20. $x - [y + z - 2x - (y - z)]$ _____

21. $3x^2 + 2x - [4x^2 - (y + x - x^2)]$ _____

22. $5 - (2a - [3b - c + a - (b - c) - (2 - a)])$ _____

KEY EXERCISES

A.   Multiply, as indicated.

1. $x^6 \cdot x^2$ _____

2. $y^4 \cdot y^3 \cdot y^2$ _____

3. $m^4 \cdot m^{10} \cdot m \cdot m^2$ _____

4. $a \cdot a^2 \cdot a^3 \cdot a^4 \cdot a^5$ _____

B.   Multiply, as indicated.

5. $(2xy)(5x^2y)$ _____

6. $(3ab)(-a^2b)(4a^2)$ _____

7. $(2uv^2)(3u^2v)(10u^5v)$ _____

8. $(5abc^2d)(4ab^3c)(2ac^2d^3)(-c^3d^2)$ _____

C.   Multiply $2m + n$ by $m + 3n$.

SOLUTION.

$$
\begin{array}{l}
2m + n \\
\underline{m + 3n} \\
2m^2 + mn \\
\underline{ + 6mn + 3n^2} \\
2m^2 + 7mn + 3n^2
\end{array}
$$

D.   Determine (a) $(x + 3)^2$,   (b) $(x + 3)(x - 3)$.

SOLUTION.

$$(a)\quad (x + 3)^2 = x^2 + 2 \cdot 3x + 3^2$$

$$= x^2 + 6x + 9$$

$$(b)\quad (x + 3)(x - 3) = x^2 - 3^2$$

$$= x^2 - 9$$

E.   Simplify: $(x - 3)(x - 2) - (x + 2)^2$

SOLUTION.

$$
\begin{array}{l}
x - 3 \\
\underline{x - 2} \\
x^2 - 3x \\
\underline{ - 2x + 6} \\
x^2 - 5x + 6
\end{array}
\qquad
\begin{array}{l}
(x + 2)^2 = x^2 + 2 \cdot 2x + 2^2 \\
 = x^2 + 4x + 4
\end{array}
$$

$$(x - 3)(x - 2) - (x + 2)^2 = x^2 - 5x + 6 - (x^2 + 4x + 4)$$

$$= x^2 - 5x + 6 - x^2 - 4x - 4$$

$$= -9x + 2$$

C. Multiply, as indicated.

9. $(m + 1)(m + 2)$ _____

10. $(x + 5)(x - 3)$ _____

11. $(x + y + 1)(x + y)$ _____

12. $(x + y + z)(x + y - z)$ _____

13. $(a + b + c)(x + y)$ _____

D. Determine each polynomial.

14. $(x + 1)^2$ _____   15. $(x - 1)^2$ _____

16. $(y + 4)^2$ _____   17. $(a - 2)^2$ _____

18. $(x + 5)(x - 5)$ _____

19. $(z - 10)(z + 10)$ _____

E. Simplify:

20. $(x + 4)^2 - (x + 2)(x - 2)$ _____

21. $(x + 6)(x - 3) + (x - 6)(x + 3)$ _____

22. $(x + y)^2 - (x - y)^2$ _____

23. $2x(y - 1) - y(2x + 1)$ _____

24. $x^2 - [2y - (x + y)^2 - (x + y)(x - y)]$ _____

▶ 2.5   Division (text page 61)

KEY TOPICS

A. $\dfrac{x^3}{x^2} = x^{3-2}$

$\phantom{\dfrac{x^3}{x^2}} = x$

B. $\dfrac{20a^5}{4a^3} = \dfrac{20}{4} a^{5-3}$

$\phantom{\dfrac{20a^5}{4a^3}} = 5a^2$

C. $\dfrac{9y^4}{-3y^4} = \dfrac{9}{-3} \cdot 1$

$\phantom{\dfrac{9y^4}{-3y^4}} = -3$

▶ 2.6   Degree (text page 63)

KEY TOPICS

A.   Determine the degree of each term.

    (a) 12   (b) $x^2 y$ (c) $a^4 b^2 c^3 d^7$

KEY EXERCISES

A.   Divide:

1. $\dfrac{x^4}{x^2}$ _____

2. $\dfrac{a^5}{a}$ _____

3. $\dfrac{x^{10}}{x^6}$ _____

4. $\dfrac{y^{12}}{y^7}$ _____

5. $\dfrac{z^{19}}{z^{18}}$ _____

B.   Divide:

6. $\dfrac{6x^2}{2x}$ _____

7. $\dfrac{3a^4}{3a^2}$ _____

8. $\dfrac{9m^{10}}{3m^7}$

9. $\dfrac{-14r^8}{-2r^3}$ _____

10. $\dfrac{-27x^{13}}{9x^9}$ _____

C.   Divide:

11. $\dfrac{x^6}{x^6}$ _____

12. $\dfrac{-3y^4}{3y^4}$ _____

13. $\dfrac{a^5}{3a^4}$

14. $\dfrac{-x^{10}}{-2x^{10}}$ _____

KEY EXERCISES

A.   Determine the degree of each term.

1. 20 _____

2. x^4 _____

14 RIGHT

SOLUTION.

    (a) 12 has degree 0. (The degree of a nonzero term is 0.)

    (b) $x^2 y$ has degree 3. (Add the exponents.)

    (c) $a^4 b^2 c^3 d^7$ has degree 16 $(= 4 + 2 + 3 + 7)$.

B.   Write $x^3 - x^4 + x^2 - x^5 + 1$ in standard form.

SOLUTION.

$$x^3 - x^4 + x^2 - x^5 + 1 = -x^5 - x^4 + x^3 + x^2 + 1$$

C.   Determine the degree of each polynomial:

    (a) $x^7 - x^6 + x^8$

    (b) $x^2 y - xy^2$

    (c) $x^4 - x^4 + x^3$

SOLUTION.

    (a) The highest degree term is x^8. Thus the degree of
        $x^7 - x^6 + x^8$ is 8.

    (b) Both terms are of degree 3. Thus the degree of

        $x^2 y - xy^2$ is 3.

    (c) First combine similar terms.

$$x^4 - x^4 + x^3 = x^3$$

        The degree of $x^4 - x^4 + x^3$ is 3, the degree of x^3.

3. x^2y^2 _____   4. $2r^2st$ _____

5. $4wx^2yz^6$ _____

B.   Write each polynomial in standard form.

6. $x^3 - x + 1 + x^2$ _____

7. $3y^2 - 4y^3 + 5y^4 - 2y + 1$ _____

8. $m^{10} - 7m^4 + m^9 - m^{12} + m^2 - 7$ _____

9. $x^4 - x^3 + x^4 + x^3$ _____

10. $2x^2 - 4x^5 + x^3 - x^2 + x^3 + x^6 - x^2 + 1$ _____

C.   Determine the degree of each polynomial.

11. x^5 _____

12. $x^4 - x^3 + x^2 + 3$ _____

13. $m^4 - m^3 + 5m^4 - 2m^3$ _____

14. $x^5 + x^3 - x - x^5 + x^3 - x - 2x^3$ _____

15. $x^2y^2 - x^3y^2 + 2x^2y^2 + x^3y^2$ _____

▶ 2.7   Long Division (text page 65)

KEY TOPICS

A.   Divide $8x^3 + 6x^2 - 12x$ by $2x$. Check your answer.

SOLUTION.

$$
2x \overline{\smash{\big)}\, 8x^3 + 6x^2 - 12x} \\
\, 4x^2 + 3x - 6
$$

CHECK:

$$
\begin{array}{r}
4x^2 + 3x - 6 \quad \text{quotient} \\
\times\ 2x \quad \text{divisor} \\
\hline
8x^3 + 6x^2 - 12x \quad \text{dividend}
\end{array}
$$

B.

$$
x + 3 \overline{\smash{\big)}\, x^2 + 7x + 12} \\
\, x + 4
$$

$$
\begin{array}{r}
\bar{\oplus}x^2\ \bar{\oplus}\ 3x \\
\hline
4x + 12 \\
\bar{\oplus}\ 4x\ \bar{\oplus}\ 12
\end{array}
$$

Change signs, and add. The
original sign is encircled;
the new sign lies above.

CHECK:

$$
\begin{array}{r}
x + 4 \quad \text{quotient} \\
\times\ x + 3 \quad \text{divisor} \\
\hline
x^2 + 4x \\
+ 3x + 12 \\
\hline
x^2 + 7x + 12 \quad \text{divident}
\end{array}
$$

C.   Divide $2x^3 - 8x$ by $2x + 4$.

KEY EXERCISES

A.

1. $x \overline{\smash{\big)}2x^2 + x}$ (Check.)   2. $5x \overline{\smash{\big)}25x^2 - 5x}$

3. $-2y \overline{\smash{\big)}2y^3 - 2y^2 + 4y}$ (Check.)   4. $3a^2 \overline{\smash{\big)}27a^4 - 6a^3 + 12a^2}$

CHECKS:

1.   3.

B.

5. $x + 4 \overline{\smash{\big)}x^2 + 9x + 20}$ (Check.)   6. $a - 7 \overline{\smash{\big)}a^2 - 10a + 21}$

7. $2x + 1 \overline{\smash{\big)}4x^2 - 4x - 3}$ 8. $y + 1 \overline{\smash{\big)}y^3 + 3y^2 + 3y + 1}$ (Check.)

9. $m^2 - 3m + 2 \overline{\smash{\big)}m^3 - m^2 - 4m + 4}$

CHECKS:

5.   8.

C.

10. $x + 4 \overline{\smash{\big)}x^2 - 16}$ 11. $2x + 1 \overline{\smash{\big)}2x^4 + x^3 + 2x + 1}$

16 RIGHT

SOLUTION.

Write the divisor as $2x^3 + 0x^2 - 8x$.

$$
2x + 4 \enclose{longdiv}{\begin{array}{l} x^2 - 2x \\ \hline 2x^3 + 0x^2 - 8x \\ \underline{\oplus 2x^3 \ \overline{\oplus} \ 4x^2} \\ \qquad - 4x^2 - 8x \\ \qquad \underline{- 4x^2 - 8x} \end{array}}
$$

D.   Divide $2x^4 + 2x^3 + 3x^2 + x - 2$ by $2x^2 + 1$. What is the remainder? Check the result.

SOLUTION.

Write the dividend as $2x^2 + 0x + 1$.

$$
2x^2 + 0x + 1 \enclose{longdiv}{\begin{array}{l} \qquad\qquad\quad x^2 + x + 1 + \dfrac{-3}{2x^2 + 1} \\ \hline 2x^4 + 2x^3 + 3x^2 + x - 2 \\ \underline{\overline{\oplus}\,2x^4 \qquad\quad \overline{\oplus}\ x^2} \\ \qquad 2x^3 + 2x^2 + x \\ \qquad \underline{\overline{\oplus}\ 2x^3 \qquad\quad \overline{\oplus}\ x} \\ \qquad\qquad\quad 2x^2 \qquad - 2 \\ \qquad\qquad\quad \underline{\overline{\oplus}\ 2x^2 \qquad \overline{\oplus}\ 1} \\ \qquad\qquad\qquad\qquad\qquad - 3 \end{array}}
$$

The remainder is -3.

CHECK:

$$
\begin{array}{lr}
\quad x^2 + x + 1 & \text{quotient} \\
\underline{\times\, 2x^2 \qquad\quad + 1} & \text{divisor} \\
2x^4 + 2x^3 + 2x^2 \\
\qquad\qquad\quad \underline{x^2 + x + 1} \\
2x^4 + 2x^3 + 3x^2 + x + 1 \\
+\ \underline{\qquad\qquad\qquad - 3} & \text{remainder} \\
2x^4 + 2x^3 + 3x^2 + x - 2 & \text{dividend}
\end{array}
$$

12. $3a - 1 \overline{\smash{\big)}\, 6a^4 - 2a^3 + 6a - 2}$ 13. $m^2 + 1 \overline{\smash{\big)}\, m^6 + 4m^4 + 5m^2 + 2}$

D.   In the following examples, there is a remainder.

14. $x + 4 \overline{\smash{\big)}\, x^2 + 5x + 6}$ (Check.)

15. $2x + 3 \overline{\smash{\big)}\, 2x^3 + 3x^2 + 4x + 10}$

16. $y^2 + 3y \overline{\smash{\big)}\, y^4 + 2y^3 - 2y^2 + 3y + 1}$

17. $a^2 + 1 \overline{\smash{\big)}\, a^4 - 2a^3 - a^2}$ (Check.)

18. $x^2 + 2x + 1 \overline{\smash{\big)}\, x^4 - 3x^2 - 6x - 2}$

CHECKS:

14.   17.

▶ 2.8   Synthetic Division (text page 73)

KEY TOPICS

A.   Write the first line of synthetic division if the divisor is
      $x - 3$ and the dividend is $x^3 - 7x - 6$.

SOLUTION.

      For the dividend, write:
      $$x^3 + 0x^2 - 7x - 6$$

      The first line of synthetic division is:

      $\underline{3}|$ 1   0   -7   -6

B.   Suppose the bottom line of a synthetic division example is:

      1   0   -2   3 $\underline{|-1}$

      Determine the quotient and, if there is one, the remainder.

SOLUTION.

      The quotient is $x^3 - 2x + 3$. The remainder is -1.

C.   Use synthetic division to determine the quotient:

$$x - 2 \;\Big|\; x^3 + 2x^2 - 3x - 10$$

SOLUTION.

      $\underline{2}|$ 1   2   -3   -10

                  2   8   10
          _____
            1   4   5 $\underline{|\,0}$

      The quotient is $x^2 + 4x + 5$.

KEY EXERCISES

A.   Write the first line of synthetic division if the divisor
      is given by (a) and the dividend by (b).

1.   (a) $x + 1$ (b) $x^2 + 6x + 5$ _____

2.   (a) $x - 1$ (b) $x^3 + x^2 - 5x + 3$ _____

3.   (a) $x - 2$ (b) $x^3 - x^2 - 4$ _____

4.   (a) $x - 4$ (b) $x^4 - 18x^2 + 9x - 4$ _____

B.   Suppose the bottom line of a synthetic division example is
      as indicated. Determine the quotient and, if there is one,
      the remainder.

5.   1 3 $\lfloor 0$ _____

6.   2 3 1 $\lfloor 1$ _____

7.   1 0 4 $\lfloor 0$ _____

8.   2 0 3 2 0 $\lfloor -1$ _____

C.   Use synthetic division to determine the quotient.

9. $\dfrac{x^2 + 11x + 18}{x + 2}$ _____   10. $t - 1 \overline{)t^3 + 3t^2 + t - 5}$

11. $x - 2 \overline{)x^3 - 3x - 2}$

12. $x + 2 \overline{)x^4 + 2x^3 - 2x^2 + x + 10}$

13. $y + 3 \overline{)y^4 - 6y^2 + 10y + 3}$

18 RIGHT

D.   Use synthetic division to determine the quotient and remainder:

$$x + 1 \enclose{longdiv}{x^4 + x^3 + 2x^2 + x + 2}$$

SOLUTION.

$$
\begin{array}{r|rrrrr}
-1 & 1 & 1 & 2 & 1 & 2 \\
   &   & -1 & 0 & -2 & 1 \\
\hline
   & 1 & 0 & 2 & -1 & \underline{3} \\
\end{array}
$$

The quotient is $x^3 + 2x - 1$.   The remainder is 3.

D. Use synthetic division to determine the quotient and remainder.

$$ \text{remainder} \underline{}$$

14. $x + 4 \overline{\smash{)}\, x^2 + 7x + 10}$

$$ \text{remainder} \underline{}$$

15. $y + 2 \overline{\smash{)}\, y^3 + 3y^2 + 3y + 3}$

$$ \text{remainder} \underline{}$$

16. $x - 2 \overline{\smash{)}\, x^4 - 6x}$

▶ 3.1   Prime Factors (text page 81)

KEY TOPICS

A.   Which of the following are primes?

(a) 13   (b) 15   (c) 17   (d) 19

SOLUTION.

13, 17, and 19 are the primes.

B.   Determine the prime factorization of:

(a) 24   (b) 54   (c) 90   (d) −5000

SOLUTION.

(a) $24 = 2^3 \cdot 3$ (b) $54 = 2 \cdot 3^3$

(c) $90 = 2 \cdot 3^2 \cdot 5$ (d) $-5000 = -(2^3 \cdot 5^4)$

C.   Determine the greatest common divisor of (a) 18 and 24, and (b) 72 and 108.

SOLUTION.

(a) GCD (18, 24) = 6

(b) $72 = 2^3 \cdot 3^2$

$108 = 2^2 \cdot 3^3$

GCD (72, 108) $= 2^2 \cdot 3^2 = 4 \cdot 9 = 36$

D.   Determine the greatest common divisor of the coefficients of $20x^2 - 16x + 12$.

SOLUTION.

Consider the coefficients.

GCD (20, −16, 12) = 4

KEY EXERCISES

A.   Which of the following are primes?

1.   7 _____   2.   27 _____   3.   37 _____

4.   47 _____   5.   57 _____   6.   67 _____

B.   Determine the prime factorization of each number.

7.   28 _____   8.   32 _____   9.   -48 _____

10. 98 _____   11. 990 _____   12. 14 400 _____

C.   Determine the greatest common divisor of the indicated
      integers.

13. 30 and 40 _____   14. 30 and 42 _____

15. 64 and 96 _____   16. 144 and 216 _____

D.   Determine the greatest common divisor of the coefficients
      of each polynomial.

17. $2x^2 + 4x + 10$ _____

18. $t^2 + 9t + 12$ _____

▶ 3.2   Common Factors (text page 86)

KEY TOPICS

A.   Isolate the common factor of each polynomial.

(a) $12a + 18b$ 　　　　　(b) $5x^2 + 12x$

(c) $x^2y^2z - x^2yz^2$ 　　　(d) $12x^3 + 36x^2 - 60x$

SOLUTION.

(a) $12a + 18b = 6(2a + 3b)$

(b) $5x^2 + 12x = x(5x + 12)$

(c) $x^2y^2z - x^2yz^2 = x^2yz(y - z)$

(d) $12x^3 + 36x^2 - 60x = 12x(x^2 + 3x - 5)$

▶ 3.3   Factoring: An Overall View (text page 89)

(no exercises)

▶ 3.4   Difference of Squares (text page 90)

KEY TOPICS

A.   Factor each polynomial.

(a) $x^2 - 9$ 　　　　　(b) $2y^2 - 2a^2$

(c) $16x^2 - 25y^2$ 　　　(d) $a^4 - 16$

SOLUTION.

(a) $x^2 - 9 = (x + 3)(x - 3)$

19. $10y^2 - 20y + 25$ _____

20. $12x^3 - 18x^2 + 36x - 24$ _____

KEY EXERCISES

A.   Isolate the common factor of each polynomial.

1. $2a + 6b$ _____   2. $5x - 10y$ _____

3. $3x^2 + 5x$ _____   4. $a^2b - ab^2$ _____

5. $9x + 12$ _____   6. $4x^2 - 8x$ _____

7. $8a^2b + 12ab$ _____   8. $20x^3 + 10x$ _____

9. $m^2n^2 + mn^3 - m^2n$ _____

10. $x^8y^9 + x^4y^{10} - xy^{12}$ _____

11. $30x^2 - 18x + 100$ _____

12. $18a^2b^2c^2 - 27ab^2c + 30a^2bc^2$ _____

KEY EXERCISES

A.   Factor each polynomial.

1. $a^2 - 16$ _____   2. $x^2 - 81$ _____

3. $1 - y^2$ _____   4. $a^2 - b^2$ _____

5. $9x^2 - 100y^2$ _____

6. $64a^2 - 36c^2$ _____

(b) $2y^2 - 2a^2 = 2(y^2 - a^2)$

$$= 2(y + a)(y - a)$$

(c) $16x^2 - 25y^2 = (4x + 5y)(4x - 5y)$

(d) $a^4 - 16 = (a^2 + 4)(a^2 - 4)$

$$= (a^2 + 4)(a + 2)(a - 2)$$

▶ 3.5   Factoring Quadratic Trinomials, I (text page 94)

KEY TOPICS

A.   Factor each polynomial.

(a) $x^2 + 4x + 3$ (b) $y^2 + 2y - 8$

(c) $a^2 - 10a + 25$ (d) $3x^2 + 24x + 45$

SOLUTION.

(a)
$$
\begin{array}{r}
x + 3 \\
\underline{x + 1} \\
x^2 + 3x \\
\underline{x + 3} \\
x^2 + 4x + 3
\end{array}
$$

$x^2 + 4x + 3 = (x + 3)(x + 1)$

(b)
$$
\begin{array}{r}
y + 4 \\
\underline{y - 2} \\
y^2 + 4y \\
\underline{- 2y - 8} \\
y^2 + 2y - 8
\end{array}
$$

$y^2 + 2y - 8 = (y + 4)(y - 2)$

7. $5x^2 - 45z^2$ _____

8. $a^3 - a$ _____   9. $x^4 - y^4$ _____

10. $a^6 - b^8$ _____

11. $16x^4 - 1$ _____

12. $(a - b)^2 - 49$ _____

13. $(a^2 - b^2)^3$ _____

14. $6ax^2 - 54a$ _____

KEY EXERCISES

A.   Factor each polynomial.

1. $x^2 + 6x + 5$ _____   2. $x^2 - 6x + 5$ _____

3. $x^2 + 4x - 5$ _____   4. $x^2 - 4x - 5$ _____

5. $a^2 + 5a + 6$ _____   6. $b^2 + 9b + 14$ _____

7. $z^2 - 6z + 8$ _____   8. $m^2 - 7m + 10$ _____

9. $t^2 - 4t - 12$ _____   10. $t^2 - 8t + 16$ _____

11. $a^2x^2 - 5a^2x + 4a^2$ _____

12. $5z^2 - 30z - 35$ _____

13. $x^3 - 9x^2 + 18x$ _____

14. $4 + 3a - a^2$ _____

(c) $a - 5$
        $a - 5$
        $\overline{a^2 - 5a}$
        $- 5a + 25$
        $\overline{a^2 - 10a + 25}$

$a^2 - 10a + 25 = (a - 5)^2$

(d) $3x^2 + 24x + 45 = 3(x^2 + 8x + 15)$

        $x + 5$
        $x + 3$
        $\overline{x^2 + 5x}$
        $3x + 15$
        $\overline{x^2 + 8x + 15}$

$3x^2 + 24x + 45 = 3(x + 5)(x + 3)$

▶ 3.6   Factoring Quadratic Trinomials, II (text page 97)

KEY TOPICS

A.   Factor each polynomial.

(a) $2a^2 + 5a + 2$ (b) $4x^2 + 8x + 3$

(c) $6y^2 + y - 2$ (d) $8a^2 + 14ab + 3b^2$

SOLUTION.

(a) $2a + 1$
        $a + 2$
        $\overline{2a^2 + a}$
        $4a + 2$
        $\overline{2a^2 + 5a + 2}$

$2a^2 + 5a + 2 = (2a + 1)(a + 2)$

KEY EXERCISES

A.   Factor each polynomial.

1. $2x^2 + 7x + 3$ _____

2. $3y^2 + 7y + 2$ _____

3. $2x^2 + 7x + 5$ _____

4. $4a^2 + 16a + 15$ _____

5. $4x^2 - 4x - 3$ _____

6. $3y^2 - 5y + 2$ _____

7. $7b^2 + 8b + 1$ _____

(b) $\begin{array}{r} 2x + 3 \\ 2x + 1 \\ \hline 4x^2 + 6x \\ 2x + 3 \\ \hline 4x^2 + 8x + 3 \end{array}$

$4x^2 + 8x + 3 = (2x + 3)(2x + 1)$

(c) $\begin{array}{r} 3y + 2 \\ 2y - 1 \\ \hline 6y^2 + 4y \\ - 3y - 2 \\ \hline 6y^2 + y - 2 \end{array}$

$6y^2 + y - 2 = (3y + 2)(2y - 1)$

(d) $\begin{array}{r} 2a + 3b \\ 4a + b \\ \hline 8a^2 + 12ab \\ 2ab + 3b^2 \\ \hline 8a^2 + 14ab + 3b^2 \end{array}$

$8a^2 + 14ab + 3b^2 = (2a + 3b)(4a + b)$

▶ 3.7   Factoring by Grouping (text page 103)

KEY TOPICS

A.   Factor each polynomial.

(a) $mx + my + nx + ny$

(b) $a^2 + 5a + ab + 5b$

(c) $2a^2 - 2b^2 - a^2x + b^2x$

(d) $a^2x^2 + 100 - 4a^2 - 25x^2$

(e) $a^2x^2 + 3a^2x + 2a^2 - x^2 - 3x - 2$

8. $5a^2 - 11a + 2$ _____

9. $12z^2 + 10z + 2$ _____

10. $2a^3 - a^2 - 15a$ _____

11. $2x^2 + 5xy + 2y^2$ _____

12. $3a^2 - 5ab - 2b^2$ _____

13. $10m^2 + 3mn - n^2$ _____

14. $6y^2 - 17yz + 12z^2$ _____

KEY EXERCISES

A.   Factor each polynomial.

1. $cx + cy + dx + dy$ _____

2. $am - an - bm + bn$ _____

3. $ax - ay + 3x - 3y$ _____

4. $ac + bc + ad + bd$ _____

5. $ax - bx + 2ay - 2by$ _____

6. $as + 5bs + at + 5bt$ _____

SOLUTION.

(a) $mx + my + nx + ny = (mx + my) + (nx + ny)$

$$= m(x + y) + n(x + y)$$

$$= (m + n)(x + y)$$

(b) $a^2 + 5a + ab + 5b = (a^2 + 5a) + (ab + 5b)$

$$= a(a + 5) + b(a + 5)$$

$$= (a + b)(a + 5)$$

(c) $2a^2 - 2b^2 - a^2x + b^2x = (2a^2 - 2b^2) - (a^2x - b^2x)$

$$= 2(a^2 - b^2) - x(a^2 - b^2)$$

$$= (2 - x)(a^2 - b^2)$$

$$= (2 - x)(a + b)(a - b)$$

(d) $a^2x^2 + 100 - 4a^2 - 25x^2 = (a^2x^2 - 25x^2) + (100 - 4a^2)$

$$= x^2(a^2 - 25) + 4(25 - a^2)$$

$$= x^2(a^2 - 25) - 4(a^2 - 25)$$

$$= (x^2 - 4)(a^2 - 25)$$

$$= (x + 2)(x - 2)(a + 5)(a - 5)$$

(e) $a^2x^2 + 3a^2x + 2a^2 - x^2 - 3x - 2 = a^2x^2 + 3a^2x + 2a^2 - (x^2 + 3x + 2)$

$$= a^2(x^2 + 3x + 2) - (x^2 + 3x + 2)$$

$$= (a^2 - 1)(x^2 + 3x + 2)$$

$$= (a + 1)(a - 1)(x + 2)(x + 1)$$

7. $xy + x + y + y^2$ _____

8. $m^3 + m^2 + mn + n$ _____

9. $ax^2 - a + bx^2 - b$ _____

10. $a^2x^2 - a^2 - 9x^2 + 9$ _____

11. $s^2t^2 - 4t^2 - 9s^2 + 36$ _____

12. $a^2x^2 - 3a^2x + 2a^2 + x^2 - 3x + 2$ _____

13. $a^2m^2 + 8a^2m + 16a^2 - b^2m^2 - 8b^2m - 16b^2$ _____

14. $x^2y^2 - xy^2 - 6y^2 - x^2z^2 + xz^2 + 6z^2$ _____

▶ 3.8   Sums and Differences of Cubes (text page 105)

KEY TOPICS

A.   Factor each polynomial.

(a) $x^3 - 8$ (b) $y^3 + 27$

(c) $b^3 - 27a^3$ (d) $ab^3 + b^3 + ac^3 + c^3$

SOLUTION.

(a) $x^3 - 8 = (x - 2)(x^2 + 2x + 4)$

(b) $y^3 + 27 = (y + 3)(y^2 - 3y + 9)$

(c) $b^3 - 27a^3 = (b - 3a)(b^2 + 3ab + 9a^2)$

(d) $ab^3 + b^3 + ac^3 + c^3 = (ab^3 + b^3) + (ac^3 + c^3)$

$$= b^3(a + 1) + c^3(a + 1)$$

$$= (b^3 + c^3)(a + 1)$$

$$= (b + c)(b^2 - bc + c^2)(a + 1)$$

KEY EXERCISES

A.   Factor each polynomial.

1. $a^3 - 1$ _____

2. $b^3 + 64$ _____

3. $x^3 + 125$ _____

4. $a^3 b^3 - 1000$ _____

5. $x^3 y^3 - 8$ _____

6. $1000x^3 - 27a^3$ _____

7. $a^6 - b^3$ _____

8. $c^9 + d^3$ _____

9. $a^3 b^3 + a^3 c^3$ _____

10. $a^3 b^3 c^3 - a^3 b^3$ _____

11. $a^2 x^3 - 125a^2$ _____

12. $(x + 1)^3 + (a + 2)^3$ _____

13. $a^3 x^2 - 4a^3 + 4 - x^2$ _____

14. $a^3 b^2 - a^3 c^2 + b^2 - c^2$ _____

CHAPTER 4

RATIONAL EXPRESSIONS

▶ 4.1   Simplifying Fractions (text page 111)

KEY TOPICS

A.   Express positive fractions without minus signs; express
     negative fractions in standard form.

   (a) $\frac{1}{-4}$ (b) $-\frac{3}{5}$ (c) $-\frac{-\pi}{2}$ (d) $-\frac{-2}{-7}$

SOLUTION.

   (a) $\frac{1}{-4} = \frac{-1}{4}$ (b) $-\frac{3}{5} = \frac{-3}{5}$

   (c) $-\frac{-\pi}{2} = \frac{\pi}{2}$ (d) $-\frac{-2}{-7} = \frac{-2}{7}$

B.   Simplify each fraction.

   (a) $\frac{3}{12}$ (b) $\frac{6}{-10}$ (c) $\frac{-12}{-16}$ (d) $\frac{60}{225}$

SOLUTION.

   (a) $\frac{3}{12} = \frac{1}{4}$ (b) $\frac{6}{-10} = \frac{-3}{5}$

   (c) $\frac{-12}{-16} = \frac{3}{4}$ (d) $\frac{60}{225} = \frac{2^2 \cdot 3 \cdot 5}{3^2 \cdot 5^2} = \frac{2^2}{3 \cdot 5} = \frac{4}{15}$

C.   Simplify each fraction. (Multiply out the resulting
     numerator and denominator.)

   (a) $\frac{3^5}{3^2}$ (b) $\frac{2 \cdot 5^4 \cdot 7}{2 \cdot 5 \cdot 7^2}$

SOLUTION.

   (a) $\frac{3^5}{3^2} = 3^3 = 27$ (b) $\frac{2 \cdot 5^4 \cdot 7}{2 \cdot 5 \cdot 7^2} = \frac{5^3}{7} = \frac{125}{7}$

KEY EXERCISES

A.   Express positive fractions without minus signs; express
     negative fractions in standard form.

1. $\dfrac{3}{-5}$ _____   2. $\dfrac{-3}{-5}$ _____   3. $-\dfrac{-5}{8}$ _____

4. $\dfrac{2}{-\pi}$ _____   5. $-\dfrac{-3}{-4}$ _____   6. $-\dfrac{2}{-9}$ _____

B.   Simplify each fraction.

7. $\dfrac{4}{8}$ _____   8. $\dfrac{5}{25}$ _____   9. $\dfrac{-6}{-18}$ _____

10. $\dfrac{21}{-30}$ _____   11. $-\dfrac{14}{35}$ _____   12. $\dfrac{22}{99}$ _____

13. $\dfrac{48}{64}$ _____   14. $\dfrac{-75}{135}$ _____   15. $\dfrac{144}{160}$ _____

C.   Simplify each fraction.   (Multiply out the resulting
     numerator and denominator.)

16. $\dfrac{2^4}{2^2}$ _____   17. $\dfrac{5^3}{5^3}$ _____

18. $\dfrac{-3^9}{3^{11}}$ _____   19. $\dfrac{2^2 \cdot 5}{2^2 \cdot 7}$ _____

▶ 4.2   Evaluating Rational Expressions (text page 119)

KEY TOPICS

A.   Evaluate $\dfrac{2x - 1}{x^2 + x + 1}$ when x = 2.

SOLUTION.

Replace x by 2, and obtain $\dfrac{2 \cdot 2 - 1}{2^2 + 2 + 1}$, or $\dfrac{3}{7}$.

B.   Evaluate $\dfrac{3t + 5}{t^2 - 5}$ when (a) t = 1, (b) t = 5.

SOLUTION.

(a) $\dfrac{3 \cdot 1 + 5}{1^2 - 5} = \dfrac{8}{-4} = -2$

(b) $\dfrac{3 \cdot 5 + 5}{5^2 - 5} = \dfrac{20}{20} = 1$

20. $\dfrac{2 \cdot 3 \cdot 7}{3 \cdot 7^2}$ _____

21. $\dfrac{3 \cdot 5^2 \cdot 11}{3^4 \cdot 5 \cdot 11}$ _____

22. $\dfrac{5^{18} \cdot 11^{16}}{5^{16} \cdot 11^{18}}$ _____

23. $\dfrac{-2^4 \cdot 3^9 \cdot 7^{10}}{2^6 \cdot 3^8 \cdot 7^9}$ _____

24. $\dfrac{-5^{10} \cdot 13^{15}}{-5^8 \cdot 13^{16}}$ _____

KEY EXERCISES

A.

1. Evaluate $\dfrac{x + 4}{5}$ when x = 1. _____

2. Evaluate $\dfrac{t - 3}{t + 2}$ when t = 4. _____

3. Evaluate $\dfrac{y + 1}{y^2}$ when y = -10. _____

4. Evaluate $\dfrac{u^3 - u^2 + 2u - 1}{10}$ when u = 2. _____

5. Evaluate $\dfrac{x^2 - 3x + 5}{x^2 - 5}$ when x = 3. _____

B.

6. Evaluate $\dfrac{x + 2}{x - 2}$ when (a) x = 1, (b) x = 3. _____

7. Evaluate $\dfrac{4}{t + 6}$ when (a) t = -1, (b) t = 2. _____

8. Evaluate $\dfrac{y^2 + 1}{10}$ when (a) y = 0, (b) y = 3. _____

9. Evaluate $\dfrac{3 - y}{1 - y^2}$ when (a) y = 2, (b) y = -2. _____

10. Evaluate $\dfrac{t^2 + 2t + 5}{t + 3}$ when (a) t = 0, (b) t = 4. _____

C.   Evaluate $\dfrac{xy - 3}{x^2 + xy + 1}$ when x = 2 and y = -1.

SOLUTION.

Replace x by 2 and y by -1: $\dfrac{2(-1) - 3}{2^2 + 2(-1) + 1} = \dfrac{-5}{3}$

D.   Evaluate $\dfrac{xyz}{2 + x - y + z}$ when (a) x = 1, y = -1, z = 1, and

(b) x = 2, y = 3, z = 1.

SOLUTION.

(a) $\dfrac{(1)(-1)(1)}{2 + 1 - (-1) + 1} = \dfrac{-1}{5}$

(b) $\dfrac{2 \cdot 3 \cdot 1}{2 + 2 - 3 + 1} = \dfrac{6}{2} = 3$

▶ 4.3   Dividing Monomials (text page 123)

KEY TOPICS

A.   Simplify each rational expression.

(a) $\dfrac{10a^2}{2}$ (b) $\dfrac{abc^2d}{ab^2c}$

29 LEFT

C.

11. Evaluate $\frac{xy}{3}$ when x = 1 and y = 2. _____

12. Evaluate $\frac{x + y}{x + 1}$ when x = 5 and y = 2. _____

13. Evaluate $\frac{4}{s + t}$ when s = 3 and t = 6. _____

14. Evaluate $\frac{u - v}{u^2 + v}$ when u = 6 and v = 5. _____

15. Evaluate $\frac{x^2 - 3xy + 1}{y^2 + 2}$ when x = -1 and y = -3. _____

D.

16. Evaluate $\frac{x + y}{3}$ when (a) x = 1 and y = 1, (b) x = 2 and y = -3.

17. Evaluate $\frac{s + t + 1}{t - 2}$ when (a) s = 1 and t = -1,

(b) s = 4 and t = 4. _____

18. Evaluate $\frac{y^2 - z^2}{y + z + 1}$ when (a) y = 5 and z = -5,

(b) y = 10 and z = 1. _____

19. Evaluate $\frac{x + y + z}{xyz}$ when (a) x = 1, y = 2, z = 3,

(b) x = -4, y = -2, z = 1. _____

20. Evaluate $\frac{u + v - w}{1 + w^2}$ when (a) u = 1, v = -1, w = 2,

(b) u = 4, v = 3, w = 3. _____

KEY EXERCISES

A.   Simplify each rational expression.

1. $\frac{6a}{2}$ _____   2. $\frac{12x^2}{4}$ _____

(c) $\dfrac{-48x^2}{36x}$ (d) $\dfrac{40x^2y^3z^6}{25xy^4z^6}$

(e) $\dfrac{(a+b)^4}{(a+b)^3}$ (f) $\dfrac{(m+n)^5(x+y)^2}{(m+n)^4(x+y)^2(x-y)}$

SOLUTION.

(a) $\dfrac{10a^2}{2} = 5a^2$ (b) $\dfrac{abc^2d}{ab^2c} = \dfrac{cd}{b}$

(c) $\dfrac{-48x^2}{36x} = \dfrac{-4x}{3}$ (d) $\dfrac{40x^2y^3z^6}{25xy^4z^6} = \dfrac{8x}{5y}$

(e) $\dfrac{(a+b)^4}{(a+b)^3} = a+b$ (f) $\dfrac{(m+n)^5(x+y)^2}{(m+n)^4(x+y)^2(x-y)} = \dfrac{m+n}{x-y}$

3. $\dfrac{36xy}{6}$ _____

4. $\dfrac{-20ab^3}{8}$ _____

5. $\dfrac{ab}{b}$ _____

6. $\dfrac{xy^2}{xy^3}$ _____

7. $\dfrac{-mn^3}{m^2n^2}$ _____

8. $\dfrac{a^2bcd^2}{bcd}$ _____

9. $\dfrac{x^3y^{10}z^7}{x^4y^8z}$ _____

10. $\dfrac{14a^2}{7a}$ _____

11. $\dfrac{-36a^4b}{-9a^3}$ _____

12. $\dfrac{12xy^3z^2}{18xz^3}$ _____

13. $\dfrac{44a^2x^3}{55ax^2y}$ _____

14. $\dfrac{30x^2yz^{10}}{45xz^9}$ _____

15. $\dfrac{24a^4b^7c^{10}d}{42a^3b^4c^{12}d}$ _____

16. $\dfrac{-54m^2n^4p^9}{72m^4n^3p^3}$ _____

17. $\dfrac{x+y}{(x+y)^2}$ _____

18. $\dfrac{(x-y)^3}{(x-y)^2}$ _____

19. $\dfrac{4(x+y)^3}{8(x+y)}$ _____

20. $\dfrac{(a+b)(y+z)}{(a+b)^2}$ _____

21. $\dfrac{a^2(x-y)}{a^3(x-y)}$ _____

22. $\dfrac{m^2(m+n)^2(m-n)}{m(m+n)(m-n)^2}$ _____

23. $\dfrac{(a+b)^3(x+y)}{(a+b)^2(x-y)}$ _____

24. $\dfrac{49c^2(a+b)(c-d)}{28c^3(a+b)^4(c+d)^4}$ _____

▶ 4.4   Dividing by Monomials (text page 128)

KEY TOPICS

A.   Simplify each rational expression.

(a) $\dfrac{x^2y + xy^2}{x}$

(b) $\dfrac{12xy - 16x^3}{4}$

(c) $\dfrac{a^2b^3 + a^3b^2}{ab}$

(d) $\dfrac{20a^2b^3 - 25a^2b^2}{5a^2b}$

(e) $\dfrac{12x^3y^2 + 18xy^4 - 15x^3y^3}{6x^2y^2}$

(f) $\dfrac{40a^6b^2c^3 - 25a^4b^4c^4 + 60a^3b^2c^6}{20a^3b^2c}$

SOLUTION.

(a) $\dfrac{x^2y + xy^2}{x} = \dfrac{xy(x + y)}{x} = y(x + y)$

(b) $\dfrac{12xy - 16x^3}{4} = \dfrac{4x(3y - 4x^2)}{4} = x(3y - 4x^2)$

(c) $\dfrac{a^2b^3 + a^3b^2}{ab} = \dfrac{a^2b^2(b + a)}{ab} = ab(b + a)$

(d) $\dfrac{20a^2b^3 - 25a^2b^2}{5a^2b} = \dfrac{5a^2b^2(4b - 5)}{5a^2b} = b(4b - 5)$

(e) $\dfrac{12x^3y^2 + 18xy^4 - 15x^3y^3}{6x^2y^2} = \dfrac{3xy^2(4x^2 + 6y^2 - 5x^2y)}{6x^2y^2}$

$\qquad = \dfrac{4x^2 + 6y^2 - 5x^2y}{2x}$

(f) $\dfrac{40a^6b^2c^3 - 25a^4b^4c^4 + 60a^3b^2c^6}{20a^3b^2c} = \dfrac{5a^3b^2c^3(8a^3 - 5ab^2c + 12c^3)}{20a^3b^2c}$

$\qquad = \dfrac{c^2(8a^3 - 5ab^2c + 12c^3)}{4}$

KEY EXERCISES

A.   Simplify each rational expression.

1. $\dfrac{a^3b + a^2b^2}{a}$ _____

2. $\dfrac{xy^3 - x^2y}{y}$ _____

3. $\dfrac{a^6b^2 - a^4b^4}{a^3}$ _____

4. $\dfrac{x^2yz^3 - xyz^2}{z^2}$ _____

5. $\dfrac{8xy + 12x}{4}$ _____

6. $\dfrac{9abc + 15ab}{3}$ _____

7. $\dfrac{12m^2n^3 - 16mn^2}{8}$ _____

8. $\dfrac{ab^2 + a^2b}{ab}$ _____

9. $\dfrac{xyz^2 + x^2yz}{xyz}$ _____

10. $\dfrac{ab^2c^3 + a^3b^2c}{a^2b^2}$ _____

11. $\dfrac{x^2y^4z - x^3yz^5}{xy^2z}$ _____

12. $\dfrac{20abc + 50a^2b}{10ab}$ _____

13. $\dfrac{4m^2n^2 - 6mn^4}{8m^2n}$ _____

14. $\dfrac{24x^4y^2z + 32xy^4}{8x^2y^2}$ _____

15. $\dfrac{9ab + 12a^2 - 18b}{3ab}$ _____

16. $\dfrac{12xy - 6x + 24}{6x}$ _____

B.   Simplify: $\dfrac{4ab}{8a^2b + 4ab^2}$

SOLUTION.

$$\frac{4ab}{8a^2b + 4ab^2} = \frac{4ab}{4ab(2a + b)} = \frac{1}{2a + b}$$

▶ 4.5   Simplifying by Factoring (text page 131)

KEY TOPICS

A.   Simplify, if possible.   Leave the answers in factored form.

(a) $\dfrac{8x + 8y}{4x - 4y}$

(b) $\dfrac{a^2 - 9}{a - 3}$

(c) $\dfrac{a^2 + 9}{a + 3}$

(d) $\dfrac{x^2 + 9x + 20}{x^2 + 8x + 16}$

(e) $\dfrac{xy + x^2y}{x^2 + 2x + 1}$

(f) $\dfrac{a^4 - b^4}{a^2 - b^2}$

SOLUTION.

(a) $\dfrac{8x + 8y}{4x - 4y} = \dfrac{8(x + y)}{4(x - y)} = \dfrac{2(x + y)}{x - y}$

17. $\dfrac{36x^2yz^3 + 48x^2y^2z^2 + 24xy^2z^2}{12xyz^2}$ _____

18. $\dfrac{20abc^3 - 40a^4bc + 16ab^3c^2}{8ab^2c}$ _____

19. $\dfrac{49x^3y^4z^3 + 14x^5y^2 + 35xy^3z^3}{14xy^2}$ _____

20. $\dfrac{-36a^2b^3c^7d^4 + 90a^2b^3c^4d^5 - 24ad^2 + 48ad}{12abcd}$ _____

B. Simplify each rational expression.

21. $\dfrac{x^2}{x^2y^2 + x^2}$ _____ 22. $\dfrac{2a}{a^2b + 4a}$ _____

23. $\dfrac{5xy}{x^2y^2 - xy^2}$ _____

24. $\dfrac{3m^2n^2}{9m^4n^5 - 6m^3n^3 + 18m^2n^2}$ _____

KEY EXERCISES

A. Simplify, if possible. Leave the answers in factored form.

1. $\dfrac{4a + 4b}{2a + 2b}$ _____ 2. $\dfrac{15x - 15y}{5x + 5y}$ _____

3. $\dfrac{36x - 6}{12x + 6}$ _____ 4. $\dfrac{9a - 9b}{18a + 18b}$ _____

5. $\dfrac{x^2 - y^2}{x + y}$ _____ 6. $\dfrac{u + v}{2u^2 - 2v^2}$ _____

7. $\dfrac{a + b}{a^2 + b^2}$ _____ 8. $\dfrac{a - b}{a^2 - b^2}$ _____

9. $\dfrac{c^2 - 25}{c - 5}$ _____ 10. $\dfrac{a^2 - 36}{18 - 3a}$ _____

32 RIGHT

(b) $\dfrac{a^2 - 9}{a - 3} = \dfrac{(a + 3)(a - 3)}{a - 3} = a + 3$

(c) $\dfrac{a^2 + 9}{a + 3}$ cannot be simplified because the numerator

cannot be factored (by the present methods).

(d) $\dfrac{x^2 + 9x + 20}{x^2 + 8x + 16} = \dfrac{(x + 5)(x + 4)}{(x + 4)^2} = \dfrac{x + 5}{x + 4}$

(e) $\dfrac{xy + x^2 y}{x^2 + 2x + 1} = \dfrac{xy(1 + x)}{(x + 1)^2} = \dfrac{xy}{x + 1}$

(f) $\dfrac{a^4 - b^4}{a^2 - b^2} = \dfrac{(a^2 + b^2)(a^2 - b^2)}{a^2 - b^2} = a^2 + b^2$

11. $\dfrac{a^2 + 3a + 2}{a^2 + 2a + 1}$ _____ 12. $\dfrac{x^2 - 4}{x^2 + 4x + 4}$ _____

13. $\dfrac{u^2 - 100}{u^3 - 10u^2}$ _____ 14. $\dfrac{z + z^2}{1 - z^2}$ _____

15. $\dfrac{a^2 - 5a + 6}{a^2 + 5a + 6}$ _____ 16. $\dfrac{m^2 + m - 12}{m^2 - 7m + 12}$ _____

17. $\dfrac{ab + a}{b^2 - 1}$ _____ 18. $\dfrac{x^3 + 3x^2}{x^3 - 9x}$ _____

19. $\dfrac{1 - u^4}{1 + u^2}$ _____ 20. $\dfrac{x^3 - y^3}{4x - 4y}$ _____

CHAPTER 5

ARITHMETIC OF RATIONAL EXPRESSIONS

▶ 5.1   Multiplication and Division (text page 136)

KEY TOPICS

A.   Multiply, as indicated. Simplify the resulting fractions.

(a) $\dfrac{2}{3} \cdot \dfrac{1}{5}$ (b) $\dfrac{4}{9} \cdot \dfrac{3}{2}$ (c) $\dfrac{-5}{8} \cdot \dfrac{-2}{15}$

SOLUTION.

(a) $\dfrac{2}{3} \cdot \dfrac{1}{5} = \dfrac{2}{15}$ (b) $\dfrac{\overset{2}{\cancel{4}}}{\underset{3}{\cancel{9}}} \cdot \dfrac{\overset{1}{\cancel{3}}}{\underset{1}{\cancel{2}}} = \dfrac{2}{3}$

(c) $\dfrac{\overset{-1}{\cancel{-5}}}{\underset{4}{\cancel{8}}} \cdot \dfrac{\overset{-1}{\cancel{-2}}}{\underset{3}{\cancel{15}}} = \dfrac{1}{12}$

B.   Multiply, as indicated. Simplify, and leave the answers in factored form.

(a) $\dfrac{a}{b} \cdot \dfrac{x}{y}$ (b) $\dfrac{x^2 y}{ab} \cdot \dfrac{a^2 b^2}{x^2 y^2}$

(c) $\dfrac{4(x + a)}{3(x - a)} \cdot \dfrac{x - a}{2(x + a)^2}$ (d) $\dfrac{3x^2 - 3y^2}{x^2 - 1} \cdot \dfrac{x + 1}{9x + 9y}$

SOLUTION.

(a) $\dfrac{a}{b} \cdot \dfrac{x}{y} = \dfrac{ax}{by}$ (b) $\dfrac{\cancel{x^2}\,y}{\cancel{ab}} \cdot \dfrac{\overset{a}{\cancel{a^2}}\,\overset{b}{\cancel{b^2}}}{\underset{y}{\cancel{x^2}\,\cancel{y^2}}} = \dfrac{ab}{y}$

(c) $\dfrac{\overset{2}{\cancel{4(x + a)}}}{3(x - a)} \cdot \dfrac{x - a}{\underset{x + a}{\cancel{2(x + a)^2}}} = \dfrac{2}{3(x + a)}$

(d) $\dfrac{3x^2 - 3y^2}{x^2 - 1} \cdot \dfrac{x + 1}{9x + 9y} = \dfrac{3(x + y)(x - y)}{(x + 1)(x - 1)} \cdot \dfrac{\cancel{x + 1}}{\underset{3}{\cancel{9(x + y)}}}$

$= \dfrac{x - y}{3(x - 1)}$

KEY EXERCISES

A. Multiply, as indicated. Simplify the resulting fractions, if possible.

1. $\frac{1}{2} \cdot \frac{1}{4}$ _____

2. $\frac{-2}{3} \cdot \frac{1}{7}$ _____

3. $\frac{-3}{4} \cdot \frac{-2}{9}$ _____

4. $\frac{3}{20} \cdot \frac{5}{9}$ _____

5. $\frac{-6}{77} \cdot \frac{121}{36}$ _____

6. $\frac{420}{81} \cdot \frac{27}{80}$ _____

B. Multiply, as indicated. Simplify, and leave your answers in factored form.

7. $\frac{3}{x} \cdot \frac{1}{y}$ _____

8. $\frac{x}{a} \cdot \frac{a}{x^2}$ _____

9. $\frac{a^2 b}{xy^3} \cdot \frac{xy}{a^2 b^2}$ _____

10. $\frac{x + a}{x - a} \cdot \frac{(x - a)^2}{4(x + a)}$ _____

11. $\frac{x^2 - a^2}{3x - 3y} \quad \frac{x^2 - y^2}{2x + 2a}$ _____

12. $\frac{a^2 + 7a + 12}{a^2 + 2ab + b^2} \cdot \frac{5a + 5b}{a^2 - 9}$ _____

34 RIGHT

C.   Divide, as indicated. Simplify the resulting fractions.

(a) $\dfrac{-1}{3} \div \dfrac{2}{5}$ (b) $\dfrac{3}{8} \div \dfrac{9}{16}$ (c) $\dfrac{24}{25} \div \dfrac{16}{45}$

SOLUTION.

(a) $\dfrac{-1}{3} \div \dfrac{2}{5} = \dfrac{-1}{3} \cdot \dfrac{5}{2} = \dfrac{-5}{6}$ (b) $\dfrac{3}{8} \div \dfrac{9}{16} = \dfrac{\overset{1}{\cancel{3}}}{\underset{1}{\cancel{8}}} \cdot \dfrac{\overset{2}{\cancel{16}}}{\underset{3}{\cancel{9}}} = \dfrac{2}{3}$

(c) $\dfrac{24}{25} \div \dfrac{16}{45} = \dfrac{24}{25} \cdot \dfrac{45}{16} = \dfrac{\overset{3}{\cancel{2^3}} \cdot 3}{\underset{5}{\cancel{5^2}}} \cdot \dfrac{3^2 \cdot \overset{}{\cancel{5}}}{\underset{2}{\cancel{2^4}}}$

$= \dfrac{3^3}{10}$

$= \dfrac{27}{10}$

D.   Divide, as indicated. Simplify, and leave the answers in factored form.

(a) $\dfrac{xy^2}{a} \div \dfrac{b}{c}$ (b) $\dfrac{a^2 b^3 c}{xy} \div \dfrac{a^2 b^4}{x^2 y^2}$

(c) $\dfrac{x^2 - 9}{2a + 2b} \div \dfrac{x^2 + 5x + 6}{a^2 - b^2}$

SOLUTION.

(a) $\dfrac{xy^2}{a} \div \dfrac{b}{c} = \dfrac{xy^2}{a} \cdot \dfrac{c}{b} = \dfrac{xy^2 c}{ab}$

(b) $\dfrac{a^2 b^3 c}{xy} \div \dfrac{a^2 b^4}{x^2 y^2} = \dfrac{\cancel{a^2} \overset{}{\cancel{b^3}} c}{\cancel{xy}} \cdot \dfrac{\overset{x\,\,y}{\cancel{x^2 y^2}}}{\underset{b}{\cancel{a^2 b^4}}} = \dfrac{cxy}{b}$

(c) $\dfrac{x^2 - 9}{2a + 2b} \div \dfrac{x^2 + 5x + 6}{a^2 - b^2} = \dfrac{(x + 3)(x - 3)}{2(a + b)} \cdot \dfrac{(a + b)(a - b)}{(x + 3)(x + 2)}$

$= \dfrac{(x - 3)(a - b)}{2(x + 2)}$

35 LEFT

C.   Divide, as indicated. Simplify the resulting fractions.

13. $\frac{1}{2} \div \frac{1}{3}$ _____

14. $\frac{1}{4} \div \frac{1}{2}$ _____

15. $\frac{-2}{5} \div \frac{-3}{10}$ _____

16. $\frac{12}{25} \div \frac{18}{35}$ _____

17. $\frac{121}{144} \div \frac{77}{96}$ _____

18. $\frac{1400}{27} \div \frac{7000}{81}$ _____

D.   Divide, as indicated. Simplify, and leave your answers in factored form.

19. $\frac{a}{3} \div \frac{b}{4}$ _____

20. $\frac{x}{y} \div \frac{c}{d}$ _____

21. $\frac{x - y}{2} \div \frac{x + y}{6}$ _____

22. $\frac{x + y}{a^2 - b^2} \div \frac{x^2 - y^2}{a - b}$ _____

23. $\frac{a^2 - 6a + 8}{x^2 - 4x + 3} \div \frac{a^2 - 4}{x^2 - 2x - 3}$ _____

24. $\frac{y^2 + 6y + 9}{x^3 - z^3} \div \frac{y^2 + 8y + 15}{x^2 - 2xz + z^2}$ _____

E.   What polynomial must be divided by $a^2 - 16$ to obtain $\dfrac{1}{a-4}$?

SOLUTION.

$$\frac{?}{a^2 - 16} = \frac{1}{a - 4}$$

$$\frac{?}{(a + 4)(a - 4)} = \frac{1}{a - 4}$$

Observe that

$$\frac{\overset{1}{\cancel{a + 4}}}{\cancel{(a + 4)}(a - 4)} = \frac{1}{a - 4} .$$

Thus $a + 4$ must be divided by $a^2 - 16$ to obtain $\dfrac{1}{a-4}$.

▶ 5.2   Least Common Multiples (text page 144)

KEY TOPICS

A.   Determine the LCM of the indicated integers.

(a) 10, 15   (b) 24, 30

SOLUTION.

(a) LCM (10, 15) = 30

(b) $24 = 2^3 \cdot 3$

$30 = 2 \cdot 3 \cdot 5$

LCM (24, 30) $= 2^3 \cdot 3 \cdot 5 = 120$

B.   Determine an LCM of the indicated polynomials.

(a) x^2y, xy^2z (b) $x^2 - 2x + 1, x^2 - 1$

SOLUTION.

(a) LCM $(x^2y, xy^2z) = x^2y^2z$

E.

25. Divide $\dfrac{m^2 - n^2}{m + 5}$ by $\dfrac{m + n}{m^2 - 25}$. _____

26. The quotient of $\dfrac{x + 1}{x - 1}$ divided by $\dfrac{x^2 + 2x + 1}{x^2 - 6x + 5}$ is multiplied

by x + 1. Determine the resulting product. _____

27. What polynomial must be divided by $x^2 + 8x + 16$ to obtain $\dfrac{1}{x + 4}$?

_____

28. What rational expression must be divided by $\dfrac{x + 1}{x + 3}$ to obtain

$\dfrac{(x + 1)^3}{x + 3}$? _____

KEY EXERCISES

A.   Determine the LCM of the indicated integers.

1. 14, 21 _____   2. 30, 50 _____

3. 72, 96 _____   4. 4, 6, 8 _____

5. 24, 30, 42 _____

B.   Determine the LCM of the indicated polynomials.

6. xy^2, x^2yz^3 _____   7. x + a, x - a _____

8. $x^2 - 4$, $x^2 - 5x + 6$ _____

9. a^2b^3c, abc^3, a^4 _____

10. $x^2 - 9$, $x^2 + 6x + 9$, $x^2 + 7x + 12$ _____

(b) $\quad x^2 - 2x + 1 = (x - 1)^2$

$$x^2 - 1 = (x + 1)(x - 1)$$

$$\text{LCM } (x^2 - 2x + 1, \ x^2 - 1) = (x - 1)^2 (x + 1)$$

C. Determine LCD $\left(\dfrac{5}{18} , \dfrac{7}{48} \right)$.

Then determine equivalent fractions with this LCD as denominator.

SOLUTION.

$$18 = 2 \cdot 3^2$$

$$48 = 2^4 \cdot 3$$

$$\text{LCM } (18, 48) = 2^4 \cdot 3^2 = 144$$

$$\text{LCD } \left(\dfrac{5}{18} , \dfrac{7}{48} \right) = 144$$

$$\dfrac{5}{18} = \dfrac{5 \cdot 8}{18 \cdot 8} = \dfrac{40}{144}$$

$$\dfrac{7}{48} = \dfrac{7 \cdot 3}{48 \cdot 3} = \dfrac{21}{144}$$

D. Determine LCD $\left(\dfrac{x}{x^2 - y^2} , \dfrac{-1}{2x + 2y} \right)$.

Then determine equivalent rational expressions with this LCD as denominator.

SOLUTION.

$$x^2 - y^2 = (x + y)(x - y)$$

$$2x + 2y = 2(x + y)$$

$$\text{LCM } (x^2 - y^2, \ 2x + 2y) = 2(x + y)(x - y)$$

$$\text{LCD } \left(\dfrac{x}{x^2 - y^2} , \dfrac{-1}{2x + 2y} \right) = 2(x + y)(x - y)$$

C.   (a) Determine the LCD of the indicated fractions.

      (b) Then determine equivalent fractions with this LCD as denominator.

11. $\dfrac{1}{8}$, $\dfrac{1}{12}$ (a) _____ (b) _____

12. $\dfrac{5}{16}$, $\dfrac{3}{40}$ (a) _____ (b) _____

13. $\dfrac{-5}{18}$, $\dfrac{2}{45}$ (a) _____ (b) _____

14. $\dfrac{3}{20}$, $\dfrac{1}{25}$, $\dfrac{7}{30}$ (a) _____ (b) _____

15. $\dfrac{5}{54}$, $\dfrac{-1}{72}$, $\dfrac{11}{144}$ (a) _____ (b) _____

D.   (a) Determine the LCD of the indicated rational expressions.

      (b) Then determine equivalent rational expressions with this LCD as denominator.

16. $\dfrac{a}{x}$, $\dfrac{b}{y}$ (a) _____ (b) _____

17. $\dfrac{1}{x-2}$, $\dfrac{2}{x-3}$ (a) _____ (b) _____

18. $\dfrac{2}{x^2-4}$, $\dfrac{x}{x^2+4x+4}$ (a) _____ (b) _____

19. $\dfrac{a}{xy^2}$, $\dfrac{-b}{x^2y}$, $\dfrac{ab}{x^2y^2}$ (a) _____ (b) _____

$$\frac{x}{x^2 - y^2} = \frac{x}{(x + y)(x - y)} \cdot \frac{\cdot\ 2}{\cdot\ 2} = \frac{2x}{2(x + y)(x - y)}$$

$$\frac{-1}{2x + 2y} = \frac{(-1)(x - y)}{2(x + y)(x - y)} = \frac{y - x}{2(x + y)(x - y)}$$

▶ 5.3   Addition and Subtraction (text page 151)

KEY TOPICS

A.   Combine, as indicated.

(a) $\dfrac{1}{4} + \dfrac{3}{4}$ (b) $\dfrac{5}{6} - \dfrac{1}{9}$ (c) $\dfrac{3}{25} + \dfrac{7}{50} - \dfrac{1}{20}$

SOLUTION.

(a) $\dfrac{1}{4} + \dfrac{3}{4} = \dfrac{1 + 3}{4} = \dfrac{4}{4} = 1$

(b) $6 = 2 \cdot 3$

$9 = 3^2$

$\text{LCD} \left(\dfrac{5}{6}, \dfrac{1}{9}\right) = \text{LCM } (6,\ 9) = 2 \cdot 3^2 = 18$

$\dfrac{5}{6} = \dfrac{5 \cdot 3}{6 \cdot 3} = \dfrac{15}{18}$

$\dfrac{1}{9} = \dfrac{1 \cdot 2}{9 \cdot 2} = \dfrac{2}{18}$

$\dfrac{5}{6} - \dfrac{1}{9} = \dfrac{15 - 2}{18} = \dfrac{13}{18}$

(c) $25 = 5^2$

$50 = 2 \cdot 5^2$

$20 = 2^2 \cdot 5$

$\text{LCD} \left(\dfrac{3}{25}, \dfrac{7}{50}, \dfrac{1}{20}\right) = \text{LCM } (25,\ 50,\ 20)$

$= 2^2 \cdot 5^2$

$= 100$

20. $\dfrac{2}{x^2 + 6x + 8}$, $\dfrac{x}{x^2 - 16}$, $\dfrac{-3x}{x^2 - 2x - 8}$ (a) _____

(b) _____

KEY EXERCISES

A.   Combine, as indicated.

1. $\dfrac{1}{2} + \dfrac{1}{2}$ _____

2. $\dfrac{1}{5} + \dfrac{3}{5}$ _____

3. $\dfrac{4}{7} - \dfrac{1}{7}$ _____

4. $\dfrac{5}{6} - \dfrac{1}{6} + \dfrac{7}{6}$ _____

5. $\dfrac{1}{2} + \dfrac{1}{4}$ _____

6. $\dfrac{3}{8} - \dfrac{1}{4}$ _____

7. $\dfrac{9}{10} - \dfrac{1}{5} + \dfrac{1}{2}$ _____

8. $\dfrac{1}{27} + \dfrac{4}{9} + \dfrac{1}{18}$ _____

9. $\dfrac{5}{64} - \left(\dfrac{3}{32} + \dfrac{1}{48} \right)$ _____

10. $\dfrac{7}{20} + \dfrac{3}{50} - \dfrac{9}{75}$ _____

$$\frac{3}{25} = \frac{3 \cdot 4}{25 \cdot 4} = \frac{12}{100}$$

$$\frac{7}{50} = \frac{7 \cdot 2}{50 \cdot 2} = \frac{14}{100}$$

$$\frac{1}{20} = \frac{1 \cdot 5}{20 \cdot 5} = \frac{5}{100}$$

$$\frac{3}{25} + \frac{7}{50} - \frac{1}{20} = \frac{12 + 14 - 5}{100} = \frac{21}{100}$$

B.   Combine, as indicated.

(a) $\dfrac{3}{x} + \dfrac{5}{x}$ 　　　　　　　　　　(b) $\dfrac{1}{a} - \dfrac{2}{b}$

(c) $\dfrac{1}{x^2 - a^2} + \dfrac{x}{x + a} - \dfrac{1}{x^2 + 2ax + a^2}$

SOLUTION.

(a) $\dfrac{3}{x} + \dfrac{5}{x} = \dfrac{3 + 5}{x} = \dfrac{8}{x}$

(b) LCD $\left(\dfrac{1}{a} , \dfrac{2}{b}\right)$ = LCM (a, b) = ab

$$\frac{1}{a} - \frac{2}{b} = \frac{1 \cdot b}{a \cdot b} - \frac{2 \cdot a}{b \cdot a} = \frac{b - 2a}{ab}$$

(c) $x^2 - a^2 = (x + a)(x - a)$

$x + a \quad = x + a$

$x^2 + 2ax + a^2 = (x + a)^2$

LCD $\left(\dfrac{1}{x^2 - a^2} , \dfrac{x}{x + a} , \dfrac{1}{x^2 + 2ax + a^2}\right) =$

　　　　LCM $(x^2 - a^2, x + a, x^2 + 2ax + a^2) =$

　　　　$(x + a)^2 (x - a)$

$\dfrac{1}{x^2 - a^2} + \dfrac{x}{x + a} - \dfrac{1}{x^2 + 2ax + a^2} =$

B.   Combine, as indicated.

11. $\dfrac{1}{x} + \dfrac{2}{x}$ _____

12. $\dfrac{4}{a} - \dfrac{3}{a}$ _____

13. $\dfrac{a}{y} + \dfrac{b}{y}$ _____

14. $\dfrac{a}{xy} + \dfrac{bc}{xy} - \dfrac{1}{xy}$ _____

15. $\dfrac{1}{x} + \dfrac{1}{y}$ _____

16. $\dfrac{1}{a} - \dfrac{2}{a^2}$ _____

17. $\dfrac{a}{x^2 y} + \dfrac{b}{xy^2}$ _____

18. $\dfrac{1}{x - a} + \dfrac{2}{x + a}$ _____

19. $\dfrac{1}{x^2 - 4} + \dfrac{1}{x + 2} - \dfrac{1}{x - 2}$ _____

20. $\dfrac{x}{x^2 + 6x + 9} + \dfrac{1}{x^2 - 9} + \dfrac{3}{x^2 - 6x + 9}$ _____

21. $\dfrac{1}{x^2 - 25} + \dfrac{1}{x^2 + x - 20} - \dfrac{1}{x^2 - 9x + 20}$ _____

22. $\dfrac{a}{x^3 - a^2 x} - \dfrac{1}{x^2 - ax} + \dfrac{1}{x + a}$ _____

$$\frac{1 \cdot (x + a)}{(x + a)(x - a) \cdot (x + a)} + \frac{x \cdot (x + a)(x - a)}{(x + a) \cdot (x + a)(x - a)} - \frac{1(x - a)}{(x + a)^2(x - a)}$$

$$= \frac{x + a + x^3 - a^2x - (x - a)}{(x + a)^2(x - a)}$$

$$= \frac{x^3 - a^2x + 2a}{(x + a)^2(x - a)}$$

▶ 5.4 Complex Expressions (text page 156)

KEY TOPICS

A.   Simplify:

(a) $\dfrac{\dfrac{3}{4}}{6}$

(b) $\dfrac{\dfrac{1}{4} - \dfrac{3}{8}}{\dfrac{1}{2} + \dfrac{1}{16}}$

SOLUTION.

(a) $\dfrac{\dfrac{3}{4}}{6} = \dfrac{3}{4} \div 6$

$$= \frac{3}{4} \cdot \frac{1}{\overset{6}{\underset{2}{\cancel{6}}}}$$

$$= \frac{1}{8}$$

(b) $\dfrac{\dfrac{1}{4} - \dfrac{3}{8}}{\dfrac{1}{2} + \dfrac{1}{16}} = \left(\dfrac{1}{4} - \dfrac{3}{8}\right) \div \left(\dfrac{1}{2} + \dfrac{1}{16}\right)$

$$= \frac{2 - 3}{8} \div \frac{8 + 1}{16}$$

$$= \frac{-1}{\underset{1}{\cancel{8}}} \cdot \frac{\overset{2}{\cancel{16}}}{9}$$

$$= \frac{-2}{9}$$

KEY EXERCISES

A.   Simplify:

1. $\dfrac{\frac{1}{2}}{4}$ _____

2. $\dfrac{3}{\frac{1}{6}}$ _____

3. $\dfrac{\frac{1}{2}}{\frac{1}{6}}$ _____

4. $\dfrac{\frac{-3}{4}}{\frac{1}{12}}$ _____

5. $\dfrac{1 + \frac{1}{2}}{1 - \frac{3}{4}}$ _____

6. $\dfrac{\frac{1}{2} + \frac{3}{4}}{\frac{1}{8} - \frac{1}{4}}$ _____

7. $\dfrac{\frac{1}{20} + \frac{1}{5}}{\frac{1}{10} - \frac{3}{20}}$ _____

8. $\dfrac{\frac{7}{12} - \frac{2}{3}}{\frac{1}{8} - \frac{3}{4}}$ _____

B.   Simplify:

(a) $\dfrac{\dfrac{a}{x}}{\dfrac{b}{x^2}}$

(b) $\dfrac{\dfrac{1}{x^2 + x} - \dfrac{1}{x^2}}{\dfrac{x}{x + 1} + \dfrac{1}{x}}$

SOLUTION.

(a) $\dfrac{\dfrac{a}{x}}{\dfrac{b}{x^2}} = \dfrac{a}{x} \div \dfrac{b}{x^2}$

$= \dfrac{a}{\cancel{x}} \cdot \dfrac{\cancel{x^2}^{\,x}}{b}$

$= \dfrac{ax}{b}$

(b) $\dfrac{\dfrac{1}{x^2 + x} - \dfrac{1}{x^2}}{\dfrac{x}{x + 1} + \dfrac{1}{x}} = \left(\dfrac{1}{x^2 + x} - \dfrac{1}{x^2}\right) \div \left(\dfrac{x}{x + 1} + \dfrac{1}{x}\right)$

$= \left(\dfrac{1}{x(x + 1)} - \dfrac{1}{x^2}\right) \div \left(\dfrac{x}{x + 1} + \dfrac{1}{x}\right)$

$= \dfrac{x - (x + 1)}{x^2(x + 1)} \div \dfrac{x^2 + (x + 1)}{x(x + 1)}$

$= \dfrac{-1}{\cancel{x^2}_{\,x}\,\cancel{(x + 1)}} \cdot \dfrac{\cancel{x}\cancel{(x + 1)}}{x^2 + x + 1}$

$= \dfrac{-1}{x(x^2 + x + 1)}$

B.   Simplify:

9. $\dfrac{\dfrac{x}{y}}{z}$ _____

10. $\dfrac{\dfrac{-a}{b}}{c}$ _____

11. $\dfrac{\dfrac{1}{x}}{\dfrac{1}{y}}$ _____

12. $\dfrac{\dfrac{a}{x^2}}{\dfrac{b}{x}}$ _____

13. $\dfrac{\dfrac{2ab}{x^2 y}}{\dfrac{4a^2 b}{xy^2}}$ _____

14. $\dfrac{\dfrac{1}{a} - \dfrac{1}{b}}{\dfrac{a}{b} - \dfrac{b}{a}}$ _____

15. $\dfrac{\dfrac{1}{x + 1} + \dfrac{1}{x - 1}}{\dfrac{1}{x^2 - 1}}$ _____

16. $\dfrac{\dfrac{1}{x^2 - 4} + \dfrac{1}{x + 2}}{\dfrac{1}{x - 2} - \dfrac{1}{x + 2}}$ _____

▶ 5.5   Calculating with Decimals (text page 160)

KEY TOPICS

A.   Add: .345
              .827
             .932

SOLUTION.

              .345
              .827
              .932
             2.104

B.   Subtract the bottom expression from the top one:

                      2.08xy
                      1.65xy

SOLUTION.

                      2.08xy
                     −1.65xy
                       .43xy

C.   Multiply: 4.28
                  1.02

SOLUTION.

                  4.28
                  1.02
                   856
                 4280
                4.3656

      Each factor has 2 decimal places. The product has 4 (= 2 + 2)
      decimal places.

D.   Determine $(.02)^3$.

SOLUTION.

              $(.02)^3$ = .000 008

      Here, .02 is a 2-placed decimal and the exponent is 3. The
      result is a 6-placed decimal (6 = 2 · 3).

KEY EXERCISES

A.   Add:

1. .8   2.   .538   3.   .62   4.   .23x
    .7   .491   1.4   .48x
                                    .953   .52x
                                    .01

B.   Subtract the bottom expression from the top one:

5.   .34   6.   .08   7.   −4.93   8. 1.94xy
     .12   .81   −3.77   2.49xy

C.   Multiply:

9.   75   10.   .023   11.   .414x
     1.1   .25   .09x^2

12. (.2) × (.5) × (.4) _____

D.   Determine each number:

13. $(.1)^4$ _____   14. $(.05)^3$ _____

15. $(.2)^2 + (.01)^2$ _____

16. $(.1)^2 − (.1)^3$ _____

E.   Evaluate $x^2 + 5x$ when $x = .1$.

SOLUTION.

Replace each occurrence of x by .1.

$$(.1)^2 + 5(.1) = .01 + .5$$
$$= .01 + .50$$
$$= .51$$

F.   Divide: $.17 \overline{) 1.02}$

SOLUTION.

$$.17. \overline{)\overset{\textstyle 6.}{1.02.}}$$
$$\underline{1\ 02}$$

The quotient is 6.

E. Evaluate each polynomial for the specified values of the variables.

17. 5x + 2   [x = .2] _____

18. $x^2 + x$ [x = .1] _____

19. $2xy + y^2$ [x = .1, y = .2] _____

20. $s^2 + 4st - 2t^2$ [s = .01, t = .1] _____

F. Divide:

21. $.2\overline{)4.48}$ 22. $.002\overline{)4848}$ 23. $.23\overline{).0046}$

24. $7.04\overline{).352}$

CHAPTER 6

FIRST-DEGREE EQUATIONS

▶ 6.1   Roots of Equations (text page 169)

KEY TOPICS

A.   (a) $4 + 3 = 9 - 2$

is a true statement involving only constants.

(b) $5x = 10$

is a first-degree equation in a single variable.

B.   (a) 5 is a root of

$$2x + 3 = 13$$

because

$$2 \cdot 5 + 3 = 13.$$

(b) 4 is not a root of

$$\frac{1}{x} = 4$$

because

$$\frac{1}{4} \neq 4.$$

(c) $\frac{1}{3}$ is a root of $\frac{1}{x} = 3$ because

$$\frac{1}{\frac{1}{3}} = 1 \div \frac{1}{3} = 1 \cdot 3 = 3.$$

44 LEFT

KEY EXERCISES

A. Does the given statement involve only constants?

    (i) If so, is it true or false?

    (ii) If not, is it a first-degree equation in a single variable?

1. $9 - 6 = 1 + 2$ (i) _____ (ii) _____

2. $x + 1 = 3x - 2$ (i) _____ (ii) _____

3. $5 + 4 = 2 \cdot 5$ (i) _____ (ii) _____

4. $y = x + 1$ (i) _____ (ii) _____

5. $x^2 = 4$ (i) _____ (ii) _____

B. Check whether the number in the box is a root of the given equation.

6. $x + 4 = 9$ $\boxed{5}$ _____

7. $3y = 12$ $\boxed{4}$ _____

8. $2x - 9 = x + 2$ $\boxed{10}$ _____

9. $\dfrac{1}{x} = 4x$ $\boxed{\dfrac{1}{2}}$ _____

10. $\dfrac{x + 1}{3} - 1 = 0$ $\boxed{2}$ _____

11. $\dfrac{1}{2t} = 1$ $\boxed{\dfrac{1}{2}}$ _____

12. $\dfrac{1}{x} = 0$ $\boxed{0}$ _____

13. $\dfrac{1}{x} = -1$ $\boxed{-1}$ _____

▶ 6.2   Solving Equations (text page 173)

KEY TOPICS

A.   Solve each equation.

   (a)   x – 4 = 9

   (b)   3x + 1 = 10

   (c)   (3x + 5) – (2x – 1) = 10

SOLUTION.

   (a)   x – 4 = 9   Add 4 to both sides.

         x   = 13

   (b)   3x + 1 = 10   First subtract 1 from both sides.

         3x   = 9   Now divide both sides by 3.

         x   = 3

   (c)   (3x + 5) – (2x – 1) = 10   First remove parentheses.

         3x + 5 – 2x + 1   = 10   Simplify the left side.

              x + 6   = 10   Subtract 6 from both sides.

                x   = 4

B.   Solve and check.

                 5(y – 2) = –25

SOLUTION.

           5(y – 2) = –25   First remove parentheses.

           5y – 10 = –25   Add 10 to both sides.

               5y   = –15   Divide both sides by 5.

               y   = –3

14. $5z = z$ $\boxed{\dfrac{1}{5}}$ _____

15. $\dfrac{1}{x} - \dfrac{1}{2} = 0$ $\boxed{\dfrac{1}{2}}$ _____

KEY EXERCISES

A. Solve each equation.

1. $2x = 16$ _____ 2. $x + 3 = 8$ _____

3. $x - 5 = -4$ _____ 4. $\dfrac{x}{2} = 6$ _____

5. $2t + 1 = 5$ _____ 6. $\dfrac{u}{3} - 1 = 3$ _____

7. $2y - 3 = 5y + 12$ _____

8. $z - (2z - 1) = 4$ _____

9. $2(x + 1) + 3(x - 2) = 11$ _____

10. $2x + 1 = \dfrac{1}{3}$ _____

11. $4 - [2 - (x - 1)] = 3$ _____

12. $(x + 5)(x + 2) = x(x - 2)$ _____

B. Solve and check.

13. $2x + 9 = 17$ _____ 14. $\dfrac{x}{5} = -4$ _____

15. $3x - 2 = 5x + 4$ _____ 16. $\dfrac{x + 3}{6} = \dfrac{1}{3}$ _____

CHECK:

$$5(-3 - 2) \overset{?}{=} -25$$

$$5(-5) \overset{?}{=} -25$$

$$-25 \overset{\checkmark}{=} -25$$

▶ 6.3   Equations with Rational Expressions (text page 179)

KEY TOPICS

A.   Solve each equation.

(a) $\dfrac{x}{2} = \dfrac{x + 6}{4}$

(b) $\dfrac{y}{4} - \dfrac{y}{6} = \dfrac{y - 4}{2} - 3$

(c) $\dfrac{3}{x - 2} + \dfrac{7}{x + 2} = \dfrac{2}{x^2 - 4}$

SOLUTION.

(a) $\dfrac{x}{2} = \dfrac{x + 6}{4}$ First cross-multiply.

$4x = 2x + 12$

$2x = 12$

$x = 6$

(b) LCD $\left[\dfrac{y}{4} , \dfrac{y}{6} , \dfrac{y - 4}{2} , 3 \right] = 12$

$\dfrac{y}{4} - \dfrac{y}{6} = \dfrac{y - 4}{2} - 3$ First multiply both sides by 12.

$3y - 2y = 6y - 24 - 36$

$y = 6y - 60$

$60 = 5y$

$12 = y$

CHECKS:

13.   14.

15.   16.

KEY EXERCISES

A.   Solve each equation.

1. $\dfrac{2y}{12} = \dfrac{1}{2}$ _____   2. $\dfrac{4}{x} = \dfrac{8}{3}$ _____

3. $\dfrac{x + 1}{5} = \dfrac{x - 3}{3}$ _____

4. $\dfrac{2x + 1}{3} = \dfrac{x + 3}{2}$ _____

5. $\dfrac{x - 4}{2} + \dfrac{3x + 4}{4} = \dfrac{3x - 4}{4}$ _____

6. $\dfrac{t - 1}{3} + \dfrac{t + 1}{4} = \dfrac{t + 5}{6} + \dfrac{t - 3}{2}$ _____

7. $\dfrac{24}{x} = -3$ _____   8. $\dfrac{3}{1 - x} = \dfrac{1}{2}$ _____

9. $\dfrac{5y}{y + 1} = 4$ _____   10. $\dfrac{u}{u + 3} = \dfrac{4}{7}$ _____

11. $\dfrac{3}{x} + \dfrac{4}{x - 2} = \dfrac{78}{x^2 - 2x}$ _____

12. $\dfrac{6}{x - 1} + \dfrac{9}{x + 1} = \dfrac{27}{x^2 - 1}$ _____

(c) $x^2 - 4 = (x + 2)(x - 2)$

$$\text{LCD} \left[\frac{3}{x - 2} , \frac{7}{x + 2} , \frac{2}{x^2 - 4} \right] = (x + 2)(x - 2)$$

$$\left[\frac{3}{x - 2} + \frac{7}{x + 2} \right] (x + 2)(x - 2) = \frac{2}{x^2 - 4} (x + 2)(x - 2)$$

$$3(x + 2) + 7(x - 2) = 2$$
$$3x + 6 + 7x - 14 \quad = 2$$
$$10x - 8 \quad = 2$$
$$10x \quad = 10$$
$$x \quad = 1$$

B.   Solve and check:

$$\frac{4t - 2}{5} + \frac{7t - 3}{6} = \frac{t + 1}{2} + t$$

SOLUTION.

$$\text{LCD} \left[\frac{4t - 2}{5} , \frac{7t - 3}{6} , \frac{t + 1}{2} , t \right] = 30$$

$$30 \left[\frac{4t - 2}{5} + \frac{7t - 3}{6} \right] = 30 \left[\frac{t + 1}{2} + t \right]$$

$$6(4t - 2) + 5(7t - 3) = 15(t + 1) + 30t$$

$$24t - 12 + 35t - 15 \quad = 15t + 15 + 30t$$

$$59t - 27 \quad = 45t + 15$$

$$14t \quad = 42$$

$$t \quad = 3$$

CHECK:

$$\frac{4 \cdot 3 - 2}{5} + \frac{7 \cdot 3 - 3}{6} \overset{?}{=} \frac{3 + 1}{2} + 3$$

$$2 \quad + \quad 3 \quad \overset{\checkmark}{=} \quad 2 \quad + 3$$

B.   Solve and check.

13. $\dfrac{x + 2}{3} = \dfrac{x - 2}{2}$ _____   14. $\dfrac{1}{t + 2} = \dfrac{3}{4}$ _____

15. $\dfrac{y}{y + 2} = \dfrac{2}{3}$ _____   16. $\dfrac{1}{x} + \dfrac{1}{2x} = 3$ _____

CHECKS:

13.   14.

15.   16.

KEY TOPICS

A.   Assume a and b are constants. Solve for x and check the
result.

$$ax - 3 = bx + 2$$

SOLUTION.

$$ax - 3 = bx + 2 \qquad \text{First add } 3 - bx \text{ to both sides.}$$

$$ax - bx = 5$$

$$(a - b)x = 5$$

$$x = \frac{5}{a - b}$$

CHECK:

$$a\left(\frac{5}{a - b}\right) - 3 \stackrel{?}{=} b\left(\frac{5}{a - b}\right) + 2$$

$$\frac{5a - 3(a - b)}{a - b} \stackrel{?}{=} \frac{5b + 2(a - b)}{a - b}$$

$$\frac{2a + 3b}{a - b} \stackrel{\checkmark}{=} \frac{3b + 2a}{a - b}$$

B.   Solve $4x + y = \dfrac{1}{t}$ (a) for x, (b) for t.

SOLUTION.

(a) $4x + y = \dfrac{1}{t}$

$4x \quad = \dfrac{1}{t} - y$

(b) $4x + y = \dfrac{1}{t}$

$t = \dfrac{1}{4x + y}$

KEY EXERCISES

Assume a, b, c are constants.

A.   Solve for x and check your result.

1. $10x = 3a$ _____   2. $5x - 2b = 4x + 1$ _____

3. $\dfrac{x + 1 - a}{b} = 4c$ _____

4. $4x - (2x + a) = 3a - b$ _____

5. $\dfrac{5 - a}{2x} = c$ _____   6. $\dfrac{2x - 3}{a + 2} = bx$ _____

CHECKS:

1.   2.

3.   4.

5.   6.

B.

7. Solve $2x - 3t = 1$

   (a) for x, _____   (b) for t. _____

8. Solve $5x - 3y + 4z = 10$

   (a) for x, _____   (b) for y. _____

$$4x = \frac{1 - yt}{t}$$

$$x = \frac{1 - yt}{4t}$$

C. Solve $x = \dfrac{2 - ar}{5 - r}$ for r.

SOLUTION.

$$x = \frac{2 - ar}{5 - r}$$

$$(5 - r)x = 2 - ar$$

$5x - rx = 2 - ar$ Bring terms containing r to the left, all other terms to the right.

$ar - rx = 2 - 5x$ Factor the left side.

$$r(a - x) = 2 - 5x$$

$$r = \frac{2 - 5x}{a - x} \ , \ \text{if } a \neq x$$

▶ 6.5 Other Types of Equations (text page 189)

KEY TOPICS

A. (a) The equation

$$|x| = 5$$

has 2 roots: 5 and −5 .

(b) The equation

$$x^2 = 9$$

has 2 roots: 3 and −3 .

9. Solve $2x - 5y = \dfrac{4}{t}$

    (a) for y, _____ (b) for t. _____

10. Solve $\dfrac{x + a}{y + b} = \dfrac{1}{t - c}$

    (a) for x, _____ (b) for t. _____

11. Solve $2x + xy + a = 3cy$

    (a) for x, _____ (b) for y. _____

12. Solve $2y + zy = 3z - 2$

    (a) for y, _____ (b) for z. _____

C.

13. Solve $\dfrac{a + x}{4 - 3x} = 1$ for x. _____

14. Solve $\dfrac{a + 2t}{1 - t} = -1$ for t. _____

15. Solve $\dfrac{u^2 + au}{u - 1} = u + 2$ for u. _____

16. Solve $\dfrac{1}{x} + \dfrac{1}{a} = \dfrac{1}{b}$ for x. _____

KEY EXERCISES

A.   Determine the number of (real) roots of the given equation.

1. $4x + 7 = 5 - 3x$ _____

2. $y^2 - 16 = 0$ _____

3. $t^2 + 16 = 0$ _____ 4. $x^2 = 0$ _____

5. $|x| = 7$ _____ 6. $|x| + 7 = 0$ _____

7. $|x| = 0$ _____

8. $(x - 2)(x - 3)(x + 4)(x + 5) = 0$ _____

(c) The equation

$$x^2 = -4$$

has no (real) root because the square of a real number is nonnegative.

(d) The equation

$$(x - 1)(x - 2)(x + 3) = 0$$

has 3 roots: 1, 2, and -3 .

B. $$2x + 8 = 6 + 2x$$

has no solution.   To see this, subtract 2x from both sides: You obtain

$$8 \overset{?}{=} 6 ,$$

which is false.

C. $$7x - 4 = 3(2x - 1) - (1 - x)$$

is an identity.   When you simplify this equation, you obtain

$$7x - 4 \overset{?}{=} 7x - 4$$

and

$$-4 \overset{\checkmark}{=} -4$$

Every real number is a root of the given equation.

B.   Show that each of these equations has no solution.

9. $5x - 3 = 5x + 3$ 10. $t(t - 2) = (t - 1)^2$

11. $4u - [3 - (2u + 5)] = 3u - (7 - 3u)$

C.   Show that each of these equations is an identity.

12. $5u + 5(u - 3) = 7(u - 2) + 3u - 1$

13. $(y + 2)(y + 3) - 3 = y(y + 5) + 3$

D.   (a) $3x + 1 = 10$

has a single root, 3.

(b) $x + 1 = x + 2$

has no root.

(c) $(z + 1)(z + 2) = z^2 + 3z + 2$

is an identity.

14. $(x + 1)^2 - (x - 1)^2 = 4x$

D. Determine (a) which equations have a single root, (b) which
    have no root, (c) which are identities.

15. $(x + 1)^2 = (x + 2)^2$ _____

16. $(x + 3)^2 - 9 = x(x + 6)$ _____

17. $(x + 4)^2 = x(x + 8)$ _____

18. $\dfrac{4x + 1}{4} + 5 = x - 5$ _____

CHAPTER 7

WORD PROBLEMS

▶ 7.1   Integer and Age Problems (text page 196)

KEY TOPICS

A.

(a)   Let x be an integer. The next consecutive integer is x + 1.

(b)   Suppose y is an odd integer. The next consecutive odd integer is y + 2.

(c)   Suppose z is an integer. Five more than twice this integer is 2z + 5.

B.   One-third of an integer plus half the next consecutive integer equals 23. Determine the integers.

SOLUTION.

Let x be the smaller integer. Then x + 1 is the next consecutive integer. Translate the problem.

One-third of an integer plus half the next consecutive integer equals 23.

$$\frac{x}{3} + \frac{(x + 1)}{2} = 23$$

Solve the equation. First multiply both sides by 6, which is LCD $\left(\frac{x}{3} , \frac{x + 1}{2} \right)$.

KEY EXERCISES

A.

1. Suppose x is an integer. What are the next 3 consecutive
    integers?

    _____

2. Suppose y is an <u>even</u> integer. What are the next 2
    consecutive <u>even</u> integers?

    _____

3. Suppose t is an integer. Express 3 more than twice this
    integer.

    _____

4. Suppose n is an integer. Express three times two more than
    this integer.

    _____

5. Suppose s is an <u>even</u> integer. Express the sum of s and the
    next 2 consecutive <u>even</u> integers.

    _____

B.

6. Determine three consecutive integers whose sum is 33.

    _____

7. Determine three consecutive <u>odd</u> integers whose sum
    is 33.

    _____

8. Five less than four times an integer is 19. Determine this
    integer.

    _____

9. One-third of an integer plus one-fifth of the next consecutive
    integer equals 5. Determine these integers.

    _____

$$2x + 3(x + 1) = 138$$

$$2x + 3x + 3 = 138$$

$$5x = 135$$

$$x = 27$$

$$x + 1 = 28$$

The integers are 27 and 28.

C.   Let x be a man's age <u>now</u>. <u>Three years ago</u> his age was $x - 3$. <u>In five years</u> his age will be $x + 5$. His wife is 4 years younger than he is. Her <u>present age</u> is $x - 4$.

D.   Frank is 4 years older than Stan. Four years ago, Stan was $\frac{3}{4}$ as old as Frank. How old is Frank?

SOLUTION.

     Let x be Frank's age.
     Thus $x - 4$ is Stan's age.
     Four years ago, Frank's age was $x - 4$.
     Four years ago, Stan's age was $(x - 4) - 4$, or $x - 8$.
     Reword the problem.

Four years ago, Stan's age was $\frac{3}{4}$ Frank's age (four years ago).

$$x - 8 \quad = \quad \frac{3}{4} \quad (x - 4)$$

Solve the equation.

$$4(x - 8) = 3(x - 4)$$

$$4x - 32 = 3x - 12$$

$$x = 20$$

Frank is now 20 years old.

10. The sum of two integers is 48. The larger is 8 more than the smaller. Determine these integers.

_____

C. Suppose x is a woman's age now.

11. What will her age be in 5 years? _____

12. What was her age 10 years ago? _____

13. Suppose her son is half as old as she is. What is her son's age?

_____

14. Four years ago her daughter was $\frac{1}{3}$ as old as the mother. What is the daughter's age now?

_____

D.

15. A man is three times as old as his son. Five years ago he was five times as old as his son. How old is the man?

_____

16. A husband is six years older than his wife. Sixteen years ago he was twice her age. How old is the husband?

_____

17. Sam is three years younger than his brother. In four years he will be three-fourths as old as his brother. How old is Sam?

_____

KEY TOPICS

A.   (a)   A dime is worth 10 cents.
              6 dimes are worth 60 cents.

        (b)   A nickel is worth 5 cents.
              x nickels are worth 5x cents.

        (c)   A quarter is worth 25 cents.   x + 3 quarters are worth
              25(x + 3) cents.

B.   Bill has 8 more nickels than dimes and 2 less dimes than
        quarters. Altogether his coins are worth $2.50 .   How many
        of each coin does he have?

SOLUTION.

        Let x be the number of dimes. Then x + 8 is the number of
        nickels. Note that Bill has 2 <u>more</u> quarters than dimes.
        Thus x + 2 is the number of quarters.

                   Cents per Coin • Number of Coins = Total Amount in Cents

dimes	10	x	10x
nickels	5	x + 8	5(x + 8)
quarters	25	x + 2	25(x + 2)

        The value of dimes, nickels, and quarters equals 250 (cents).

$$10x + 5(x + 8) + 25(x + 2) \quad = \quad 250$$
$$10x + 5x + 40 + 25x + 50 \quad = \quad 250$$
$$40x + 90 \quad = \quad 250$$
$$40x \quad = \quad 160$$
$$x \quad = \quad 4$$
$$x + 8 \quad = \quad 12$$
$$x + 2 \quad = \quad 6$$

        Bill has 4 dimes, 12 nickels, and 6 quarters.

KEY EXERCISES

A.

1. Find the value of 8 nickels, 3 dimes and 2 quarters. _____

2. Joe has two more dimes than nickels. Suppose he has x nickels. Express the value of his coins in terms of x.

    _____

3. Marie has twice as many dimes as quarters. Suppose she has x quarters. Express the value of her coins in terms of x.

    _____

B.

4. Amy has three times as many dimes as quarters. Altogether she has $5.50 in these coins. How many quarters does she have?

    _____

5. Jose has two more pennies than nickels, and twice as many nickels as dimes. Altogether he has $2.22. How many pennies does he have?

    _____

6. Brenda has the same number of nickels as dimes. If she had two more dimes and two fewer nickels, she would have a dollar. How many nickels does she have?

    _____

C.   (a)   Chocolate sells for 70 cents per pound.
            4 pounds of chocolate cost 4 · 70 cents, or $2.80 .

     (b)   Peppermints sell for 60 cents per pound.
            x pounds of peppermints sell for 60x cents.

    (2x + 1) pounds of peppermint sell for 60(2x + 1) cents.

D.   Coffee at 90 cents per pound is blended with coffee at $1.30 per pound. How much of each must be used to make 60 pounds of a mixture at $1.20 per pound?

SOLUTION.

    Let x be the number of pounds of the 90 cents per pound coffee. Then (60 − x) pounds of the $1.30 per pound coffee must be used.

	Cents per Pound ·	Number of Pounds =	Total Amount in Cents
90¢ per pound coffee	90	x	90x
$1.30 per pound coffee	130	60 − x	130(60 − x)
Mixture ($1.20 per pound)	120	60	7200

The value of the 90¢ per pound coffee	+	the value of the $1.30 per pound coffee	=	the value of the mixture.
90x	+	130(60 − x)	=	7200
90x	+	7800 − 130x	=	7200
		600	=	40x
		15	=	x
		45	=	60 − x

15 pounds of the 90¢ per pound coffee and 45 pounds of the $1.30 per pound coffee must be used.

C.

7. Potatoes sell for 28 cents per pound.

   (a) How much do 6 pounds of potatoes cost? _____

   (b) How much do x pounds of potatoes cost? _____

8. Peaches sell for 45 cents per pound and plums for 40 cents per pound. Sara buys 6 pounds of peaches and plums altogether. If she buys x pounds of peaches, express the cost of her purchase in terms of x.

   _____

D.

9. A store buys melons for 50 cents apiece, and sells them for 79 cents each. One melon spoils. If a profit of $5.30 is made on the remaining melons, how many melons did the store purchase?

   _____

10. Ten pounds of coffee at $1.00 per pound are blended with coffee at $1.30 per pound. How many pounds of the more expensive coffee must be used if the mixture is to sell at $1.18 per pound?

    _____

11. Eight pounds of almonds at 90 cents per pound are mixed with 12 pounds of filberts at $1.00 per pound. What should be the price of the mixture?

    _____

KEY TOPICS

A.   Rate • time = Distance

      r • t   =   d

   (a)   A car travels at the constant rate of 50 miles per hour.
         In 4 hours it travels

$$4 \cdot 50 \text{ miles,}$$

   or 200 miles.

   (b)   A train traveling at a constant rate covers 600 miles
         in 8 hours. Its rate is

$$\frac{600}{8} \text{ miles per hour,}$$

   or 75 miles per hour.

   (c)   A bicycle travels at the constant rate of 12 miles per
         hour. In t hours it goes

$$12t \text{ miles.}$$

   In (t + 3) hours it goes

$$12(t + 3) \text{ miles.}$$

B.   Two cars leave a gas station at the same time traveling along
      a straight road in opposite directions. One car leaves an
      hour earlier than the other and travels at the constant rate
      of 55 miles per hour. The second car goes at the constant
      rate of 60 miles per hour. How many hours after the second
      car leaves are they 515 miles apart?

SOLUTION.

   Let t be the time (in hours) the second car travels. Then
   the first car travels for (t + 1) hours.

	r	•	t	=	d
First car	55		t + 1		55(t + 1)
Second car	60		t		60t

The cars travel in <u>opposite</u> directions.

KEY EXERCISES

(All rates are <u>constant</u>.)

A.

1.   Joe walks $10\frac{1}{2}$ miles in 3 hours. How fast is he walking?

_____

2.   An airplane traveling at the rate of 450 miles per hour covers a distance of 1800 miles. How many hours does it travel?

_____

3.   (a) Bob drives for t hours at the rate of 60 miles per hour. How many miles does he cover?

_____

    (b) Ralph leaves 2 hours after Bob and drives at the rate of 70 miles per hour. If he stops at the same time Bob does, how many miles does he cover?

_____

B.

4.   An automobile travels for 2 hours at the rate of 50 miles per hour. It then speeds up to 65 miles per hour (traveling in the same direction) for 3 hours. How far has it traveled?

_____

5.   Two joggers leave a spot at the same time going in the same direction along a straight trail. One jogs at the rate of 8 miles per hour, the other at the rate of 6 miles per hour. How far apart are they after 45 minutes?

_____

The distance the first car travels	+	the distance the second car travels	=	their distance apart.
$55(t + 1)$	+	$60t$	=	515
		$115t + 55$	=	515
		$115t$	=	460
		t	=	4

The cars are 515 miles apart 4 hours after the second car leaves.

▶ 7.4   Interest Problems (text page 211)

KEY TOPICS

A.   Percent means hundredths.

    (a) $12\% = .12$

    (b) $5\% = .05$

    (c) $\frac{1}{2}\% = \frac{.01}{2} = \frac{.010}{2} = .005$

    (d) $7\frac{1}{2}\% = 7\% + \frac{1}{2}\%$

            $= .07 + .005$

            $= .075$

    (e)   6% of $400

        means multiply:

        6% × $400

$$
\begin{array}{r}
400 \\
.06 \\
\hline
24.00
\end{array}
$$

        Thus 6% of $400 is $24.

B.   The interest earned for one year is given by the formula:

$$\text{RATE} \cdot \text{PRINCIPAL} = \text{INTEREST}$$

$$R \cdot P = I$$

6. Two cars approach one another along a straight highway. They start out at the same time from points 195 miles apart. One travels at the rate of 60 miles per hour, the other at the rate of 70 miles per hour. How far has the slower car gone when they pass each other?

_____

7. A canoe goes upstream at the rate of 8 miles per hour. It returns downstream at the rate of 12 miles per hour. If the round trip takes 5 hours, how far upstream does it go?

_____

KEY EXERCISES

A.

1. Write as a decimal:

   (a) 14% _____   (b) 9% _____   (c) 40% _____

2. Write as a decimal:

   (a) $\frac{1}{2}$% _____   (b) $5\frac{1}{2}$% _____   (c) $5\frac{1}{4}$% _____

3. Convert the following to percent:

   (a) .07 _____   (b) .19 _____   (c) .065 _____

4. Find 5% of $800. _____

5. Find $10\frac{1}{2}$% of $620. _____

B.

6. $500 is invested for one year at 6%. How much interest is earned?

_____

(a) $200 invested for one year at 7% earns

.07(200) dollars,

or 14 dollars.

(b) x dollars invested for one year at 8% earns

.08x dollars.

(c) (2000 - x) dollars invested for one year at $7\frac{1}{2}\%$ earns

.075(2000 - x) dollars.

C. Part of a sum of $6000 is invested at 8% and the remainder is invested in 6% tax-free bonds. The combined annual interest from these investments is $418. How much is invested at 8%?

SOLUTION.

Let x be the amount invested at 8%. Then 6000 - x is the amount invested at 6%.

	R	·	P	=	I
at 8%	.08		x		.08x
at 6%	.06		6000 - x		.06(6000 - x)

The combined annual interest is $408.

.08 + .06(6000 - x) = 408

To eliminate decimals multiply both sides by 100.

$$8x + 6(6000 - x) = 40\ 800$$

$$2x + 36\ 000 = 40\ 800$$

$$2x = 4800$$

$$x = 2400$$

$2400 is invested at 8% (and $3600 at 6%).

7. Suppose that x dollars is invested at 9% interest and (4000 - x) dollars is invested at 8%. How much is earned in a year from these two investments?

_____

8. $238 interest is earned in a year from a single investment of $3400. What is the annual interest rate?

_____

C.

9. A sum of $4800 is left for 2 years in a bank that pays 6% interest annually. How much interest is earned?

_____

10. Part of a sum of $8000 is invested at 7.5% and the remainder at 9%. The combined annual interest from these investments is $645. How much is invested at 7.5%?

_____

11. A man invests $1000 more at 8% than at 7%, and receives an annual interest income from these investments of $380. How much is invested at 8%?

_____

12. A man invests $1000 more at 9% than at 6%. He earns the same as if the entire amount was invested at 8%. How much did he invest at 6%?

_____

▶ 7.5   Mixture Problems (text page 214)

KEY TOPICS

A.   Fraction of the   .   Amount of   =   Amount of Substance
      Substance   Mixture

   (a)   In 5 gallons of a 16% salt solution there are

                    .16 (5) gallons of salt,

         or .8 gallons of salt.

   (b)   If an alloy is 40% gold, in x ounces of the alloy
         there are

                    .4x ounces of gold.

   (c)   If an alloy is 1 part copper to 4 parts tin, then

              $\frac{1}{1 + 4}$, or $\frac{1}{5}$ of the alloy is copper.

         In 10 pounds of the alloy there are

         $\frac{1}{5}$ · 10 pounds of copper, or 2 pounds of copper.

B.   How many pounds of an alloy containing 50% silver must be
      added to 60 pounds of an alloy containing 40% silver to
      obtain an alloy containing 42% silver?

SOLUTION.

      Here silver is the substance. Let x be the number of pounds
      of the 50% alloy.

	Fraction of Silver	.	Pounds of Alloy	=	Pounds of Silver
50% alloy	.50		x		.50x
40% alloy	.40		60		24
42% alloy	.42		x + 60		.42(x + 60)

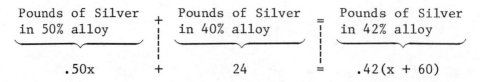

Pounds of Silver in 50% alloy	+	Pounds of Silver in 40% alloy	=	Pounds of Silver in 42% alloy
.50x	+	24	=	.42(x + 60)

KEY EXERCISES

A.

1.   If an alloy is 60% copper, how much copper is there in 20 pounds of the alloy?

2.   If a solution is $\frac{1}{4}$ alcohol, how much alcohol is there in x gallons of the solution?

_____

3.   If 5 gallons of a 12% salt solution are added to 10 gallons of a 10% salt solution, how many gallons of salt are there in the mixture?

_____

B.

4.   How many gallons of a 12% salt solution must be combined with 20 gallons of an 18% salt solution to obtain a 16% solution?

_____

5.   How much pure alcohol must be added to 12 gallons of a 40% alcohol solution to obtain a 60% solution?

_____

6.   How many pounds of an alloy containing 20% platinum must be melted with an alloy containing 30% platinum to obtain 10 pounds of an alloy containing 22% platinum?

_____

7.   Alloy A is 1 part zinc to 1 part copper. Alloy B is 1 part zinc to 3 parts copper. How much of each alloy should be used to make 100 tons of an alloy that is 2 parts zinc to 3 parts copper?

_____

59 RIGHT

Multiply both sides by 100 to eliminate decimals.

$$50x \quad + \quad 2400 \quad = \quad 42(x + 60)$$
$$50x \quad + \quad 2400 \quad = \quad 42x + 2520$$
$$8x \quad = \quad 120$$
$$x \quad = \quad 15$$

15 pounds of the 50% alloy must be used.

▶ 7.6   Work Problems (text page 217)

KEY TOPICS

A.   Fraction of Work • Time = Fraction of Work done in 1 time unit

(a)   A man can paint a room in 3 hours. In 1 hour he paints $\frac{1}{3}$ of the room. In 2 hours he paints

$$\frac{1}{3} \cdot 2,$$

or $\frac{2}{3}$ of the room.

(b)   A secretary stuffs a batch of envelopes in 5 hours. In x hours she completes

$$\frac{x}{5}$$

of the job.

(c)   Let x be the number of hours it takes Bill to do a job. In 1 hour Bill does $\frac{1}{x}$ of the job. In 3 hours he does

$$\frac{1}{x} \cdot 3,$$

or $\frac{3}{x}$ of the job.

KEY EXERCISES

A.

1. A student can do his homework in 4 hours. What part of the homework can be completed in an hour and a half?

   _____

2. A lawyer prepares a brief in 6 hours. In x hours, what part of the work is done?

   _____

3. It takes Alice x hours to memorize her part in a play. How much of her part does she memorize in 2 hours?

   _____

B.   Fred can mow a lawn in 6 hours. It takes Tom 8 hours to complete this task. How long does it take these men to do the work together?

SOLUTION.

Let x be the number of hours to mow the lawn together. In 1 hour Fred does $\frac{1}{6}$ of the job and Tom does $\frac{1}{8}$ of the job.

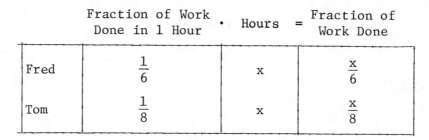

	Fraction of Work Done in 1 Hour	Hours	Fraction of Work Done
Fred	$\frac{1}{6}$	x	$\frac{x}{6}$
Tom	$\frac{1}{8}$	x	$\frac{x}{8}$

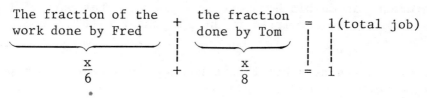

The fraction of the work done by Fred $+$ the fraction done by Tom $=$ 1(total job)

$$\frac{x}{6} \quad + \quad \frac{x}{8} \quad = \quad 1$$

Multiply both sides by the LCD, 24.

$$4x \quad + \quad 3x \quad = \quad 24$$
$$7x \quad = \quad 24$$
$$x \quad = \quad \frac{24}{7}$$

It takes $\frac{24}{7}$ hours (about 3 hours and 26 minutes) to complete the work together.

B.

4. Janet can paint her apartment in 4 days. It takes her son Jim 8 days to do this work. How long does it take them if they work together?

_____

5. Two soldiers clean up their barracks together in 6 hours. One works twice as fast as the other. How long does it take the slower one to do the work alone?

_____

6. Three men paint a house together. Working separately, one can complete the painting in 3 days, one in 4 days, and one in 6 days. How long does it take them to paint the house together?

_____

7. The hot water faucet fills a tub in 15 minutes. The cold water faucet fills the tub in 10 minutes. How long does it take for both faucets to fill the tub?

_____

CHAPTER 8

FUNCTIONS AND GRAPHS

▶ 8.1   Sets and Functions (text page 222)

KEY TOPICS

A.   Use braces to indicate the set consisting of the first
      seven even positive integers.

SOLUTION.

{2, 4, 6, 8, 10, 12, 14}

B.   Which of these correspondences represents functions?

(a) 1 → 4   (b) 1 ────→ 1   (c) 1 ◄──── 1

     2 → 3   2   2

     3 → 4   3   3

     4 → 3   4   4

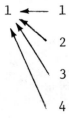

SOLUTION.

(a) and (b). Note that (c) does not represent a function
because more than one number of the range corresponds to
the number 1 of the domain.

KEY EXERCISES

A.   Use braces to indicate each set.

1.   The set consisting of Joe, Barry and Alex. _____

2.   The set consisting of Greenland, Alaska, Canada, and Mexico.

                              _____

3.   The set consisting of the first five <u>odd</u> positive integers.

                                       _____

4.   The set consisting of all <u>even</u> positive integers less than 21.

                              _____

B.   Which of these correspondences represent functions?

5.   1 → 1   _____   6.   1 → 6   _____

       2 → 2   2 → 5

       3 → 3   3 → 4

       4 → 4   4 → 3

       5 → 5   5 → 2

                                          6 → 1

7.   1 → 8   _____   8.   7 → 1   _____
                                            ↘
       2 → 7   2

       3 → 8   8 → 3
                                            ↘
       4 → 7   4

C.   Determine   i. the domain and   ii. the range of each function.

(a) $5 \rightarrow 1$ (b) $1 \rightarrow 1$

$10 \rightarrow 2$ $2 \rightarrow 2$

$15 \rightarrow 3$ $3 \rightarrow 1$

$20 \rightarrow 4$ $4 \rightarrow 2$

$5 \rightarrow 1$

SOLUTION.

(a) i . $\{5, 10, 15, 20\}$, ii . $\{1, 2, 3, 4\}$

(b) i . $\{1, 2, 3, 4, 5\}$, ii . $\{1, 2\}$

9. 11 → 2 _____

12 → 1

13 → 2

14 → 4

10. 11 → 1 _____

12 → 5

13 → 6

11 → 4

C.   Determine (a) the domain, (b) the range of each function.

11.   1 → 2   (a) _____

2 → 4   (b) _____

3 → 6

12.   -1 → 1   (a) _____

-2 → 2   (b) _____

-3 → 3

-4 → 4

13.   1 → 2   (a) _____

2 → 2   (b) _____

3 → 2

4 → 2

14.   1 → 5   (a) _____

2 → 6   (b) _____

3 → 5

4 → 6

5 → 5

6 → 6

15.   10 → 1   (a) _____

20 → 2   (b) _____

30 → 3

40 → 4

16.   10 → 1   (a) _____

20 → 1   (b) _____

30 → 1

40 → 1

50 → 1

60 → 1

KEY TOPICS

A.   Suppose f is the function defined by the correspondence:

$$1 \to 10$$

$$2 \to 20$$

$$3 \to 10$$

$$4 \to 20$$

(a) What are the arguments of f?

(b) Determine the value of f at 1.

(c) Determine the value of f at 4.

SOLUTION.

(a)   The arguments of f are 1, 2, 3, 4.

(b)   The value of f at 1 is 10.

(c)   The value of f at 4 is 20.

B.   Let g(x) = 3x − 1.

Determine: (a)   g(1)   (b)   g(2)

(c) $g\left(\dfrac{1}{3}\right)$ (d) $g\left(\dfrac{4}{3}\right)$

SOLUTION.

(a)   g(1) = 3 · 1 − 1 = 2

(b)   g(2) = 3 · 2 − 1 = 5

(c) $g\left(\dfrac{1}{3}\right) = 3 \cdot \dfrac{1}{3} - 1 = 1 - 1 = 0$

(d) $g\left(\dfrac{4}{3}\right) = 3 \cdot \dfrac{4}{3} - 1 = 4 - 1 = 3$

KEY EXERCISES

A. Suppose f is the function defined by the indicated
    correspondence. (a) What are the arguments of f? (b)
    Determine the value of f at 1. (c) Determine the value of
    f at 3.

1. 1 → 4 (a)_____   2. 1 → 10 (a)_____

    2 → 3 (b)_____   2 → 20 (b)_____

    3 → 2 (c)_____   3 → 10 (c)_____

    4 → 1   4 → 20

                                   5 → 10

B.

3. Let f(x) = 5x. Determine:

    (a) f(1) _____   (b) f(2) _____

    (c) f(3) _____   (d) f(4) _____

4. Let g(x) = x + 8. Determine:

    (a) g(0) _____   (b) g(2) _____

    (c) g(-1) _____   (d) g(-6) _____

5. Let h(x) = 2x - 3. Determine:

    (a) h(1) _____   (b) h(4) _____

    (c) h(0) _____   (d) h(-1) _____

C.   An encyclopedia salesman receives a salary of $150 per week.
     He also receives a $20 commission on each set of encyclopedias
     he sells.

     (a)   Determine his earnings for a week as a function of s,
           the number of sets of encyclopedias he sells.

     (b)   How much does he earn in a week in which he makes 9 sales?

SOLUTION.

     (a)   Let $f(s)$ be the salesman's earnings for a week (in
           dollars). Then

           $$f(s) = 150 + 20s$$

     (b)   Replace s by 9.

           $$f(9) = 150 + 20 \cdot 9$$
           $$= 150 + 180$$
           $$= 330$$

He earns $330 that week.

6. Let $F(x) = 3 - 2x$. Determine:

    (a) $F(1)$ _____   (b) $F(4)$ _____

    (c) $F(0)$ _____   (d) $F(-1)$ _____

7. Let $G(x) = 10$ for all x. Determine:

    (a) $G(1)$ _____   (b) $G(5)$ _____

    (c) $G(10)$ _____   (d) $G(-10)$ _____

8. Let $H(x) = x^2 + 4$. Determine:

    (a) $H(1)$ _____   (b) $H(-1)$ _____

    (c) $H(2)$ _____   (d) $H(-3)$ _____

C.

9. A factory produces 200 tractors a month.

    (a) Determine the number of tractors produced as a function of the number of months of production.

             _____

    (b) How many tractors are produced in a year?

             _____

10. A movie theater charges $3 admission for all tickets. There is a fixed operation cost of $900 per week.

    (a) Determine the weekly profit (or loss) as a function of the number of tickets sold.

             _____

    (b) How many tickets must be sold for the theater to break even?

             _____

11. A merchant buys apples for 20 cents a pound and sells them for 35 cents a pound.

    (a) Describe his profit from apples as a function of the number of pounds sold.

             _____

    (b) If he sells 80 pounds of apples, what is his profit?

             _____

D.   Determine the largest possible domain of the function given by

$$f(x) = \frac{x + 4}{x - 4}.$$

SOLUTION.

The function can be defined except when the denominator, x − 4, is 0. Because

$$x - 4 = 0$$

when

$$x = 4,$$

the domain of the function is the set of all real numbers other than 4.

▶ 8.3   Cartesian Coordinates (text page 233)

KEY TOPICS

A.   Determine the pair of coordinates of each point.

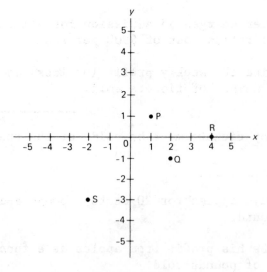

Figure 8.1

SOLUTION.

P = (1, 1)   Q = (2, −1)   R = (4, 0)   S = (−2, −3)

D. Determine the largest possible domain of the function given by each equation.

12. $f(x) = \dfrac{5}{x - 5}$ _____

13. $g(x) = \dfrac{x + 2}{x + 4}$ _____

14. $F(x) = \dfrac{x^2 + 1}{x^2 + 9}$ _____

15. $G(x) = \dfrac{x}{5}$ _____

KEY EXERCISES

A.

1. Determine the pair of coordinates of each point.

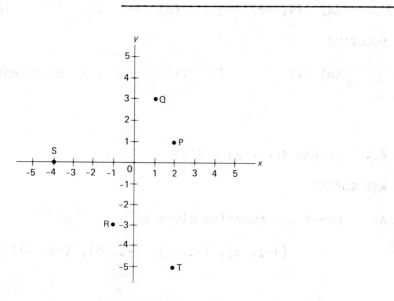

Figure 8.2

B.   On a coordinate system plot the following pairs:

   (a)   P = (4, 3)   (b)   Q = (-2, 4)

   (c)   R = (-3, -2)   (d)   S = (5, -5)

SOLUTION.

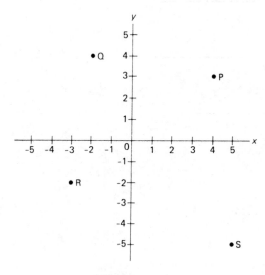

Figure 8.3

C.   Determine the quadrant of each point, or indicate that the
     point lies on a coordinate axis.

   (a)   (4, -5)   (b)   (-5, 2)   (c)   (0, -6)

SOLUTION.

   (a)   IV   (b)   III   (c)   coordinate axis

▶ 8.4   Graphs (text page 238)

KEY TOPICS

A.   Graph the function given by

          {(-1, 2), (-2, 4), (-3, 6), (-4, 8)}.

B.   On a coordinate system plot the following pairs.

2. P = (1, 4)

3. Q = (6, 4)

4. R = $\left(\frac{1}{2}, 1\right)$

5. S = (0, 2)

6. T = (-2, 1)

7. U = (-3, -4)

8. V = (-2, 2)

9. W = $\left(-5, \frac{-1}{2}\right)$

C.   Determine the quadrant of each point, or indicate that the point lies on a coordinate axis.

10. (1, 4) _____   11. (-2, 2) _____

12. (2, -2) _____   13. (9, 0) _____

14. (-15, -16) _____   15. $\left(\frac{1}{2}, -1\right)$ _____

16. (0, -1) _____   17. (0, 0) _____

KEY EXERCISES

A.   Graph the indicated function.

1. {(1, 3), (2, 6), (3, 4)}

2. {(1, 5), (2, 4), (3, 3), (4, 2), (5, 1)}

SOLUTION.

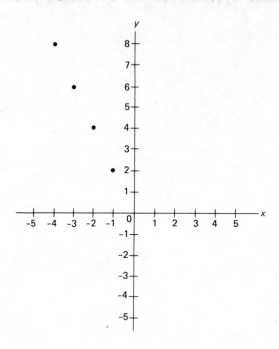

Figure 8.4

B.   Which diagrams represent graphs of functions?

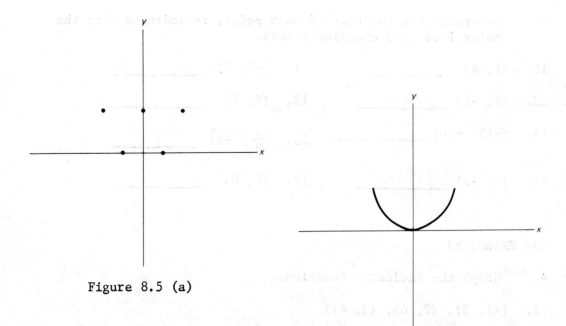

Figure 8.5 (a)

Figure 8.5 (b)

3. {(1, 0), (2, 1), (3, 0), (4, 1), (5, 0), (6, 1)}

4. {(1, 4), (2, 4), (3, 4), (4, 4)}

B.   Which diagrams represent graphs of functions?

5-10.

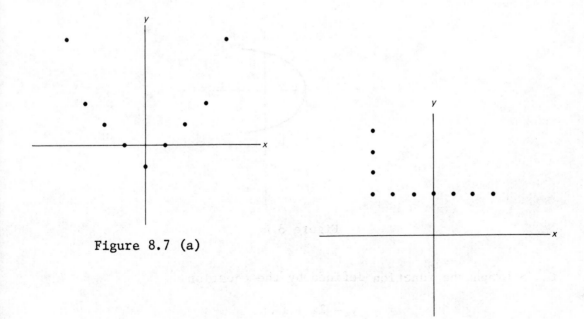

Figure 8.7 (a)

Figure 8.7 (b)

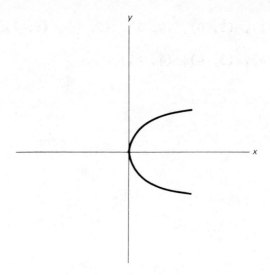

Figure 8.5 (c)

SOLUTION.

(a) and (b) represent graphs of functions. (c) does not because here there are <u>vertical</u> lines that intersect the graph of the function more than once. (See Figure 8.6.)

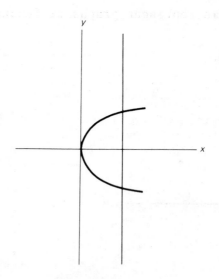

Figure 8.6

C.   Graph the function defined by the equation

$$y = 2x + 1.$$

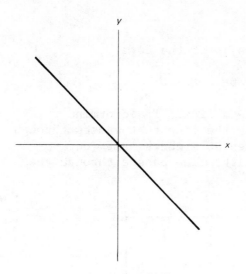

Figure 8.7 (c)

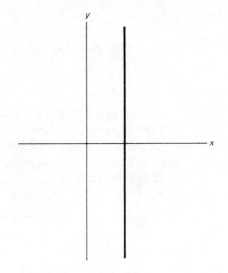

Figure 8.7 (d)

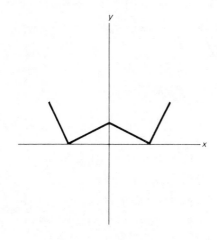

Figure 8.7 (e)

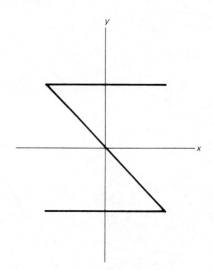

Figure 8.7 (f)

C.   Graph the function defined by each equation.

11.   y = x + 3

12.   y = -2x

SOLUTION.

The defining equation is of the form

$$y = mx + b.$$

The graph of this function is a line. To determine this line, plot 2 points, and draw the line that passes through them. (A third point is given as a check. If your plotting is accurate, a straight line passes through the three points.)

x	0	1	2
y = 2x + 1	1	3	5

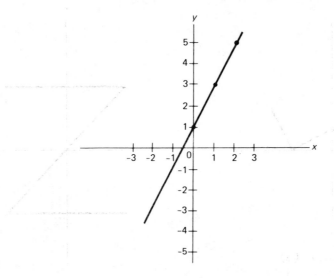

Figure 8.8   The graph of

$$y = 2x + 1$$

D.   Graph the function defined by

$$y = x^2 + 2.$$

SOLUTION.

The defining equation is <u>not</u> of the form y = mx + b. Plot several points to determine the graph.

13. $y = 3x - 1$

14. $y = 5 - x$

D. Graph the function indicated by each equation.

15. $y = x^2 - 1$ 16. $y = x^2 + 3$

17. $y = 2x^2$ 18. $y = \dfrac{x^2}{2}$

x	0	$\dfrac{1}{4}$	$\dfrac{-1}{4}$	$\dfrac{1}{2}$	$\dfrac{-1}{2}$	$\dfrac{3}{4}$	$\dfrac{-3}{4}$	1	-1	2	-2
x^2	0	$\dfrac{1}{16}$	$\dfrac{1}{16}$	$\dfrac{1}{4}$	$\dfrac{1}{4}$	$\dfrac{9}{16}$	$\dfrac{9}{16}$	1	1	4	4
$y = x^2 + 2$	2	$2\dfrac{1}{16}$	$2\dfrac{1}{16}$	$2\dfrac{1}{4}$	$2\dfrac{1}{4}$	$2\dfrac{9}{16}$	$2\dfrac{9}{16}$	3	3	6	6

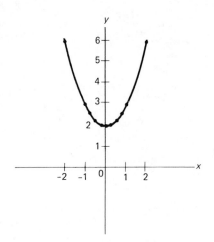

Figure 8.9   The graph of

$$y = x^2 + 2$$

▶ 8.5   Inverse of a Function (text page 247)

KEY TOPICS

A.   Which diagrams represent one-one functions?

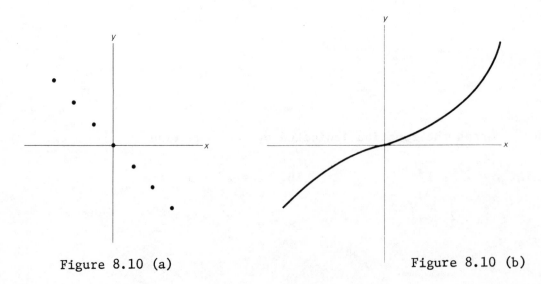

Figure 8.10 (a)   Figure 8.10 (b)

KEY EXERCISES

A.   Which diagrams represent one-one functions?

1-5.

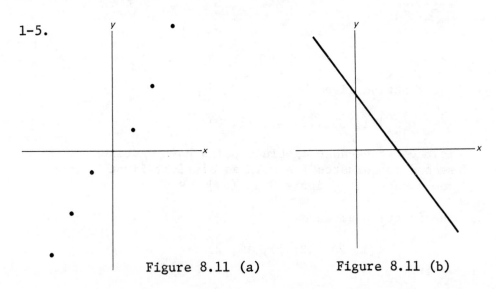

Figure 8.11 (a)   Figure 8.11 (b)

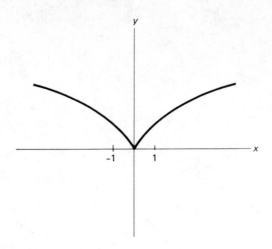

Figure 8.10 (c)

SOLUTION.

    (a) and (b) represent one-one functions; (c) does not. Observe that in (c) the same y-value corresponds to the x-values 1 and -1.

B.   (a) The function given by

$$\{(1, 3), (2, 4), (3, 0)\}$$

is one-one because distinct pairs have distinct second coordinates (as well as distinct first coordinates). [Figure 8.12 (a)]

    (b) The function given by

$$\{(1, 2), (2, 5), (3, 2)\}$$

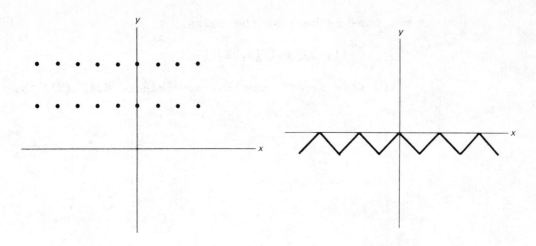

Figure 8.11 (c) Figure 8.11 (d)

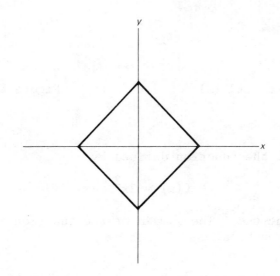

Figure 8.11 (e)

B.   Which of the indicated functions are one-one?

6. {(1, 2), (2, 3), (3, 4)} _____

7. {(1, 2), (2, 1), (3, 3)} _____

8. {(1, 2), (2, 1), (3, 1), (4, 1)} _____

9. {(1, 10), (2, 10), (3, 10), (4, 10)} _____

10. {(1, 5), (2, 4), (3, 3), (4, 2), (5, 1)} _____

is not one-one because the pairs

$$(1, 2) \text{ and } (3, 2)$$

have the same second coordinate. [Figure 8.12 (b)]

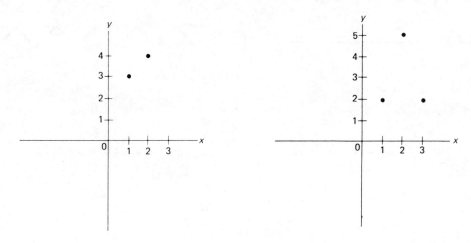

Figure 8.12 (a)   Figure 8.12 (b)

C.   Show that the function defined by

$$f(x) = 2x^2$$

is not one-one. The domain of the function is the set of all real numbers.

SOLUTION.

You must find two different arguments that have the same function values.

$$f(1) = 2 \cdot 1^2 = 2$$

$$f(-1) = 2 \cdot (-1)^2 = 2$$

Therefore, this function is not one-one.

D.   Determine the inverse of the indicated one-one function:

(a) $\{(1, 6), (2, 5), (3, 4)\}$

(b) $y = 2x + 1$

C. Show that the function defined by each equation is <u>not</u> one-
    one. The domain of each function is the set of all real
    numbers.

11. f(x) = 10 _____

12. f(x) = 5x^2 _____

13. f(x) = 1 - x^2 _____

D. Determine the inverse of the indicated one-one function.

14. {(1, 6), (2, 3), (3, 1)} _____

15. {(1, 10), (2, 1), (3, 8), (4, 3)} _____

SOLUTION.

(a) Interchange the coordinates of each pair:

$$\{(6, 1), (5, 2), (4, 3)\}$$

(b) Interchange x and y. Then solve for y in terms of x.

$$x = 2y + 1$$

$$x - 1 = 2y$$

$$\frac{x - 1}{2} = y$$

or

$$y = \frac{x - 1}{2}$$

16. {(1, 1), (2, 2), (3, 6), (4, 5), (5, 4), (6, 3)}

_____

17. y = 3x _____

18. y = x + 5 _____

19. y = 1 − x _____

20. y = 6x + 5 _____

CHAPTER 9

LINES

▶ 9.1   Proportion (text page 260)

KEY TOPICS

A.   Determine the ratio of y to x, x ≠ 0, in the equation:

$$4y = 6x .$$

SOLUTION.

Suppose x ≠ 0 .

4y = 6x   Divide both sides by 4x.

$$\frac{y}{x} = \frac{6}{4}$$

$$\frac{y}{x} = \frac{3}{2}$$

B.   Find the value of b:

$$\frac{5}{b} = \frac{15}{60}$$

SOLUTION.

Cross–multiply:

5 · 60 = 15b

b = 20

C.   A batter has 3 hits for every 11 times at bat. If he keeps
up this rate how many times must he come to bat in order to
have 99 hits?

SOLUTION.

Let d be the number of at–bats. Set up the proportion:

$$\frac{3}{11} = \frac{99}{d}$$

3d = 99 · 11

d = 363

75 LEFT

KEY EXERCISES

A.   Determine the ratio of y to x, x ≠ 0, in each equation.

1.   y = 4x _____   2.   x = 5y _____

3.   2x = 7y _____   4.   -x = 3y _____

B.   Find all possible values of a, b, c, or d in each proportion.

5. $\frac{a}{3} = \frac{15}{5}$ _____   6. $\frac{2}{b} = \frac{-1}{4}$ _____

7. $\frac{5}{9} = \frac{c}{45}$ _____   8. $\frac{3}{7} = \frac{9}{d}$ _____

9. $\frac{\frac{1}{4}}{2} = \frac{c}{4}$ _____   10. $\frac{a}{9} = \frac{4}{a}$ _____

C.

11.   If 3 pounds of onions cost one dollar, how many pounds of
       onions can you buy for three dollars?

                                        _____

12.   If 5 students can eat 18 frankfurters, how many frankfurters
       should be prepared for 25 students?

                                        _____

13.   A team wins three games for every two it loses. If it has
       won 36 games, how many has it lost?

                                        _____

D.   In Figure 9.1 the triangles are similar. Corresponding
sides are marked with the same number of bars. Determine
the lengths of the indicated sides.

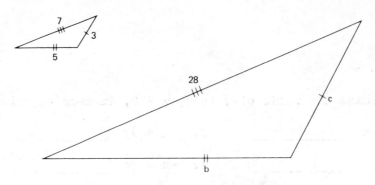

Figure 9.1

SOLUTION.

$$\frac{b}{5} = \frac{28}{7} \qquad\qquad \frac{c}{3} = \frac{28}{7}$$

$$b = 5 \cdot \frac{28}{7} \qquad\qquad c = 3 \cdot 4$$

$$b = 5 \cdot 4 \qquad\qquad c = 12$$

$$b = 20$$

▶ 9.2   Point-Slope Equation of a Line (text page 266)

KEY TOPICS

A.   Determine the slope of the line through (3, 2) and (5, −2).

SOLUTION.

$$slope = \frac{-2 - 2}{5 - 3}$$

$$= \frac{-4}{2}$$

$$= -2$$

D.   In each of the exercises 14-16, the triangles are similar.
      Corresponding sides are marked with the same number of bars.
      Determine the lengths of the indicated sides.

14.

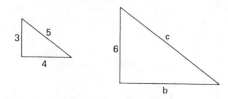

       Figure 9.2 (a)

                                          15.

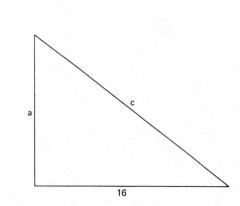

16.

                                          Figure 9.2 (b)

       Figure 9.2 (c)

                    14. b = _____   c = _____

                    15. a = _____   c = _____

                    16. a = _____   b = _____

KEY EXERCISES

A.   Determine the slope of the line through the given points.

1.   (2, 5) and (4, 7) _____

2.   (1, 4) and (2, 1) _____

3.   (-4, 8) and (2, 2) _____

4.   (3, -5) and (5, -1) _____

5.   (0, -6) and (3, 0) _____

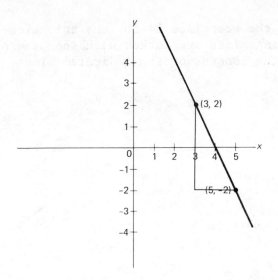

Figure 9.3   slope = $\dfrac{\text{rise}}{\text{run}} = \dfrac{-4}{2} = -2$

B.   A line L has slope 3 and passes through (1, 2). Determine
the y-coordinate of the point on L with x-coordinate 3.

SOLUTION.

In the point-slope form of the equation of a line,

$$y - y_1 = m(x - x_1) .$$

Take m = 3, x_1 = 1, y_1 = 2.

$$y - 2 = 3(x - 1)$$

$$y = 3x - 3 + 2$$

$$y = 3x - 1$$

Replace x by 3 in this equation.

$$y = 3 \cdot 3 - 1$$

$$y = 8$$

B.

6. A line L has slope 3 and passes through (2, 1). Determine the x-coordinate of the point on L with y-coordinate 4.

_____

7. A line L has slope −2 and passes through (3, 5). Determine the y-coordinate of the point on L with x-coordinate 1.

_____

8. A line L passes through (1, −2) and (2, 3). Determine the x-coordinate of the point on L with y-coordinate 8.

_____

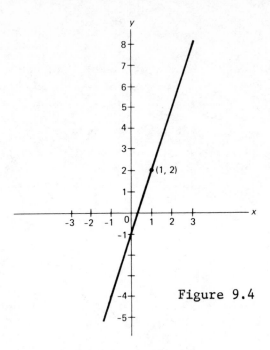

Figure 9.4

C. Determine the equation of the line that has slope −4 and that passes through the point (1, −5).

SOLUTION.

$$y - (-5) = -4(x - 1)$$

$$y + 5 = -4(x - 1)$$

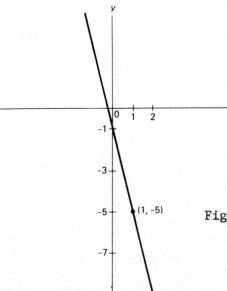

Figure 9.5 The line given by

$$y + 5 = -4(x - 1)$$

C. Determine the equation of the line that has slope m and that passes through the point P.

9.   m = 2, P = (4, 4) _____

10. m = -1, P = (0, 3) _____

11. m = 5, P = (-1, -2) _____

12. m = $\frac{1}{2}$, P = (1, 6) _____

D. Determine the equation of the vertical line that passes through (6, −3).

SOLUTION.

The equation is

$$x = 6.$$

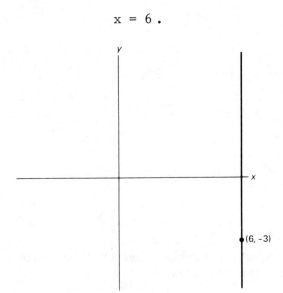

Figure 9.6   The line given by

$$x = 6$$

▶ 9.3   Alternate Forms of Linear Equations (text page 275)

KEY TOPICS

A. Determine (a) the x-intercept, (b) the y-intercept of the line given by the equation

$$y - 2 = 3(x - 1).$$

SOLUTION.

(a) To find the x-intercept, let y = 0 in the above equation.

$$-2 = 3(x - 1)$$

$$\frac{-2}{3} = x - 1$$

D.

13. Determine the equation of the vertical line that passes through (1, 2).

   _____

14. Determine the equation of the horizontal line that passes through (1, 2).

   _____

15. Determine the equation of the vertical line that passes through (-1, 7).

   _____

16. Determine the equation of the horizontal line that passes through $\left(\frac{1}{2}, \frac{1}{4}\right)$. _____

KEY EXERCISES

A. Determine (a) the x-intercept, (b) the y-intercept of the line given by each equation.

1. $y - 1 = 4x$ (a) _____ (b) _____

2. $y + 2 = 2(x - 5)$ (a) _____ (b) _____

3. $y = 5x + 3$ (a) _____ (b) _____

4. $x + 3y + 4 = 0$ (a) _____ (b) _____

$$1 - \frac{2}{3} = x$$

$$\frac{1}{3} = x$$

The x-intercept is $\frac{1}{3}$.

(b) To find the y-intercept, let x = 0 in the given equation.

$$y - 2 = 3(0 - 1)$$

$$y = 2 - 3$$

$$y = -1$$

The y-intercept is -1.

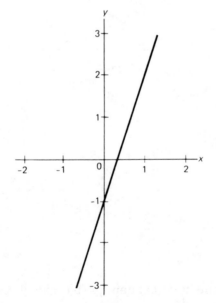

Figure 9.7   The line given by

$$y - 2 = 3(x - 1)$$

has x-intercept $\frac{1}{3}$ and y-intercept -1.

B.   Determine the slope-intercept form of the equation of the line given by

$$y - 4 = -3(x + 1).$$

B.   Determine the slope-intercept form of the equation of the
      indicated line L.

5.   y + 1 = 2(x - 5) _____

SOLUTION.

$$m = -3$$

To find b, the y-intercept, let x = 0 in the given equation.

$$y - 4 = -3(0 + 1)$$
$$y = 4 - 3$$
$$y = 1$$

Thus b, the y-intercept, is 1.

The slope-intercept form,

$$y = mx + b \, ,$$

is therefore

$$y = -3x + 1 \, .$$

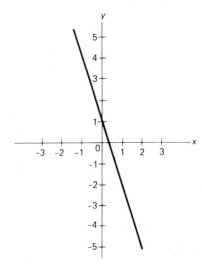

Figure 9.8

The line given by

$$y = -3x + 1$$

C.   Determine the 2-point form of the equation of the line that passes through (2, -5) and (-1, 1).

SOLUTION.

The 2-point form is

$$y - y_1 = \frac{y_2 - y_1}{x_2 - x_1} (x - x_1) \, .$$

6. x + y + 1 = 0 _____

7. L has x-intercept 2 and y-intercept -3. _____

8. L passes through (1, 4) and (2, 6). _____

C. Determine the 2-point form of the equation of the indicated line L.

9. L passes through (1, 6) and (2, 2). _____

10. L passes through (0, 3) and (-2, -4). _____

11. L has x-intercept 4 and y-intercept -2. _____

12. L passes through (4, -3) and has x-intercept 10. _____

Let $(x_1, y_1) = (2, -5)$, $(x_2, y_2) = (-1, 1)$.

$$y - (-5) = \frac{1 - (-5)}{-1 - 2} \ (x - 2)$$

$$y + 5 = \frac{6}{-3} \ (x - 2)$$

$$y + 5 = -2 \ (x - 2)$$

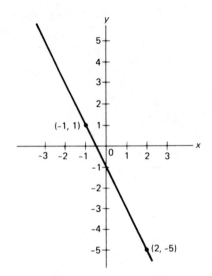

Figure 9.9   The line given by

$$y + 5 = -2(x - 2)$$

D.   Determine the general form of the equation of the line that has slope 2 and that passes through $(1, -4)$.

SOLUTION.

First write the equation in the point-slope form:

$$y + 4 = 2(x - 1)$$

Now rewrite this in the general form,

$$Ax + By + C = 0.$$

$$y + 4 = 2x - 2$$

$$-2x + y + 6 = 0$$

D.   Determine the general form of the equation of the indicated
     line L.

13. L: y − 3 = 2x + 1 _____

14. L passes through (2, 10) and (1, −5). _____

15. L is the vertical line through (3, 6). _____

16. L is the horizontal line through (2, −2). _____

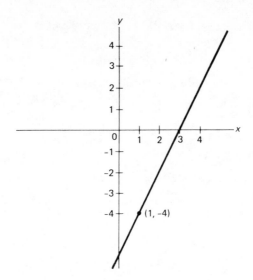

Figure 9.10   The line given by

$$-2x + y + 6 = 0$$

▶ 9.4   Parallel and Perpendicular Lines (text page 283)

KEY TOPICS

A.   (a)   The lines given by

$$y = 2x + 5 \text{ and } y = 2x + 1$$

are parallel. Both have the same slope, 2. The lines
are different because one has y-intercept 5, the other
y-intercept 1 [Figure 9.11(a)].

(b)   The lines given by

$$y = 3x + 4 \text{ and } y = \frac{-x}{3} - 2$$

are perpendicular. Their slopes, 3 and $\frac{-1}{3}$, are
negative reciprocals [Figure 9.11b].

(c)   The lines given by

$$y = 2x \text{ and } y = -2x$$

are neither parallel nor perpendicular. Their
slopes, 2 and -2, are not equal. Nor are they
negative reciprocals [Figure 9.11(c)].

KEY EXERCISES

A.   Determine whether the given lines are (a) parallel,
     (b) perpendicular, (c) neither parallel nor perpendicular.

1. $y = 3x - 1$ and $y = 3x + 1$ _____

2. $y = x + 1$ and $y = 1 - x$ _____

3. $y = 5x + 4$ and $y = 4 - 5x$ _____

4. $y = \frac{x}{2}$ and $2x + y = 0$ _____

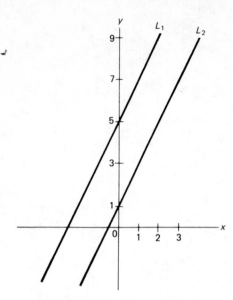

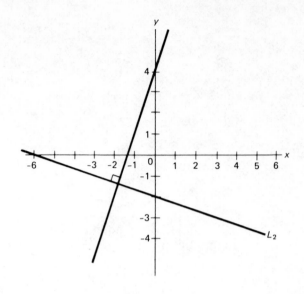

Figure 9.11 (a)

$L_1 : y = 2x + 5$

$L_2 : y = 2x + 1$

$L_1 \parallel L_2$

Figure 9.11 (b)

$L_1 : y = 3x + 4$

$L_2 : y = \dfrac{-x}{3} - 2$

$L_1 \perp L_2$

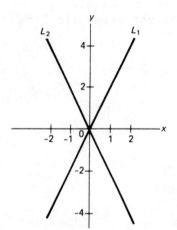

Figure 9.11 (c) $L_1 : y = 2x$

$L_2 : y = -2x$

B.   Determine whether the line through (2, 5) and (5, 2) is
(a) parallel to, (b) perpendicular to, (c) neither parallel
to, nor perpendicular to, the line through (−1, −1) and (1, 1).

B.   Determine whether the lines through P and Q and through R and
      S are (a) parallel, (b) perpendicular, (c) neither parallel
      nor perpendicular.

SOLUTION.

The slopes are

$$\frac{2 - 5}{5 - 2} = -1 \quad \text{and} \quad \frac{1 - (-1)}{1 - (-1)} = 1.$$

Because the slopes are negative reciprocals, the lines are perpendicular.

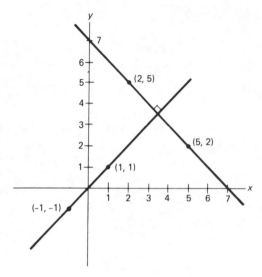

Figure 9.12

C. Determine the equation of the line that passes through (4, 2) and is (a) parallel to, (b) perpendicular to, the line L given by

$$y = 5x - 3.$$

SOLUTION.

(a) $m = 5$, $(x_1, y_1) = (4, 2)$

The line through (4, 2) that is parallel to L is given by

$$y - 2 = 5(x - 4).$$

(b) $m = \frac{-1}{5}$, $(x_1, y_1) = (4, 2)$

The line through (4, 2) that is perpendicular to L is given by $y - 2 = \frac{-1}{5}(x - 4)$.

5. P = (2, 2), Q = (4, 3);   R = (5, 5), S = (7, 6) _____

6. P = (1, -1), Q = (4, 1);   R = (2, 5), Q = (-5, 2) _____

7. P = (4, 1), Q = (6, 2);   R = (-2, 3), S = (-1, 1) _____

8. P = (4, 3), Q = (3, 4);   R = (-3, -4), S = (-4, -3) _____

C.   Determine the equation of the line that passes through P and
     is (a) parallel to, (b) perpendicular to, the given line L.

9. P = (1, 2), L: y = 3x - 4 (a) _____ (b) _____

10. P = (0, 3), L: y = x   (a) _____ (b) _____

11. P = (4, -1), L: y - 1 = 4x - 1 (a) _____ (b) _____

12. P = (0, 0), L: y = -2x + 5 (a) _____ (b) _____

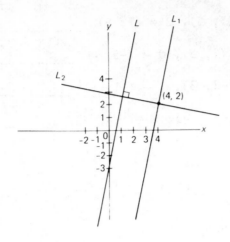

Figure 9.13

L $\quad$: $y = 5x - 3$

L_1 : $y - 2 = 5(x - 4)$

L_2 : $y - 2 = \dfrac{-1}{5} (x - 4)$

$L \parallel L_1, \quad L \perp L_2$

D. $\quad$ Determine all pairs of (a) parallel lines, (b) perpendicular lines.

L_1: $\quad y = 4x$ $\qquad$ L_2: $\quad y = -4x$ $\qquad$ L_3: $\quad 4y = x$

L_4: $\quad y = 1 - 4x$ $\qquad$ L_5: $\quad y = \dfrac{x + 1}{4}$

SOLUTION.

(a) $\quad$ L_2 and L_4 are parallel.

L_3 and L_5 are parallel.

(b) $\quad$ L_2 and L_3, $\quad$ L_2 and L_5, $\quad$ L_4 and L_3, $\quad$ L_4 and L_5 are perpendicular.

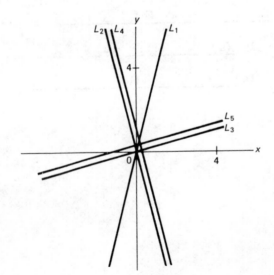

Figure 9.14

D.   Determine all pairs of (a) parallel lines, (b) perpendicular
     lines.

13. L_1: $y = x + 9$ 14. L_1: $y = \dfrac{x}{3}$

     L_2: $y - x = 2$ L_2: $y = 3x - 5$

     L_3: $x + y = 1$ L_3: $3y = x + 1$

     L_4: $y = 1 - x$ L_4: $y = 1 - 3x$

     L_5: $\dfrac{x + y}{2} = 1$ L_5: $y = \dfrac{4 - x}{3}$

     (a) _____   (a) _____

     (b) _____   (b) _____

CHAPTER 10

SYSTEMS OF LINEAR EQUATIONS

▶ 10.1   Linear Systems in Two Variables (text page 296)

KEY TOPICS

A.   Determine the intersection of L_1 and L_2 graphically.

$$L_1: \quad x + y = 5$$

$$L_2: \quad 2x + y = 6$$

SOLUTION.

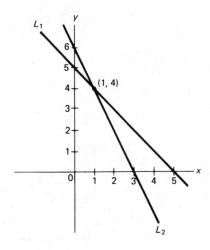

Figure 10.1 $L_1 : x + y = 5$

$$L_2 : 2x + y = 6$$

L_1 and L_2 intersect at $(1, 4)$.

The unique point of intersection is $(1, 4)$.

B.   Solve the system

$$4x + y = 12$$

$$3x - 2y = -2$$

by the substitution method.

KEY EXERCISES

A.   Determine the intersection of L_1 and L_2 graphically.

  1. L_1: $2x - y = 4$

      L_2: $x - y = 1$

  2. L_1: $x - 2y = 2$

      L_2: $2y = 8$

  3. L_1: $5x - y = 0$

      L_2: $3x + 2y = 13$

  4. L_1: $4x + 2y = 1$

      L_2: $3x - y = 2$

B.   Solve each system by the substitution method.

  5. $x + 2y = 10$ _____   6. $2x - y = 12$ _____

       $3x - 4y = 10$ $7x + 10y = 15$

SOLUTION.

From the first equation,

$$y = 12 - 4x$$

Replace y by 12 - 4x in the second equation, and simplify.

$$3x - 2(12 - 4x) = -2$$
$$3x - 24 + 8x = -2$$
$$11x = 22$$
$$x = 2$$

Replace x by 2 in the equation

$$y = 12 - 4x.$$
$$y = 12 - 4 \cdot 2$$
$$y = 4$$

The solution is (2, 4).

C.   Solve the system

$$2x + 3y = 9$$
$$4x - 5y = 29$$

by "adding equations".

SOLUTION.

Multiply both sides of the first equation by -2 and add the corresponding sides of the two equations.

$$-4x - 6y = -18$$
$$\underline{4x - 5y = 29}$$
$$-11y = 11$$
$$y = -1$$

Replace y by -1 in the first equation, and solve for x:

$$2x + 3(-1) = 9$$
$$2x - 3 = 9$$

7. $5x + 4y = 5$ _____   8. $4x + 2y = 0$ _____

    $2x\quad\ = 2$ $3x + 2y = 3$

9. $3x - 7y = 1$ _____

    $2x - 5y = 1$

C. Solve each system by "adding equations".

10. $x + y = 10$ _____   11. $3x - 2y = -1$ _____

     $x - y = 2$ $x + 2y = 13$

12. $8x - y = 1$ _____   13. $3x + 2y = 19$ _____

     $4x - 2y = -10$ $2x - 10y = 7$

14. $5x + 3y = 4$ _____

     $3x + 2y = 2$

$$2x = 12$$

$$x = 6$$

The solution is $(6, -1)$.

▶ 10.2   Linear Systems in Three Variables (text page 306)

KEY TOPICS

A.   Solve each system.

(a) $x + 2y + z = 2$

$$y - z = 5$$

$$y + 2z = -4$$

(b) $x + 3y - 7z = 3$

$$8x - 3y + 5z = -2$$

$$5x - z = 1$$

SOLUTION.

(a)   First solve the last 2 equations for y and z.
Subtract the second equation from the third to obtain:

$$3z = -9$$

$$z = -3$$

Replace z by -3 in the second equation.

$$y - (-3) = 5$$

$$y + 3 = 5$$

$$y = 2$$

Now replace y by 2 and z by -3 in the first equation.

$$x + 2(2) + (-3) = 2$$

$$x + 1 = 2$$

$$x = 1$$

The solution is $(1, 2, -3)$.

KEY EXERCISES

A.   Solve each system.   You may use any methods.

1. $2x \quad\ + z = 4$
    $\quad\ y - z = 2$
    $x + y \quad\ = 5$

    _____

2. $x + 2y \quad\ = 12$
    $\quad\ y - z = \ 2$
    $x \quad\ + z = \ 7$

    _____

3. $x - 2y \quad\ = 2$
    $x \quad\ - z = 2$
    $\quad\ 3y - z = 4$

    _____

4. $x + y + z = 4$
    $2x + 5y \quad\ = 9$
    $\quad\ 3y - 2z = 1$

    _____

5. $x \quad\ + z = \ 6$
    $\quad\ y + 2z = 11$
    $3x - y + \ z = \ 7$

    _____

6. $5x + 7y - \ z = \ 7$
    $2x + 3y - 2z = -7$
    $4x + 6y - \ z = \ 4$

    _____

7. $x + 3y + \ z = 3$
    $4x + 5y + 2z = 1$
    $2x + 6y + 3z = 1$

    _____

8. $3x + 3y + 8z = 2$
    $x + 2y + 2z = 0$
    $5x - 3y + 4z = 5$

    _____

(b) Add the corresponding sides of the first two equations
     to eliminate y:

(A) $9x - 2z = 1$

Multiply both sides of the third equation by -2.

(B) $-10x + 2z = -2$

Add the corresponding sides of equations (A) and (B).

$$-x = -1$$

$$x = 1$$

Replace x by 1 in equation (B):

$$-10(1) + 2z = -2$$

$$2z = 8$$

$$z = 4$$

Replace x by 1 and z by 4 in the first equation,

$$x + 3y - 7z = 3.$$

$$1 + 3y - 7(4) = 3$$

$$3y - 27 = 3$$

$$3y = 30$$

$$y = 10$$

The solution is (1, 10, 4).

▶ 10.3   2 × 2 Determinants and Cramer's Rule (text page 312)

KEY TOPICS

A.   Evaluate: $\begin{vmatrix} 4 & 3 \\ 2 & 5 \end{vmatrix}$

SOLUTION.

$$\begin{vmatrix} 4 & 3 \\ 2 & 5 \end{vmatrix} = 4(5) - 2(3) = 14$$

KEY EXERCISES

A. Evaluate each determinant.

1. $\begin{vmatrix} 4 & 5 \\ 2 & 1 \end{vmatrix}$ _____

2. $\begin{vmatrix} 8 & -3 \\ 2 & \frac{1}{2} \end{vmatrix}$ _____

3. $\begin{vmatrix} 4 & -7 \\ -2 & 6 \end{vmatrix}$ _____

4. $\begin{vmatrix} 1 & 5 \\ 2 & 9 \end{vmatrix}$ _____

B.   Determine x: $\begin{vmatrix} x & 8 \\ 1 & 2 \end{vmatrix} = 2$

SOLUTION.

$$\begin{vmatrix} x & 8 \\ 1 & 2 \end{vmatrix} = x(2) - 1(8)$$

$$= 2x - 8$$

Thus solve:

$$2x - 8 = 2$$

$$2x = 10$$

$$x = 5$$

C.   Indicate whether Cramer's Rule applies. If it applies, use Cramer's Rule to find the solution.

   (a) $4x + 3y = 13$ (b) $5x - y = 7$

         $3x + 2y = 11$ $-10x + 2y = 9$

SOLUTION.

   (a) $D = \begin{vmatrix} 4 & 3 \\ 3 & 2 \end{vmatrix} = 4(2) - 3(3) = -1$

         $D \neq 0$. Thus Cramer's Rule applies.

         $D_x = \begin{vmatrix} 13 & 3 \\ 11 & 2 \end{vmatrix} = 13(2) - 11(3) = -7$

         $D_y = \begin{vmatrix} 4 & 13 \\ 3 & 11 \end{vmatrix} = 4(11) - 3(13) = 5$

         $x = \dfrac{D_x}{D} = \dfrac{-7}{-1} = 7$

         $y = \dfrac{D_y}{D} = \dfrac{5}{-1} = -5$

   The solution is (7, -5).

5. $\begin{vmatrix} \dfrac{1}{2} & \dfrac{1}{3} \\ \dfrac{1}{4} & \dfrac{1}{6} \end{vmatrix}$ _____

B. Determine x:

6. $\begin{vmatrix} x & 2 \\ 4 & 3 \end{vmatrix} = 4$ _____ 7. $\begin{vmatrix} 6 & 4 \\ x & 2 \end{vmatrix} = 8$ _____

8. $\begin{vmatrix} 5 & 2 \\ 1 & -x \end{vmatrix} = -3$ _____

C. (a) Indicate whether Cramer's Rule applies. (b) If it applies, use Cramer's Rule to find the solution.

9. $3x + 2y = 12$
    $2x - y = 1$

10. $7x + 3y = 1$
    $3x + 2y = 4$

_____   _____

11. $5x + 2y = 1$
    $2x + 3y = 18$

12. $3x + y = 2$
    $9x + 3y = 5$

_____   _____

13. $x + y = 4$
    $2x - 2y = 8$

14. $x + y = 4$
    $2x + 2y = 8$

_____   _____

91 RIGHT

(b) $\quad D = \begin{vmatrix} 5 & -1 \\ -10 & 2 \end{vmatrix} = 5(2) - (-10)(-1)$

$$= 10 - 10$$

$$= 0$$

Cramer's Rule does not apply.

▶ 10.4   3 × 3 Determinants and Cramer's Rule (text page 319)

KEY TOPICS

A.   Evaluate: $\begin{vmatrix} 2 & 1 & 5 \\ 1 & 4 & 8 \\ -1 & 2 & 0 \end{vmatrix}$

SOLUTION.

$$\begin{vmatrix} 2 & 1 & 5 \\ 1 & 4 & 8 \\ -1 & 2 & 0 \end{vmatrix} = 2 \begin{vmatrix} 4 & 8 \\ 2 & 0 \end{vmatrix} - 1 \begin{vmatrix} 1 & 5 \\ 2 & 0 \end{vmatrix} + (-1) \begin{vmatrix} 1 & 5 \\ 4 & 8 \end{vmatrix}$$

$$= 2(-16) - (-10) - (-12)$$

$$= -10$$

B.   Determine x: $\begin{vmatrix} 1 & 2 & 1 \\ 0 & 4 & 1 \\ x & 1 & 3 \end{vmatrix} = 1$

SOLUTION.

$$\begin{vmatrix} 1 & 2 & 1 \\ 0 & 4 & 1 \\ x & 1 & 3 \end{vmatrix} = 1 \begin{vmatrix} 4 & 1 \\ 1 & 3 \end{vmatrix} - 0 + x \begin{vmatrix} 2 & 1 \\ 4 & 1 \end{vmatrix}$$

$$= 11 + x(-2)$$

$$= 11 - 2x$$

Thus solve

$$11 - 2x = 1 .$$

$$10 = 2x$$

$$5 = x$$

KEY EXERCISES

A.   Evaluate each determinant.

1. $\begin{vmatrix} 1 & 0 & 2 \\ 0 & 1 & 0 \\ 1 & 1 & -1 \end{vmatrix}$ _____

2. $\begin{vmatrix} 3 & 0 & 1 \\ 0 & 1 & -2 \\ 0 & 2 & 1 \end{vmatrix}$ _____

3. $\begin{vmatrix} 4 & 0 & 1 \\ 6 & 0 & 2 \\ 1 & 2 & 3 \end{vmatrix}$ _____

4. $\begin{vmatrix} 5 & 1 & 2 \\ 0 & -1 & 1 \\ -1 & -1 & 2 \end{vmatrix}$ _____

B.   Determine x:

5. $\begin{vmatrix} x & 0 & 2 \\ 0 & 2 & 3 \\ 0 & 2 & 4 \end{vmatrix} = 4$ _____

6. $\begin{vmatrix} 1 & 3 & x \\ 0 & 2 & 2 \\ 1 & -5 & -5 \end{vmatrix} = 2$ _____

C. Determine whether Cramer's Rule applies. If it applies, use Cramer's Rule to find the solution.

(a) $2x + y - 3z = 5$

$x + 2y + 2z = 4$

$3x + 3y - z = 10$

(b) $2x - y + z = 1$

$x - y + 4z = 0$

$5x - 3y + 2z = 2$

SOLUTION.

(a)
$$D = \begin{vmatrix} 2 & 1 & -3 \\ 1 & 2 & 2 \\ 3 & 3 & -1 \end{vmatrix}$$

$$= 2\begin{vmatrix} 2 & 2 \\ 3 & -1 \end{vmatrix} - 1\begin{vmatrix} 1 & -3 \\ 3 & -1 \end{vmatrix} + 3\begin{vmatrix} 1 & -3 \\ 2 & 2 \end{vmatrix}$$

$$= 2(-8) - 8 + 3(8)$$

$$= 0$$

Cramer's Rule does not apply.

(b)
$$D = \begin{vmatrix} 2 & -1 & 1 \\ 1 & -1 & 4 \\ 5 & -3 & 2 \end{vmatrix}$$

$$= 2\begin{vmatrix} -1 & 4 \\ -3 & 2 \end{vmatrix} - 1\begin{vmatrix} -1 & 1 \\ -3 & 2 \end{vmatrix} + 5\begin{vmatrix} -1 & 1 \\ -1 & 4 \end{vmatrix}$$

$$= 2(10) - 1(1) + 5(-3)$$

$$= 4$$

$$D_x = \begin{vmatrix} 1 & -1 & 1 \\ 0 & -1 & 4 \\ 2 & -3 & 2 \end{vmatrix}$$

$$= 1\begin{vmatrix} -1 & 4 \\ -3 & 2 \end{vmatrix} - 0 + 2\begin{vmatrix} -1 & 1 \\ -1 & 4 \end{vmatrix}$$

$$= 10 + 2(-3)$$

$$= 4$$

C.   (a) Determine whether Cramer's Rule applies. (b) If it applies, use Cramer's Rule to find the solution.

7. $x + y \quad\quad = 5$
        $y - z = 1$
    $x + y + 2z = 7$

8. $2x + y - z = 10$
     $x + 2y \quad\quad = 5$
    $4x + 5y - z = 13$

_____

_____

9. $2x + 5y + 9z = 15$
    $x \quad\quad\quad + 5z = 2$
        $2y + z = 3$

10. $5x - 3y - z = 1$
    $-2x + y + 6z = 4$
     $7x - 4y - 7z = 3$

_____

_____

$$D_y = \begin{vmatrix} 2 & 1 & 1 \\ 1 & 0 & 4 \\ 5 & 2 & 2 \end{vmatrix}$$

$$= 2\begin{vmatrix} 0 & 4 \\ 2 & 2 \end{vmatrix} -1\begin{vmatrix} 1 & 1 \\ 2 & 2 \end{vmatrix} + 5\begin{vmatrix} 1 & 1 \\ 0 & 4 \end{vmatrix}$$

$$= 2(-8) -0 + 5(4)$$

$$= 4$$

$$D_z = \begin{vmatrix} 2 & -1 & 1 \\ 1 & -1 & 0 \\ 5 & -3 & 2 \end{vmatrix}$$

$$= 2\begin{vmatrix} -1 & 0 \\ -3 & 2 \end{vmatrix} -1\begin{vmatrix} -1 & 1 \\ -3 & 2 \end{vmatrix} + 5\begin{vmatrix} -1 & 1 \\ -1 & 0 \end{vmatrix}$$

$$= 2(-2) -1 + 5(1)$$

$$= 0$$

$$x = \frac{D_x}{D} = \frac{4}{4} = 1$$

$$y = \frac{D_y}{D} = \frac{4}{4} = 1$$

$$z = \frac{D_z}{D} = \frac{0}{4} = 0$$

The solution is (1, 1, 0).

CHAPTER 11

EXPONENTS, ROOTS, AND RADICALS

▶ 11.1   Zero and Negative Exponents (text page 329)

KEY TOPICS

A.   Evaluate:

(a) 4^{-1} (b) 3^0 (c) $\dfrac{2^{-4}}{3^{-2}}$

SOLUTION.

(a) $4^{-1} = \dfrac{1}{4}$ (b) $3^0 = 1$ (c) $\dfrac{2^{-4}}{3^{-2}} = \dfrac{\frac{1}{2^4}}{\frac{1}{3^2}}$

$$= \frac{1}{2^4} \cdot \frac{3^2}{1}$$

$$= \frac{9}{16}$$

B.   Determine the exponent m:

(a) $\dfrac{1}{a} = a^m$ (b) $\dfrac{4}{25} = \left(\dfrac{5}{2}\right)^m$

SOLUTION.

(a) $m = -1$ because $a^{-1} = \dfrac{1}{a}$

(b) $m = -2$ because $\left(\dfrac{5}{2}\right)^{-2} = \left(\dfrac{2}{5}\right)^2 = \dfrac{4}{25}$

C.   Simplify and write your answers using negative exponents (instead of using a denominator).

(a) $\dfrac{x^{-2}}{x^6}$ (b) $\dfrac{2ab^3}{a^{-3}b^4}$

KEY EXERCISES

A.   Evaluate each expression:

1. 6^{-1} _____   2. 8^0 _____

3. $(-4)^{-2}$ _____   4. $\left(\dfrac{3}{5}\right)^{-2}$ _____

5. $(2^{-3})^{-1}$ _____

B.   Determine the exponent m.

6. $\dfrac{1}{x^2} = x^m$ _____   7. $\dfrac{1}{16} = 4^m$ _____

8. $9^m = 1$ _____   9. $\dfrac{27}{8} = \left(\dfrac{2}{3}\right)^m$ _____

C.   Simplify and write your answers using negative exponents
      (instead of using a denominator).

10. $\dfrac{b^7}{b^{10}}$ _____   11. $(a^2 x^3 y)^{-1}$ _____

SOLUTION.

(a) $\dfrac{x^{-2}}{x^6} = x^{-2-6} = x^{-8}$

(b) $\dfrac{2ab^3}{a^{-3}b^4} = 2a^{1-(-3)}b^{3-4} = 2a^4b^{-1}$

▶ 11.2   The Rules for Exponents (text page 335)

KEY TOPICS

Assume $a \neq 0$, $b \neq 0$, $x \neq 0$.

A.   Simplify, and write your answers using only positive exponents.

(a) a^8a^{-6}

(b) $\dfrac{a^{-7}b}{a^{-4}b^{-2}}$

(c) $(5ab^2)^3$

(d) $\dfrac{4abx^2}{(2x)^2}$

(e) $\left(\dfrac{a}{b}\right)^3 (ab)^2$

SOLUTION.

(a) $a^8a^{-6} = a^{8-6} = a^2$

(b) $\dfrac{a^{-7}b}{a^{-4}b^{-2}} = \dfrac{a^{-7}}{a^{-4}} \cdot \dfrac{b}{b^{-2}}$

$= a^{-7-(-4)}b^{1-(-2)}$

$= a^{-3}b^3$

$= \dfrac{b^3}{a^3}$

(c) $(5ab^2)^3 = 5^3a^3(b^2)^3 = 125a^3b^{2\cdot3} = 125a^3b^6$

96 LEFT

12. $\left(\dfrac{1}{2x^3y^2}\right)^{-2}$ _____ 13. $\left(\dfrac{x^2a}{ax^3}\right)^{-3}$ _____

14. $\dfrac{a-b}{(a-b)^{-1}}$ _____

KEY EXERCISES

Assume $a \neq 0$, $b \neq 0$, $x \neq 0$, $y \neq 0$.

A. Simplify, and write your answers using only positive exponents.

1. a^4a^6 _____ 2. a^6a^{-4} _____

3. a^4a^{-6} _____ 4. $\dfrac{a^4}{a^6}$ _____

5. $\dfrac{a^4}{a^{-6}}$ _____ 6. $(ab)^4$ _____

7. $(a^2b^3)^3$ _____ 8. $\left(\dfrac{a}{b}\right)^5$ _____

9. $\left(\dfrac{a^2}{b^3}\right)^2$ _____ 10. $\left(\dfrac{ab^2}{xy}\right)^{-1}$ _____

11. $\dfrac{(2ax^2)^4}{(2ax)^2}$ _____ 12. $\left(\dfrac{a}{b}\right)^2 \left(\dfrac{b}{a}\right)^3$ _____

13. $\dfrac{(10ax)^2}{5a^4x}$ _____ 14. $\dfrac{(a+b)^2}{a+b}$ _____

15. $\dfrac{x^{-1}+y^{-1}}{(x+y)^{-1}}$ _____

(d) $\dfrac{4abx^2}{(2x)^2} = \dfrac{4abx^2}{4x^2} = ab$

(e) $\left(\dfrac{a}{b}\right)^3 (ab)^2 = \dfrac{a^3}{b^3} \cdot a^2 b^2 = \dfrac{a^5}{b}$

▶ 11.3   Scientific Notation (text page 339)

KEY TOPICS

A.   Express each number in scientific notation.

(a) 276

(b) 639 000

(c) .0076

SOLUTION.

(a) $276 = 2.76 \times 10^2$

(b) $639\ 000 = 6.39 \times 10^5$

(c) $.0076 = 7.6 \times 10^{-3}$

B.   Convert scientific notation back to the usual decimal notation.

(a) 2.82×10^4

(b) 8.08×10^{-5}

SOLUTION.

(a) $2.82 \times 10^4 = 28\ 200$

(b) $8.08 \times 10^{-5} = .000\ 080\ 8$

C.   Find the value of $\dfrac{2400 \times 900}{40\ 000 \times 2.7}$.

Express your answer in scientific notation.

SOLUTION.

$$\frac{2400 \times 900}{40\ 000 \times 2.7} = \frac{\overset{2}{\cancel{24}} \times 10^2 \times \cancel{9} \times 10^2}{\cancel{4} \times 10^4 \times \cancel{27} \times 10^{-1}}$$

$$= 2 \times 10^{2+2-[4+(-1)]}$$

$$= 2 \times 10$$

KEY EXERCISES

A.   Express each number in scientific notation.

1. 32 _____   2. 9847 _____

3. .07 _____   4. 8 110 000 _____

5. .000 43 _____

B.   Convert scientific notation back to the usual decimal
     notation.

6. 2.46×10^2 _____   7. 8.35×10^7 _____

8. 1.01×10^{-2} _____   9. 4.13×10^{-6} _____

10. 7.171×10^{-1} _____

C.   Find the value of each number. Express your answer in
     scientific notation.

11. $10^6 \times 10^5 \times 10^{-7}$ _____

12. $3000 \times 50\ 000 \times 2000$ _____

13. $8000 \times .005$ _____

14. $\dfrac{20\ 000 \times 25\ 000}{400 \times 500\ 000}$ _____

15. $\dfrac{.0049 \times 12\ 500}{70\ 000 \times .005}$ _____

▶ 11.4 Rational Exponents (text page 344)

KEY TOPICS

A. Simplify:

(a) $64^{1/2}$ (b) $27^{2/3}$

(c) $81^{-1/2}$

SOLUTION.

(a) $64^{1/2} = 8$

(b) $27^{2/3} = (27^{1/3})^2$

$= 3^2$

$= 9$

(c) $81^{-1/2} = (81^{1/2})^{-1}$

$= 9^{-1}$

$= \frac{1}{9}$

B. Find the length of the hypotenuse of a right triangle if the lengths of the other sides are 6 and 8.

SOLUTION.

Let c be the length of the hypotenuse and let a and b be the lengths of the other sides. Then

$$c^2 = a^2 + b^2$$

$$= 6^2 + 8^2$$

$$= 36 + 64$$

$$= 100$$

$$c = 100^{1/2}$$

$$= 10$$

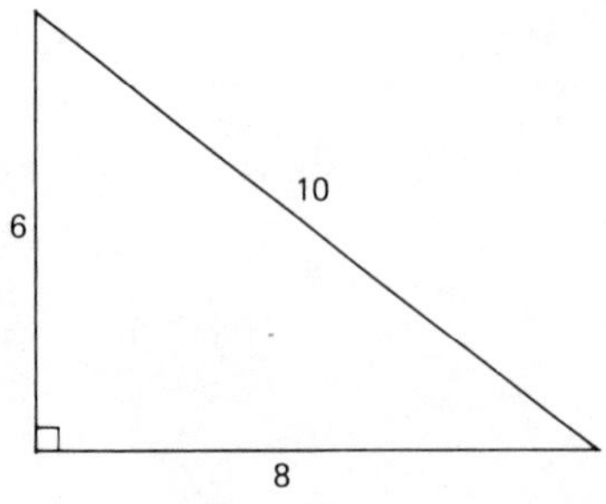

Figure 11.1

KEY EXERCISES

A.   Simplify:

1. $25^{1/2}$ _____

2. $64^{1/3}$ _____

3. $16^{3/4}$ _____

4. $100^{-1/2}$ _____

5. $144^{1/2}$ _____

6. $36^{1/2} \cdot 49^{-1/2}$ _____

7. $64^{5/6}$ _____

8. $27^{-4/3}$ _____

9. $(-1000)^{2/3}$ _____

10. $81^{-3/4}$ _____

B.   Find the length of the hypotenuse of a right triangle if the lengths of the other sides are:

11. 9 and 12 _____

12. 5 and 12 _____

KEY TOPICS

Let $a > 0$, $b > 0$, $x > 0$, $y > 0$.

A.   Simplify and express your answer using only positive exponents.

(a) $a^{1/4} \cdot a^{1/4}$

(b) $\dfrac{a^{2/3}}{a^{1/3}}$

(c) $(a^{1/2})^{1/5}$

(d) $\left(\dfrac{a^{1/2}b^2}{xy^{2/3}}\right)^{1/2}$

(e) $\dfrac{a^{1/2}b^{1/4}}{a^{3/4}b^{1/2}}$

SOLUTION.

(a) $a^{1/4} \cdot a^{1/4} = a^{1/4 + 1/4} = a^{2/4} = a^{1/2}$

(b) $\dfrac{a^{2/3}}{a^{1/3}} = a^{2/3 - 1/3} = a^{1/3}$

(c) $(a^{1/2})^{1/5} = a^{(1/2)(1/5)} = a^{1/10}$

(d) $\left(\dfrac{a^{1/2}b^2}{xy^{2/3}}\right)^{1/2} = \dfrac{(a^{1/2})^{1/2}(b^2)^{1/2}}{x^{1/2}(y^{2/3})^{1/2}}$

$= \dfrac{a^{(1/2)(1/2)}b^{2(1/2)}}{x^{1/2}y^{(2/3)(1/2)}}$

$= \dfrac{a^{1/4}b}{x^{1/2}y^{1/3}}$

(e) $\dfrac{a^{1/2}b^{1/4}}{a^{3/4}b^{1/2}} = \dfrac{a^{1/2}}{a^{3/4}} \cdot \dfrac{b^{1/4}}{b^{1/2}}$

$= a^{1/2 - 3/4} \cdot b^{1/4 - 1/2}$

KEY EXERCISES

Let $a > 0$, $b > 0$, $c > 0$, $x > 0$, $y > 0$.

A. Simplify and express your answer using only positive exponents.

1. $a^{1/2} \cdot a^{3/2}$ _____

2. $\dfrac{a^{3/2}}{a^{1/2}}$ _____

3. $a^{3/4} \cdot a^{1/2}$ _____

4. $\dfrac{a^{3/4}}{a^{1/2}}$ _____

5. $(x^{1/2})^{3/4}$ _____

6. $(a^{1/4}b)^{1/2}$ _____

7. $\left(\dfrac{a}{b^{1/2}xy^{1/3}}\right)^{1/2}$ _____

8. $\left(\dfrac{4a^{1/4}}{xy^{3/4}}\right)^{1/2}$ _____

9. $\dfrac{a^{1/4}b^{3/4}c^{1/2}}{a^{1/4}b^{1/4}c^{3/4}}$ _____

10. $(25a^{1/2}b^{4/3})^{-1/2}$ _____

$$= a^{2/4 - 3/4} \, b^{1/4 - 2/4}$$

$$= a^{-1/4} b^{-1/4}$$

$$= \frac{1}{a^{1/4} b^{1/4}}$$

B.   Simplify:

(a) $\left(\frac{81}{16}\right)^{3/4}$ (b) $\left(\frac{8}{27}\right)^{-1/3}$

SOLUTION.

(a) $\left(\frac{81}{16}\right)^{3/4} = \frac{81^{3/4}}{16^{3/4}}$ (b) $\left(\frac{8}{27}\right)^{-1/3} = \frac{8^{-1/3}}{27^{-1/3}}$

$$= \frac{(81^{1/4})^3}{(16^{1/4})^3} \qquad\qquad = \frac{(8^{1/3})^{-1}}{(27^{1/3})^{-1}}$$

$$= \frac{3^3}{2^3} \qquad\qquad\qquad = \frac{2^{-1}}{3^{-1}}$$

$$= \frac{27}{8} \qquad\qquad\qquad = \frac{\frac{1}{2}}{\frac{1}{3}}$$

$$= \frac{1}{2} \cdot \frac{3}{1}$$

$$= \frac{3}{2}$$

▶ 11.6   Radical Notation (text page 352)

KEY TOPICS

Assume a > 0, b > 0, c > 0, x > 0, y > 0.

A.   Simplify:

(a) $\sqrt{49}$ (b) $\sqrt[4]{16}$

B.   Simplify:

11. $\left(\dfrac{4}{9}\right)^{1/2}$ _____

12. $\left(\dfrac{16}{25}\right)^{3/2}$ _____

13. $\left(\dfrac{100}{49}\right)^{-1/2}$ _____

14. $25^{1/2}16^{3/4}$ _____

15. $\left(\dfrac{27}{1000}\right)^{-2/3}$ _____

KEY EXERCISES

Assume a > 0, b > 0, c > 0, x > 0, y > 0, z > 0.

A.   Simplify:

1. $\sqrt{144}$ _____

2. $\sqrt[3]{-8}$ _____

100 RIGHT

SOLUTION.

$\quad\quad$ (a) $\quad \sqrt{49} = 7$ $\quad\quad\quad\quad$ (b) $\quad \sqrt[4]{16} = 2$

B. $\quad$ Express in radical notation:

$\quad\quad$ (a) $\quad a^{3/4}$ $\quad\quad\quad\quad\quad\quad$ (b) $\quad a^{2/3}b^{1/2}$

SOLUTION.

$\quad\quad$ (a) $\quad a^{3/4} = \sqrt[4]{a^3}$ $\quad\quad$ (b) $\quad a^{2/3}b^{1/2} = \sqrt[3]{a^2}\,\sqrt{b}$

C. $\quad$ Express in terms of rational exponents.

$\quad\quad$ (a) $\quad \sqrt[5]{x}$ $\quad\quad\quad\quad\quad\quad$ (b) $\quad \sqrt[4]{xy^3}$

SOLUTION.

$\quad\quad$ (a) $\quad \sqrt[5]{x} = x^{1/5}$ $\quad\quad$ (b) $\quad \sqrt[4]{xy^3} = (xy^3)^{1/4}$

$$= x^{1/4}y^{3/4}$$

D. $\quad$ Simplify:

$\quad\quad$ (a) $\quad \sqrt{a^6 b^4 c^{10}}$ $\quad\quad\quad\quad$ (b) $\quad \sqrt[3]{27}\,\sqrt[4]{16b^4c^{12}}$

SOLUTION.

$\quad\quad$ (a) $\quad \sqrt{a^6 b^4 c^{10}} = a^3 b^2 c^5$

$\quad\quad$ (b) $\quad \sqrt[3]{27}\,\sqrt[4]{16b^4c^{12}} = 3 \cdot 2bc^3$

$$= 6bc^3$$

▶ 11.7 $\quad$ Combining Radicals (text page 356)

KEY TOPICS

A. $\quad$ Combine, as indicated.

$\quad\quad$ (a) $\quad \sqrt{5} + 2\sqrt{5}$ $\quad\quad\quad\quad$ (b) $\quad \dfrac{\sqrt{7}}{2} - \dfrac{\sqrt{7}}{3}$

3. $(\sqrt{25})^3$ _____   4. $\sqrt[5]{100\ 000}$ _____

5. $\sqrt[3]{(-1)^5}$ _____

B. Express in radical notation:

6. $a^{3/4}$ _____   7. $b^{1/2}c^{1/4}$ _____

8. $(4ab)^{1/2}$ _____   9. $(a-b)^{1/2}$ _____

10. $a - b^{1/2}$ _____

C. Express in terms of rational exponents.

11. $\sqrt{xy}$ _____   12. $\sqrt{4xy^2z^3}$ _____

13. $\sqrt{a+b}$ _____   14. $\sqrt{a} + \sqrt{b}$ _____

15. $\dfrac{5}{\sqrt{xy}}$ _____

D. Simplify:

16. $\sqrt{36a^4}$ _____   17. $\sqrt{\dfrac{a^8b^6}{c^4}}$ _____

18. $\sqrt[5]{32a^5b^{10}}$ _____   19. $\sqrt{x^2} + \sqrt{y^2}$ _____

20. $\dfrac{\sqrt[4]{16a^8b^4}}{\sqrt[3]{8a^9b^6}}$ _____

KEY EXERCISES

A. Combine, as indicated.

1. $2\sqrt{3} + 3\sqrt{3}$ _____   2. $\dfrac{\sqrt{5}}{2} - \dfrac{\sqrt{5}}{4}$ _____

101 RIGHT

SOLUTION.

(a) $\sqrt{5} + 2\sqrt{5} = 3\sqrt{5}$ (b) $\dfrac{\sqrt{7}}{2} - \dfrac{\sqrt{7}}{3} = \dfrac{3\sqrt{7} - 2\sqrt{7}}{6} = \dfrac{\sqrt{7}}{6}$

B. Multiply, as indicated.

(a) $\sqrt{2}(\sqrt{3} + \sqrt{6})$ (b) $(x^{1/2} + y^{1/2})(x^{1/2} - y^{1/2})$

SOLUTION.

(a) $\sqrt{2}(\sqrt{3} + \sqrt{6}) = \sqrt{2 \cdot 3} + \sqrt{2 \cdot 6}$

$\qquad\qquad\qquad = \sqrt{6} + \sqrt{2 \cdot 2 \cdot 3}$

$\qquad\qquad\qquad = \sqrt{6} + 2\sqrt{3}$

(b) $(x^{1/2} + y^{1/2})(x^{1/2} - y^{1/2}) = x^{1/2}x^{1/2} + x^{1/2}y^{1/2} - x^{1/2}y^{1/2} - y^{1/2}y^{1/2}$

$\qquad\qquad\qquad\qquad\qquad = x - y$

C. Factor:

(a) $\sqrt{75} - \sqrt{50}$ (b) $\sqrt{18x^3y^3} - \sqrt{8xy^5}$

SOLUTION.

(a) $\sqrt{75} - \sqrt{50} = \sqrt{3 \cdot 25} - \sqrt{2 \cdot 25}$

$\qquad\qquad\qquad = 5\sqrt{3} - 5\sqrt{2}$

$\qquad\qquad\qquad = 5(\sqrt{3} - \sqrt{2})$

(b) $\sqrt{18x^3y^3} - \sqrt{8xy^5} = \sqrt{9x^2y^2 \cdot 2xy} - \sqrt{4y^4 \cdot 2xy}$

$\qquad\qquad\qquad\qquad = 3xy\sqrt{2xy} - 2y^2\sqrt{2xy}$

$\qquad\qquad\qquad\qquad = y\sqrt{2xy}(3x - 2y)$

3. $\sqrt{25x} + \sqrt{16x}$ _____

4. $\dfrac{\sqrt{3}}{2} - \left[\dfrac{\sqrt{3}}{4} - \dfrac{\sqrt{3}}{8}\right]$ _____

5. $\dfrac{(ab)^{1/2}}{5} - \dfrac{(ab)^{1/2}}{3}$ _____

B.   Multiply, as indicated.

6. $\sqrt{2}\,(\sqrt{5} + \sqrt{2})$ _____

7. $y^{1/2}(y^{1/2} + y^{1/4})$ _____

8. $x^{1/4}(x^{3/4} - 1)$ _____

9. $(a^{1/2} + a^{1/4})a^{3/4}$ _____

10. $(x^{1/2} + x^{1/4})(x^{1/2} - x^{1/4})$ _____

C.   Factor:

11. $\sqrt{12} - \sqrt{27}$ _____

12. $\sqrt{10} + \sqrt{6}$ _____

13. $\sqrt{a^4bc^2} + \sqrt{4a^4b}$ _____

14. $x^{1/2}y^{3/2} - x^{3/2}y^{1/2}$ _____

15. $\sqrt{8x^3y^5} + \sqrt{2xy^3} - \sqrt{18x^7y^9}$ _____

D.   Simplify: $\dfrac{\sqrt{32} - \sqrt{48}}{4}$

SOLUTION.

$$\frac{\sqrt{32} - \sqrt{48}}{4} = \frac{\sqrt{16 \cdot 2} - \sqrt{16 \cdot 3}}{4}$$

$$= \frac{4\sqrt{2} - 4\sqrt{3}}{4}$$

$$= \frac{4(\sqrt{2} - \sqrt{3})}{4}$$

$$= \sqrt{2} - \sqrt{3}$$

▶ 11.8   Rationalizing the Denominator (text page 360)

KEY TOPICS

A.   Rationalize the denominator.

(a) $\dfrac{2}{\sqrt{5}}$ (b) $\dfrac{-5}{a^{3/5}}$

(c) $\dfrac{3}{1 - \sqrt{2}}$ (d) $\dfrac{a}{\sqrt{x} + \sqrt{y}}$

SOLUTION.

(a) $\dfrac{2}{\sqrt{5}} = \dfrac{2}{\sqrt{5}} \cdot \dfrac{\sqrt{5}}{\sqrt{5}} = \dfrac{2\sqrt{5}}{5}$

(b) $\dfrac{-5}{a^{3/5}} = \dfrac{-5}{a^{3/5}} \cdot \dfrac{a^{2/5}}{a^{2/5}} = \dfrac{-5a^{2/5}}{a}$

(c) $\dfrac{3}{1 - \sqrt{2}} = \dfrac{3}{1 - \sqrt{2}} \cdot \dfrac{1 + \sqrt{2}}{1 + \sqrt{2}} = \dfrac{3(1 + \sqrt{2})}{1 - 2}$

$$= \frac{3(1 + \sqrt{2})}{-1} = -3(1 + \sqrt{2})$$

D.   Simplify:

16. $\dfrac{10 - \sqrt{50}}{5}$ _____

17. $\dfrac{9x\sqrt{a} + 6y\sqrt{a}}{3\sqrt{a}}$ _____

18. $\dfrac{\sqrt{5} - \sqrt{20}}{\sqrt{45}}$ _____

19. $\dfrac{\sqrt{x^3 y^3} - \sqrt{xy}}{\sqrt{x^5 y^7}}$ _____

20. $\dfrac{\sqrt{100x^6 y^8} + \sqrt{25x^4 y^{10}}}{5x^2 y^3}$ _____

KEY EXERCISES

A.   Rationalize the denominator.

1. $\dfrac{5}{\sqrt{3}}$ _____

2. $\dfrac{3}{2^{1/2}}$ _____

3. $\dfrac{4}{3\sqrt{2}}$ _____

4. $\dfrac{10}{3\sqrt{2x}}$ _____

5. $\dfrac{-2}{\sqrt{a}\sqrt{b}}$ _____

6. $\dfrac{1}{\sqrt{x^3 y^3}}$ _____

7. $\dfrac{2}{a^{1/3}}$ _____

8. $\dfrac{1}{1 + \sqrt{3}}$ _____

9. $\dfrac{5}{1 - \sqrt{2}}$ _____

10. $\dfrac{-2}{\sqrt{a} + \sqrt{b}}$ _____

11. $\dfrac{5}{2 - 3\sqrt{x}}$ _____

12. $\dfrac{1}{2\sqrt{3} - 5\sqrt{2}}$ _____

(d) $\dfrac{a}{\sqrt{x} + \sqrt{y}} = \dfrac{a}{\sqrt{x} + \sqrt{y}} \cdot \dfrac{\sqrt{x} - \sqrt{y}}{\sqrt{x} - \sqrt{y}}$

$$= \dfrac{a(\sqrt{x} - \sqrt{y})}{x - y}$$

▶ 11.9   Complex Numbers (text page 364)

KEY TOPICS

A.   Write $\sqrt{-9}$ in the form bi.

SOLUTION.

$$\sqrt{-9} = \sqrt{9(-1)} = \sqrt{9}\sqrt{-1} = 3i$$

B.   Determine the real part, the imaginary part, and the conjugate of 4 − 2i.

SOLUTION.

The real part is 4.
The imaginary part is −2.
The conjugate of 4 − 2i is 4 + 2i.

C.   Determine each complex number in the form a + bi.

(a)   (2 + 5i) − (3 − 2i)   (b)   (4 + i)(5 − 2i)

(c) $\dfrac{3 + i}{2 + i}$

SOLUTION.

(a)   (2 + 5i) − (3 − 2i) = (2 − 3) + [5 − (−2)]i

$$= -1 + 7i$$

(b)   4 + i
         5 − 2i   Note: $-2i^2 = -2(-1) = 2$
        ‾‾‾‾‾‾
        20 + 5i
            −8i + 2
        ‾‾‾‾‾‾‾‾‾
        22 − 3i

KEY EXERCISES

A.   Write each expression in the form bi.

1. $\sqrt{-25}$ _____   2. $\sqrt{-6}$ _____

3. $\sqrt{\dfrac{-1}{4}}$ _____   4. $\sqrt{\dfrac{-9}{16}}$ _____

B.   Determine (a) the real part, (b) the imaginary part, and
     (c) the conjugate of the given complex number.

5. 6 + 5i   (a) _____ (b) _____ (c) _____

6. $\dfrac{3}{2}$ - 8i   (a) _____ (b) _____ (c) _____

7.   -9   (a) _____ (b) _____ (c) _____

8.   4i   (a) _____ (b) _____ (c) _____

C.   Determine each complex number in the form a + bi.

9. (6 + 7i) + (5 - 3i) _____

10. (2 - i) - (3 + 2i) _____

11. (6 + 3i)(1 - i) _____

12. $(-5i)^2$ _____   13. $\dfrac{2 + 5i}{3 + i}$ _____

14. $(2 + i)^{-1}$ _____

(c) $\dfrac{3 + i}{2 + i} = \dfrac{3 + i}{2 + i} \cdot \dfrac{2 - i}{2 - i}$

$$= \dfrac{6 - 3i + 2i - i^2}{4 - i^2}$$

$$= \dfrac{7 - i}{5}$$

$$= \dfrac{7}{5} - \dfrac{1}{5}i$$

D. Simplify i^{14}.

SOLUTION.

$$i^{14} = i^{12} \cdot i^2 = i^2 = -1$$

D.   Simplify:

15. i^{11} _____   16. i^{-3} _____

CHAPTER 12

LOGARITHMS

▶ 12.1   Definition of Logarithms (text page 375)

KEY TOPICS

A.   Express in logarithmic notation.

(a) $5^2 = 25$ (b) $.04^{1/2} = .2$

SOLUTION.

(a) $\log_5 25 = 2$ (b) $\log_{.04} .2 = \dfrac{1}{2}$

B.   Find the value of each logarithm.

(a) $\log_3 81$ (b) $\log_8 \dfrac{1}{2}$

SOLUTION.

(a) $\log_3 81 = 4$ because $3^4 = 81$

(b) $\log_8 \dfrac{1}{2} = \dfrac{-1}{3}$ because $8^{-1/3} = \dfrac{1}{8^{1/3}} = \dfrac{1}{2}$

C.   Find the value of x.

(a) $\log_7 x = 2$ (b) $\log_x 1000 = 3$

SOLUTION.

(a) $x = 49$ because $\log_7 49 = 2$

(b) $x = 10$ because $\log_{10} 1000 = 3$

KEY EXERCISES

A. Express in logarithmic notation.

1. $9^2 = 81$ _____

2. $5^3 = 125$ _____

3. $\left(\frac{1}{2}\right)^2 = \frac{1}{4}$ _____

4. $6^{-1} = \frac{1}{6}$ _____

5. $16^{1/4} = 2$ _____

B. Find the value of each logarithm.

6. $\log_8 64$ _____   7. $\log_2 32$ _____

8. $\log_{\frac{1}{2}} \frac{1}{8}$ _____   9. $\log_{25} 5$ _____

10. $\log_3 \frac{1}{9}$ _____

C. Find the value of x.

11. $\log_{10} 100 = x$ _____

12. $\log_x 36 = 2$ _____

13. $\log_3 x = 3$ _____

14. $\log_x .008 = 3$ _____

▶ 12.2   Properties of Logarithms (text page 380)

KEY TOPICS

A.   Verify the equation

$$\log_2 32 = \log_2 8 + \log_2 4$$

by evaluating both sides. Indicate which property of logarithms is illustrated.

SOLUTION.

$$\log_2 32 = \log_2 8 + \log_2 4$$

because

$$5 \quad = \quad 3 + 2$$

Recall the property

$$\log_b n_1 n_2 = \log_b n_1 + \log_b n_2.$$

Here $b = 2$, $n_1 = 8$, $n_2 = 4$

B.   Express $\log_b \sqrt{xy}$ in terms of simpler logarithms.

SOLUTION.

$$\log_b \sqrt{xy} = \log_b (xy)^{1/2}$$

$$= \log_b x^{1/2} y^{1/2}$$

$$= \log_b x^{1/2} + \log_b y^{1/2}$$

$$= \frac{1}{2}\log_b x + \frac{1}{2}\log_b y$$

15. $\log_x \frac{1}{36} = -2$ _____

KEY EXERCISES

A.   (a) Verify each equation by evaluating both sides.
      (b) Indicate which property of logarithms is illustrated.

1. $\log_2 128 = \log_2 32 + \log_2 4$

(a) _____ (b) _____

2. $\log_5 25 = \log_5 125 - \log_5 5$

(a) _____ (b) _____

3. $\log_{10} 1000 = 3 \log_{10} 10$

(a) _____ (b) _____

4. $\log_2 64 = 3 \log_2 4$

(a) _____ (b) _____

5. $\log_2 \frac{1}{16} = -2 \log_2 4$

(a) _____ (b) _____

B.   Express in terms of simpler logarithms.

6. $\log_{10} ab$ _____

7. $\log_5 \frac{ab}{c}$ _____

8. $\log_2 \sqrt{\frac{x}{y}}$ _____

9. $\log_3 \frac{\sqrt{x}}{y}$ _____

10. $\log_3 \frac{5ab}{7}$ _____

C.   Express $\log_b \dfrac{45}{32}$ in terms of $\log_b 2$, $\log_b 3$, and $\log_b 5$.

SOLUTION.

$$\log_b \frac{45}{32} = \log_b \frac{3^2 \cdot 5}{2^5}$$

$$= \log_b 3^2 \cdot 5 - \log_b 2^5$$

$$= 2\log_b 3 + \log_b 5 - 5\log_b 2$$

D.   Express $\dfrac{\log_b 10 - \log_b 3}{2}$

as a single logarithm.

SOLUTION.

$$\frac{\log_b 10 - \log_b 3}{2} = \frac{1}{2}(\log_b 10 - \log_b 3)$$

$$= \frac{1}{2}\log_b \frac{10}{3}$$

$$= \log_b \left(\frac{10}{3}\right)^{1/2}$$

$$\text{or} \qquad \log_b \sqrt{\frac{10}{3}}$$

▶ 12.3   Common Logarithms (text page 385)

KEY TOPICS

All logarithms are to the base 10 (common logarithms).

A.   Find the value of: log 3.82

C.   Express in terms of $\log_b 2$, $\log_b 3$, and $\log_b 5$.

11. $\log_b 10$ _____

12. $\log_b \dfrac{3}{5}$ _____

13. $\log_b \dfrac{27}{10}$ _____

14. $\log_b 48$ _____

15. $\log_b \dfrac{1}{30}$ _____

D.   Express as a single logarithm.

16. $\log_{10} a + \log_{10} b + \log_{10} c$ _____

17. $\log_{10} a - \log_{10} b + \log_{10} c$ _____

18. $2 \log_5 a + 3 \log_5 b$ _____

19. $\dfrac{\log_2 5 + \log_2 3}{10}$ _____

KEY EXERCISES

All logarithms are common logarithms.

A.   Find each value.

1. log 2.06 _____   2. log 4.71 _____

SOLUTION.

n	0	1	2	3	4	5	6	7	8	9
1.0	.0000	.0043	.0086	.0128	.0170	.0212	.0253	.0294	.0334	.0374
1.1	.0414	.0453	.0492	.0531	.0569	.0607	.0645	.0682	.0719	.0755
1.2	.0792	.0828	.0864	.0899	.0934	.0969	.1004	.1038	.1072	.1106
1.3	.1139	.1173	.1206	.1239	.1271	.1303	.1335	.1367	.1399	.1430
1.4	.1461	.1492	.1523	.1553	.1584	.1614	.1644	.1673	.1703	.1732
1.5	.1761	.1790	.1818	.1847	.1875	.1903	.1931	.1959	.1987	.2014
1.6	.2041	.2068	.2095	.2122	.2148	.2175	.2201	.2227	.2253	.2279
1.7	.2304	.2330	.2355	.2380	.2405	.2430	.2455	.2480	.2504	.2529
1.8	.2553	.2577	.2601	.2625	.2648	.2672	.2695	.2718	.2742	.2765
1.9	.2788	.2810	.2833	.2856	.2878	.2900	.2923	.2945	.2967	.2989
2.0	.3010	.3032	.3054	.3075	.3096	.3118	.3139	.3160	.3181	.3201
2.1	.3222	.3243	.3263	.3284	.3304	.3324	.3345	.3365	.3385	.3404
2.2	.3424	.3444	.3464	.3483	.3502	.3522	.3541	.3560	.3579	.3598
2.3	.3617	.3636	.3655	.3674	.3692	.3711	.3729	.3747	.3766	.3784
2.4	.3802	.3820	.3838	.3856	.3874	.3892	.3909	.3927	.3945	.3962
2.5	.3979	.3997	.4014	.4031	.4048	.4065	.4802	.4099	.4116	.4133
2.6	.4150	.4166	.4183	.4200	.4216	.4232	.4249	.4265	.4281	.4298
2.7	.4314	.4330	.4346	.4362	.4378	.4393	.4409	.4425	.4440	.4456
2.8	.4472	.4487	.4502	.4518	.4533	.4548	.4564	.4579	.4594	.4609
2.9	.4624	.4639	.4654	.4669	.4683	.4698	.4713	.4728	.4742	.4757
3.0	.4771	.4786	.4800	.4814	.4829	.4843	.4857	.4871	.4886	.4900
3.1	.4914	.4928	.4942	.4955	.4969	.4983	.4997	.5011	.5024	.5038
3.2	.5051	.5065	.5079	.5092	.5105	.5119	.5132	.5145	.5159	.5172
3.3	.5185	.5198	.5211	.5224	.5237	.5250	.5263	.5276	.5289	.5302
3.4	.5315	.5328	.5340	.5353	.5366	.5378	.5391	.5403	.5416	.5428
3.5	.5441	.5453	.5465	.5478	.5490	.5502	.5514	.5527	.5539	.5551
3.6	.5563	.5575	.5587	.5599	.5611	.5623	.5635	.5647	.5658	.5670
3.7	.5682	.5694	.5705	.5717	.5729	.5740	.5752	.5763	.5775	.5786
3.8	.5798	.5809	.5821	.5832	.5843	.5855	.5866	.5877	.5888	.5899
3.9	.5911	.5922	.5933	.5944	.5955	.5966	.5977	.5988	.5999	.6010

TABLE 12.1

log 3.82 = .5821

B.   Determine the characteristic of:

(a)   log 4720   (b)   log .0856

SOLUTION.

(a) $4720 = 4.720 \times 10^3$

The characteristic of log 4720 is 3.

(b) $.0856 = 8.56 \times 10^{-2}$

The characteristic of log .0856 is −2.

3. log 9.47 _____   4. log 5.08 _____

5. log 3.13 _____

B.   Determine the characteristic of each logarithm.

6. log 29.2 _____   7. log 7.43 _____

8. log 9390 _____   9. log .439 _____

10. log .000 724 _____

C.   Find the value of: log .004 19

SOLUTION.

$$.004\ 19 = 4.19 \times 10^{-3}$$

$$\log .004\ 19 = \log (4.19 \times 10^{-3})$$

$$= \log 4.19 - 3$$

	0	1	2	3	4	5	6	7	8	9
4.0	.6021	.6031	.6042	.6053	.6064	.6075	.6085	.6096	.6107	.6117
4.1	.6128	.6138	.6149	.6160	.6170	.6180	.6191	.6201	.6212	.6222
4.2	.6232	.6243	.6253	.6263	.6274	.6284	.6294	.6304	.6314	.6325
4.3	.6335	.6345	.6355	.6365	.6375	.6385	.6395	.6405	.6415	.6425
4.4	.6435	.6444	.6454	.6464	.6474	.6484	.6493	.6503	.6513	.6522
4.5	.6532	.6542	.6551	.6561	.6571	.6580	.6590	.6599	.6609	.6618
4.6	.6628	.6637	.6646	.6656	.6665	.6675	.6684	.6693	.6702	.6712
4.7	.6721	.6730	.6739	.6749	.6758	.6767	.6776	.6785	.6794	.6803
4.8	.6812	.6821	.6830	.6839	.6848	.6857	.6866	.6875	.6884	.6893
4.9	.6902	.6911	.6920	.6928	.6937	.6946	.6955	.6964	.6972	.6981
5.0	.6990	.6998	.7007	.7016	.7024	.7033	.7042	.7050	.7059	.7067
5.1	.7076	.7084	.7093	.7101	.7110	.7118	.7126	.7135	.7143	.7152
5.2	.7160	.7168	.7177	.7185	.7193	.7202	.7210	.7218	.7226	.7235
5.3	.7243	.7251	.7259	.7267	.7275	.7284	.7292	.7300	.7308	.7316
5.4	.7324	.7332	.7340	.7348	.7356	.7364	.7372	.7380	.7388	.7396
n	**0**	**1**	**2**	**3**	**4**	**5**	**6**	**7**	**8**	**9**

TABLE 12.2

$$\log 4.19 = .6222$$

Thus $\log .004\ 19 = .6222 - 3$

▶ 12.4   Antilogs (text page 394)

KEY TOPICS

A.   Find the value of:

antilog (.6776 - 3)

SOLUTION.

Locate the mantissa .6776 in the table.

C.   Find each value.

11.   log 32.1 _____   12.   log 40 400 _____

13.   log .921 _____   14.   log 354 000 _____

15.   log .007 26 _____

KEY EXERCISES

A.   Find the value of each indicated antilog.

1.   antilog .6964 _____

2.   antilog .9320 _____

3.   antilog 1.6064 _____

4.   antilog 3.9410 _____

5.   antilog .8921 − 1 _____

n	0	1	2	3	4	5	6	7	8	9
4.5	.6532	.6542	.6551	.6561	.6571	.6580	.6590	.6599	.6609	.6618
4.6	.6628	.6637	.6646	.6656	.6665	.6675	.6684	.6693	.6702	.6712
4.7	.6721	.6730	.6739	.6749	.6758	.6767	.6776	.6785	.6794	.6803
4.8	.6812	.6821	.6830	.6839	.6848	.6857	.6866	.6875	.6884	.6893
4.9	.6902	.6911	.6920	.6928	.6937	.6946	.6955	.6964	.6972	.6981
5.0	.6990	.6998	.7007	.7016	.7024	.7033	.7042	.7050	.7059	.7067
5.1	.7076	.7084	.7093	.7101	.7110	.7118	.7126	.7135	.7143	.7152
5.2	.7160	.7168	.7177	.7185	.7193	.7202	.7210	.7218	.7226	.7235
5.3	.7243	.7251	.7259	.7267	.7275	.7284	.7292	.7300	.7308	.7316
5.4	.7324	.7332	.7340	.7348	.7356	.7364	.7372	.7380	.7388	.7396

TABLE 12.3   log 4.76 = .6776 and thus
antilog .6776 = 4.76

Because the characteristic is −3, move the
decimal point 3 places to the left. Add
enough 0's.

$$\log .004\ 76 = .6776 - 3$$

$$.004\ 76 = \text{antilog } (.6776 - 3)$$

▶ 12.5   Interpolating (text page 398)

KEY TOPICS

A.   Find the value of log 45.44 by interpolating.

SOLUTION.

$$\log 45.44 = \log(4.544 \times 10^1)$$

$$= 1 + \log 4.544$$

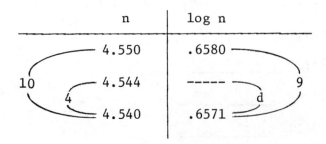

	n	log n	
	4.550	.6580	
10	4.544	-----	9
4	4.540	.6571	d

Table 12.4

111 LEFT

6. antilog .5453 - 2 _____

7. antilog .0253 - 5 _____

8. antilog 6.6618 _____

9. antilog .8463 _____

10. antilog .1523 - 4 _____

KEY EXERCISES

A.   Find the value of the common log by interpolating.

1. log 1.365 _____   2. log 2407 _____

3. log 48.19 _____   4. log .081 13 _____

5. log .000 247 2 _____

Set up the proportion:

$$\frac{4}{10} = \frac{d}{9}$$

$$\frac{36}{10} = d$$

$$3.6 = d$$

Because the digit to the right of the decimal point is 5 or more, approximate d as 4, rather than as 3.

$$
\begin{array}{r}
.6571 \\
+.0004 \\
\hline
\log 4.544 = \quad .6575
\end{array}
$$

and

$$\log 45.44 = 1.6575$$

B.   Find the value of antilog .3081 – 2 by interpolating.

SOLUTION.

First consider the mantissa, .3081. Find n such that log n = .3081.

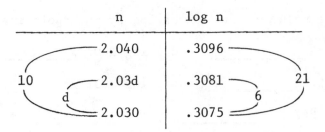

n	log n
2.040	.3096
2.03d	.3081
2.030	.3075

Table 12.5

Set up the proportion:

$$\frac{d}{10} = \frac{6}{21}$$

$$d = \frac{6 \cdot 10}{21} = \frac{60}{21} = 2\frac{18}{21}$$

B.   Find the value of the antilog by interpolating.

6.   antilog .6504 _____

7.   antilog 2.7310 _____

8.   antilog .7370 - 2 _____

9.   antilog 4.9913 _____

10. antilog .0140 - 3 _____

Because $\dfrac{18}{21} \ge \dfrac{1}{2}$, take

$$d = 3 \ .$$

Therefore

$$2.033 = \text{antilog } .3081$$

To find antilog .3081 - 2 (with characteristic -2), move the decimal point 2 places to the left. Add a 0 to the left of 2.

$$.02\underset{\smile}{\ }033 = \text{antilog } .3081 - 2$$

▶ 12.6   Computing with Logarithms (text page 404)

KEY TOPICS

A.   Compute, using common logarithms:

$$\left(\frac{971}{.0732}\right)^2$$

SOLUTION.

$$\text{Let } N = \left(\frac{971}{.0732}\right)^2$$

$$\log N = \log \left(\frac{971}{.0732}\right)^2$$

$$= 2 \log\left(\frac{971}{.0732}\right)$$

$$= 2(\log 971 - \log .0732)$$

$$= 2[\log(9.71 \times 10^2) - \log(7.32 \times 10^{-2})]$$

$$= 2[2.9872 - (.8645 - 2)]$$

$$= 2[2.9872 - .8645 + 2]$$

KEY EXERCISES

A.   Compute, using logarithms.

1. (6.54)(4.85) _____   2. $\dfrac{545}{29.2}$ _____

3. $(.872)^5$ _____   4. $186^{1/3}$ _____

5. $\sqrt{8830}$ _____   6. $\dfrac{(.001\,82)(.0829)}{743}$ _____

7. $\sqrt{(632)(.0874)}$ _____

8. $\dfrac{1960^{1/5}}{.0284^3}$ _____

```
  2.9872
- .8645
  2.1227
+2
  4.1227
×     2
  8.2454
```

$$\log N = 8.2454$$
$$N = \text{antilog } 8.2454$$

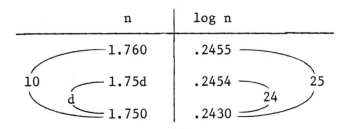

n	log n
1.760	.2455
1.75d	.2454
1.750	.2430

Table 12.6

$$\frac{d}{10} = \frac{24}{25}$$

$$d = \frac{10 \cdot 24}{25} = \frac{240}{25} = 9\frac{15}{25} = 9\frac{3}{5} \approx 10$$

$$N = 1.760 \times 10^8$$

$$= 176\ 000\ 000$$

▶ 12.7 Logarithmic and Exponential Functions (text page 413)

(no exercises)

▶ 12.8   Exponential Equations; Changing the Base (text page 416)

KEY TOPICS

A.   Solve the equation

$$8^{3x} = 494$$

to 2 places after the decimal point.

KEY EXERCISES

A.   Solve the indicated exponential equation to 2 decimal places.

1. $3^x = 30$ _____   2. $y^5 = 100$ _____

SOLUTION.

$$8^{3x} = 494$$

$$\log 8^{3x} = \log 494$$

$$3x \log 8 = \log 494$$

$$3x = \frac{\log 494}{\log 8} = \frac{2.6937}{.9031} \approx 2.983$$

$$x = .99$$

B.   Solve the equation

$$\log (x + 2) = -2 .$$

(Base 10 is understood.)

SOLUTION.

$$\log_{10} (x + 2) = -2$$

$$10^{-2} = x + 2$$

$$.01 = x + 2$$

$$-1.99 = x$$

C.   Find the value of $\log_2 5$ to 2 decimal places.

SOLUTION.

$$\log_2 5 = \frac{\log_{10} 5}{\log_{10} 2}$$

$$= \frac{.6990}{.3010}$$

$$\approx 2.32$$

D.   Use the General Change-of-Base Formula to express $\log_3 7$ to the base 2.

SOLUTION.

$$\log_3 7 = \frac{\log_2 7}{\log_2 3}$$

3. $2^{t+1} = 25$ _____ 4. $9^{-3x} = 500$ _____

5. $8^{1-2t} = 1250$ _____

B.   Solve the indicated logarithmic equation.   (Base 10 is understood.)

6. log 2x = 5 _____

7. log (x + 3) = -1 _____

8. log (-4x) = 6 _____

9. log (2x + 3) = 4 _____

10. log x + log 4 = -2 _____

C.   Find the value of the indicated logarithm to 2 decimal places.

11. $\log_2 9$ _____   12. $\log_5 15$ _____

13. $\log_7 8$ _____   14. $\log_{.4} 200$ _____

D.   Use the General Change-of-Base Formula to express the given logarithm to the indicated base.

15. $\log_3 8$, base 5 _____   16. $\log_5 12$, base 4 _____

17. $\log_8 92$, base 2 _____   18. $\log_4 242\,000$, base 3 _____

CHAPTER 13

QUADRATIC EQUATIONS

▶ 13.1   Solving by Factoring (text page 424)

KEY TOPICS

A.   Determine all roots of the quadratic equation

$$x^2 - 7x + 12 = 0 .$$

SOLUTION.

$$x^2 - 7x + 12 = 0$$

Factor the left side:

$$(x - 3)(x - 4) = 0$$

Obtain the two first-degree equations:

x − 3 = 0   x − 4 = 0

Solve these separately.

x − 3 = 0	x − 4 = 0
x = 3	x = 4

The roots of the quadratic equation

$$x^2 - 7x + 12 = 0$$

are 3 and 4.

B.   Determine a quadratic equation whose roots are 2 and −5.

SOLUTION.

If 2 and −5 are roots of the same quadratic equation, then both first-degree equations

$$x = 2 \text{ and } x = -5$$

are true.   Therefore

$$x - 2 = 0 \text{ and } x + 5 = 0 .$$

KEY EXERCISES

A.   Determine all roots of each equation.

1. $(x - 5)(x + 8) = 0$ _____

2. $(3x - 5)(2x + 9) = 0$ _____

3. $x^2 - 4x = 0$ _____

4. $t^2 - 9t + 20 = 0$ _____

5. $y^2 + 7y - 8 = 0$ _____

6. $u^2 - 3u - 18 = 0$ _____

7. $s^2 + 8s + 16 = 0$ _____

8. $u + \dfrac{2}{u} = -3$ _____

B.   Determine a quadratic equation whose roots are as indicated.

9.   1 and 6 _____

10.   3 and 8 _____

11.   −2 and −4 _____

12.   5 and −3 _____

13.   only 6 _____

Also,

$$(x - 2)(x + 5) = 0 \cdot 0 = 0$$

Consequently,

$$x^2 + 3x - 10 = 0$$

is a quadratic equation whose roots are 2 and −5.

▶ 13.2   Equations of the Form $x^2 = a$ (text page 430)

KEY TOPICS

A.   Solve each quadratic equation.

(a) $x^2 = 25$ (b) $y^2 = 24$ (c) $t^2 + 9 = 0$

SOLUTION.

(a) The roots are given by:

$$x = \pm\sqrt{25} = \pm 5$$

(b) The roots are given by:

$$y = \pm\sqrt{24}$$
$$= \pm\sqrt{4 \cdot 6}$$
$$= \pm\sqrt{4} \cdot \sqrt{6}$$
$$= \pm 2\sqrt{6}$$

(c) $t^2 + 9 = 0$

$$t^2 = -9$$

The roots are given by:

$$t = \pm\sqrt{-9}$$
$$= \pm\sqrt{9(-1)}$$
$$= \pm\sqrt{9}\sqrt{-1}$$
$$= \pm 3i$$

KEY EXERCISES

Assume $A > 0$.

A.   Solve each quadratic equation.

1. $x^2 = 16$ _____

2. $x^2 = 7$ _____

3. $x^2 = 8$ _____

4. $y^2 = 45$ _____

5. $t^2 = -4$ _____

6. $u^2 + 18 = 0$ _____

7. $9t^2 = 49$ _____

8. $x^2 = 36A^2$ _____

B.   Solve for t:

$$\left(\frac{3t + 1}{2}\right)^2 = 96$$

SOLUTION.

$$\left(\frac{3t + 1}{2}\right)^2 = 96$$

$$\frac{3t + 1}{2} = \pm\sqrt{96}$$

$$= \pm 4\sqrt{6}$$

$$3t + 1 = \pm 8\sqrt{6}$$

$$3t = -1 \pm 8\sqrt{6}$$

$$t = \frac{-1 \pm 8\sqrt{6}}{3}$$

▶ 13.3   Completing the Square (text page 434)

KEY TOPICS

A.   Solve by completing the square:

$$x^2 - 6x + 7 = 0$$

SOLUTION.

$$x^2 - 6x = -7$$

This is of the form $x^2 + Bx = -C$.

$$B = -6, \quad \frac{B}{2} = -3, \quad \left(\frac{B}{2}\right)^2 = 9$$

$$x^2 - 6x + 9 = -7 + 9$$

$$(x - 3)^2 = 2$$

$$x - 3 = \pm\sqrt{2}$$

$$x = 3 \pm \sqrt{2}$$

B.   Solve each quadratic equation.

9. $9(t - 2)^2 = 1$ _____

10. $A^2 x^2 = 81$ _____

11. $A^2 \left(\dfrac{z + 3}{2} \right)^2 = 1$ _____

12. $A^2 (y + 5)^2 = -1$ _____

KEY EXERCISES

A.   Solve each equation by completing the square.

1. $x^2 - 4x - 1 = 0$ _____

2. $x^2 + 2x - 5 = 0$ _____

3. $x^2 - 6x + 7 = 0$ _____

4. $t^2 - 10t + 21 = 0$ _____

5. $y^2 - 3y + 1 = 0$ _____

6. $u^2 + 12u + 33 = 0$ _____

7. $x^2 + 4x + 8 = 0$ _____

8. $2y^2 + 8y + 3 = 0$ _____

9. $2x^2 + 2x - 1 = 0$ _____

10. $x^2 + x + 1 = 0$ _____

KEY TOPICS

A.   For each equation, determine the discriminant. Also, without solving, state whether the equation has

   2 distinct real roots,

   exactly 1 real root,

   or

   2 complex conjugate roots.

(a) $x^2 + x - 1 = 0$ (b) $x^2 - 2x + 2 = 0$

(c) $9x^2 - 30x + 25 = 0$

SOLUTION.

(a) $B^2 - 4AC = 1^2 - 4(1)(-1) = 5$

The discriminant is positive. The equation has 2 distinct real roots.

(b) $B^2 - 4AC = (-2)^2 - 4(1)(2) = -4$

The discriminant is negative. The equation has 2 complex conjugate roots.

(c) $B^2 - 4AC = (-30)^2 - 4(9)(25) = 900 - 900 = 0$

The discriminant is 0. There is exactly 1 real root.

B.   Solve by means of the quadratic formula.

(a) $x^2 + 5x + 3 = 0$ (b) $x^2 - x + 5 = 0$

(c) $x^2 - 2x + 1 = 0$

SOLUTION.

(a) $x = \dfrac{-5 \pm \sqrt{5^2 - 4(1)(3)}}{2}$

$= \dfrac{-5 \pm \sqrt{13}}{2}$

KEY EXERCISES

A.   For each equation:

      (a) Determine the discriminant.
      (b) Without solving, state whether the equation has
                   2 distinct real roots,
                   exactly 1 real root,
              or 2 complex conjugate roots.

1. $x^2 - 8x + 16 = 0$ (a) _____ (b) _____

2. $x^2 - x + 1 = 0$ (a) _____ (b) _____

3. $x^2 + 3x + 1 = 0$ (a) _____ (b) _____

4. $4x^2 - 4x + 1 = 0$ (a) _____ (b) _____

5. $2x^2 + 3x - 1 = 0$ (a) _____ (b) _____

B.   Solve by means of the quadratic formula.

6. $x^2 + 4x + 2 = 0$ _____

7. $x^2 + 6x + 9 = 0$ _____

8. $x^2 + 3x + 1 = 0$ _____

9. $x^2 + 2x + 5 = 0$ _____

10. $x^2 + 8x + 5 = 0$ _____

(b) $\quad x = \dfrac{1 \pm \sqrt{(-1)^2 - 4(1)(5)}}{2}$

$\quad\quad = \dfrac{-1 \pm \sqrt{-19}}{2}$

$\quad\quad = \dfrac{-1}{2} \pm \dfrac{\sqrt{19}}{2} i$

(c) $\quad x = \dfrac{2 \pm \sqrt{(-2)^2 - 4(1)(1)}}{2}$

$\quad\quad = \dfrac{2 \pm \sqrt{0}}{2}$

$\quad\quad = \dfrac{2}{2}$

$\quad\quad = 1$

▶ 13.5   Word Problems (text page 442)

KEY TOPICS

A.   The sum of two numbers is 12 and the product is 35.
      Find these numbers.

SOLUTION.

Let x be one of these numbers.   Then 12 – x is the other
because

$$x + (12 - x) = 12.$$

The product of these numbers is 35.

$$x(12 - x) \quad\quad = \quad 35$$

$$12x - x^2 \quad\quad = \quad 35$$

$$0 \quad\quad\quad = \quad x^2 - 12x + 35$$

$$0 \quad\quad\quad = \quad (x - 5)(x - 7)$$

11. $2x^2 + 5x + 2 = 0$ _____

12. $3x^2 + 4x - 1 = 0$ _____

13. $4x^2 + 20x + 25 = 0$ _____

KEY EXERCISES

A.

1. The sum of two integers is 17 and the product is 66. Find these numbers.

   _____

2. Twice a certain positive number is 10 less than its square. Find this number.

   _____

3. The product of two consecutive negative integers is 90. Determine these integers.

   _____

4. The perimeter of a rectangle is 28 inches and the area is 40 square inches. Determine the dimensions of the rectangle.

   _____

5. A ball is thrown straight up from ground level. Its height, h feet after t seconds, is given by

$$h = 192t - 16t^2.$$

$$x - 5 = 0 \qquad\qquad x - 7 = 0$$

$$x = 5 \qquad\qquad x = 7$$

$$12 - x = 7 \qquad\qquad 12 - x = 5$$

In either case the two numbers are 5 and 7.

▶ 13.6   Equations with Square Roots (text page 449)

KEY TOPICS

A.   Solve and check the (supposed) roots:

$$9 - \sqrt{x - 3} = x$$

SOLUTION.

Isolate the radical on one side.

$$9 - x = \sqrt{x - 3}$$

Square both sides. (In so doing, you may <u>possibly</u> add an additional root.)

$$(9 - x)^2 = x - 3$$

$$81 - 18x + x^2 = x - 3$$

$$x^2 - 19x + 84 = 0$$

$$(x - 7)(x - 12) = 0$$

$$x = 7, 12$$

Check to see if these are roots of the given equation.

$x = 7$:	$x = 12$:
$9 - \sqrt{7 - 3} \overset{?}{=} 7$	$9 - \sqrt{12 - 3} \overset{?}{=} 12$
$9 - \sqrt{4} \quad\overset{?}{=} 7$	$9 - \sqrt{9} \quad\overset{?}{=} 12$
$9 - 2 \quad\overset{?}{=} 7$	$9 - 3 \quad\overset{?}{=} 12$
$7 \quad\overset{\checkmark}{=} 7$	$6 \quad\overset{\times}{=} 12$

Thus 7 is the only root of the given equation.

(a) How long will it take to rise 320 feet?

(b) At what time t will it be 320 feet above the ground on its way down?

<u>(a)   (b)   </u>

KEY EXERCISES

A.   Solve each equation and check the (supposed) roots.

1. $\sqrt{x + 2} = 3$ _____   2. $\sqrt{x + 10} = 5$ _____

3. $\sqrt{2y} - 4 = 0$ _____   4. $\sqrt{2t + 1} + 3 = 0$ _____

5. $x + \sqrt{x + 3} = 9$ _____   6. $x - \sqrt{x - 6} = 8$ _____

CHECKS:

1.   2.

3.   4.

5.

6.

B.   Solve and check the (supposed) roots.

$$\sqrt{2x} + \sqrt{x - 1} = 3$$

SOLUTION.

Isolate one of the radicals. For example, subtract $\sqrt{2x}$ from both sides so that only $\sqrt{x - 1}$ remains on the left.

$$\sqrt{x - 1} = 3 - \sqrt{2x}$$

Square both sides.

$$x - 1 = 9 - 6\sqrt{2x} + 2x$$

Simplify, and isolate the radical.

$$6\sqrt{2x} = x + 10$$

Square both sides.

$$36 \cdot 2x = x^2 + 20x + 100$$

$$72x = x^2 + 20x + 100$$

$$0 = x^2 - 52x + 100$$

$$0 = (x - 2)(x - 50)$$

$$x = 2, \quad 50$$

Check to see if these are roots of the given equation.

$x = 2:$

$$\sqrt{2 \cdot 2} + \sqrt{2 - 1} \overset{?}{=} 3$$

$$\sqrt{4} + \sqrt{1} \overset{?}{=} 3$$

$$2 + 1 \overset{?}{=} 3$$

$$3 \overset{\checkmark}{=} 3$$

$x = 50:$

$$\sqrt{2 \cdot 50} + \sqrt{50 - 1} \overset{?}{=} 3$$

$$\sqrt{100} + \sqrt{49} \overset{?}{=} 3$$

$$10 + 7 \overset{?}{=} 3$$

$$17 \overset{\times}{=} 3$$

Thus 3 is the only root of the given equation.

B.   Solve each equation and check the (supposed) roots.

7. $\sqrt{x} + \sqrt{x + 3} = 3$ _____

8. $\sqrt{x + 1} - \sqrt{x - 4} = 1$ _____

9. $\sqrt{x + 3} + \sqrt{x + 2} = 1$ _____

CHECKS:

7.   8.

9.

C.   Solve and check the (supposed) roots:

$$\sqrt{t + 2} \; \sqrt{t + 5} = 2$$

SOLUTION.

Square both sides.

$$(t + 2)(t + 5) = 4$$

$$t^2 + 7t + 10 = 4$$

$$t^2 + 7t + 6 = 0$$

$$(t + 1)(t + 6) = 0$$

$$t = -1, \; -6$$

Check to see if these are roots of the given equation.

t = -1:

$$\sqrt{-1 + 2} \; \sqrt{-1 + 5} \overset{?}{=} 2$$

$$\sqrt{1}\sqrt{4} \overset{?}{=} 2$$

$$1 \cdot 2 \overset{?}{=} 2$$

$$2 \overset{\checkmark}{=} 2$$

t = -6:

$$\sqrt{-6 + 2} \; \sqrt{-6 + 5} \overset{?}{=} 2$$

$$\sqrt{-4}\sqrt{-1} \overset{?}{=} 2$$

$$2i \cdot i \overset{?}{=} 2$$

$$2(-1) \overset{?}{=} 2$$

$$-2 \overset{\times}{\cong} 2$$

Thus -1 is the only root.

C.   Solve each equation and check the (supposed) roots.

10. $\sqrt{x}\sqrt{x + 8} = 3$ _____ 11. $\sqrt{x} - 2\sqrt{x + 3} = 6$ _____

12. $\sqrt{4x + 1}\sqrt{x - 1} = 3$ _____

CHECKS:

10.

11.

12.

CHAPTER 14

INEQUALITIES AND ABSOLUTE VALUE

▶ 14.1   Intervals (text page 456)

KEY TOPICS

A.   (a)   (2, 5) is an open interval.

             (b)   [2, 5] is a closed interval.

             (c)   (3, ∞) is an open right ray.

             (d)   [3, ∞) is a closed right ray.

             (e)   (-∞, 3) is an open left ray.

             (f)   (-∞, 3] is a closed left ray.

B.   (a)   5 is in (1, 8) because 1 < 5 < 8.

             (b)   -2 is in [-2, -1] because $-2 \leq -2 \leq -1$.

             (c)   -4 is not in (-3, -2) because -3 < -4 is false.

C.   (a)   4 < x < 7 can be written in the form (4, 7).

             (b) $-3 \leq x \leq 2$ can be written in the form [-3, 2].

             (c) $x \leq 4$ can be written in the form (-∞, 4].

KEY EXERCISES

A. Describe each set of numbers as either

                    (a) an open interval,
                    (b) a closed interval,
                    (c) an open right ray,
                    (d) a closed right ray,
                    (e) an open left ray,
                    (f) a closed left ray.

1. $(-4, 8)$ _____ 2. $(-4, \infty)$ _____ 3. $(-\infty, -2)$ _____

4. $[-6, -3]$ _____ 5. $[100, \infty)$ _____

B. Answer "true" or "false".

6. 10 is in $(1, 10)$. _____

7. 0 is in $(-\infty, 0]$. _____

8. -2.5 is in $[-3, -2]$. _____

9. -3 is in $(-3, -2)$. _____

10. 0 is in $(0, \infty)$. _____

C. Describe each indicated set of numbers in one of the forms
    $[a, b]$, (a, b), (a, ∞), $[a, \infty)$, $(-\infty, b)$, or $(-\infty, b]$.

11. $4 < x < 12$ _____ 12. $2 \leq x \leq 8$ _____

13. $x < -12$ _____ 14. $x > \frac{1}{2}$ _____

15. $x \geq 5$ _____

D.   Graph the function given by

$$y = x + 3 , \qquad 0 \leq x \leq 3.$$

What is the domain of this function?

SOLUTION.

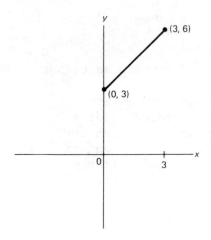

Figure 14.1   The function given by

$$y = x + 3, \ 0 \leq x \leq 3$$

(0, 3) and (3, 6) are included.

The domain of this function is [0, 3].

▶ 14.2   Arithmetic of Inequalities (text page 461)

KEY TOPICS

A.   Fill in < or >:

        (a) 3 + c   6 + c

        (b) If c > 0, then −2c   −5c

        (c) If c < 0, then 3c   4c

SOLUTION.

        (a) 3 + c < 6 + c

        (b) c > 0. Thus −2c > −5c because −2 > −5

        (c) c < 0. Thus 3c > 4c because 3 < 4

D.   (a) Graph the indicated function.   (b)   What is the domain
          of the function?

16.   y = x, 0 $\leq$ x $\leq$ 5   (b) _____

17.   y = x − 2, 1 $\leq$ x $\leq$ 3   (b) _____

18.   y = 2x, 1 < x < 4   (b) _____

19.   y = 2x + 1, −2 $\leq$ x $\leq$ 1   (b) _____

20.   y = $\frac{x}{2}$, x $\geq$ 1   (b) _____

KEY EXERCISES

A.   Fill in "<" or ">".

1.   10 + c   20 + c

2.   c − 2   c − 4

3.   If c > 0, 5c   6c

4.   If c < 0, 3c   7c

5.   5(−4)   8(−4)

6.   If a < b, then a − b   0

B.   Show that if x ≤ 3, then 4x ≤ 12.

SOLUTION.

Suppose x ≤ 3.

Then $4x \le 4 \cdot 3$

Thus 4x ≤ 12

▶ 14.3   Solving Inequalities (text page 466)

KEY TOPICS

A.   Solve the inequalities:

(a) $\dfrac{x}{2} \ge \dfrac{3}{4}$ (b)   3 ≤ 4x + 1 ≤ 13

SOLUTION.

(a) $\dfrac{x}{2} \ge \dfrac{3}{4}$

Multiply both sides by 2.

$x \ge \dfrac{3}{2}$

The solution set is $\left[\dfrac{3}{2},\ \infty \right)$.

(b) 3 ≤ 4x + 1 ≤ 13

Subtract 1 from each expression.

2 ≤ 4x ≤ 12

Divide each expression by 4.

$\dfrac{1}{2} \le x \le 3$

The solution set is $\left[\dfrac{1}{2},\ 3 \right]$.

B.

7. Show that if $x < 2$, then $x + 2 < 4$.

8. Show that if $x \leq 5$, then $3x \leq 15$.

9. Show that if $x < -2$, then $-2x > 4$.

10. Show that if $x < 6$, then $\frac{x}{3} < 2$.

KEY EXERCISES

A.　　Solve the indicated inequalities.

1. $x + 3 < 8$ _____

2. $x - 2 > 12$ _____

3. $\frac{x}{3} \leq 5$ _____

4. $\frac{-x}{2} \geq 3$ _____

5. $2x + 1 < 5$ _____

6. $\frac{y}{5} + 2 \leq 12$ _____

7. $\frac{1 - t}{4} > 2$ _____

8. $\frac{z}{2} - \frac{1}{4} < \frac{3}{4}$ _____

9. $1 < x + 3 < 4$ _____

10. $-3 < x - 2 < -1$

11. $2 \leq \frac{y}{5} \leq 3$ _____

12. $1 < 1 - 5t < 6$ _____

▶ 14.4   Graphing Inequalities (text page 472)

KEY TOPICS

A.   Consider the inequality:

$$y < 3x + 2$$

(a)   (1, 4) satisfies this inequality because

$$4 < 3 \cdot 1 + 2.$$

(b)   (2, 8) does not satisfy this inequality because

$$8 = 3 \cdot 2 + 2.$$

B.   Graph the inequality:

$$y \leq x - 3$$

SOLUTION.

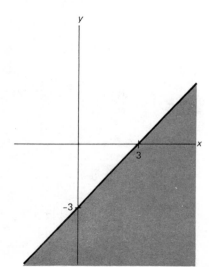

Figure 14.2   The graph of the inequality

$$y \leq x - 3$$

The line is included.

KEY EXERCISES

A.   Indicate which points satisfy the given inequality.

1. $y < x + 4$ _____

    (a) (0, 3), (b) (3, 0), (c) (1, 5), (d) (2, 5)

2. $y \leq 4x$ _____

    (a) (0, 0), (b) (1, 3), (c) (3, 1), (d) (1, 6)

3. $y > 1 - 2x$ _____

    (a) (1, 1), (b) (2, -2), (c) (0, 0), (d) $\left(\frac{1}{2}, 0\right)$

4. $x \leq 4$ _____

    (a) (1, 5), (b) (4, 5), (c) (5, 3), (d) (3, 5)

5. $3y \geq 4x$ _____

    (a) (1, 1), (b) (3, 4), (c) (4, 3), (d) (-1, -1)

B.   Graph each inequality.

6. $y < x + 2$

7. $y \geq x - 3$

8. $y \leq 2x$

9. $y \geq 2x + 1$

10. $y > 1 - 2x$

▶ 14.5   Quadratic Inequalities (text page 477)

KEY TOPICS

A.   Solve the inequality:

$$x^2 + 3x + 2 < 0$$

SOLUTION.

Factor the left side to obtain

$$(x + 1)(x + 2) < 0.$$

Observe that

$(x + 1)(x + 2) = 0$ when $x = -1$ and when $x = -2$.

The points -1 and -2 divide the x-axis into three regions. In each region $(x + 1)(x + 2)$ is either positive throughout the region or else negative.

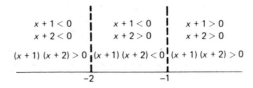

Figure 14.3

Figure 14.3 indicates that

$$(x + 1)(x + 2) < 0$$

in the middle region, where one factor is positive and the other negative. Thus the solution set of

$$x^2 + 3x + 2 < 0$$

is the open interval $(-2, -1)$.

B.   Solve:

$$\frac{2}{x} \geq 3$$

KEY EXERCISES

A. Solve each inequality.

1. $(x + 2)(x - 4) < 0$ _____

2. $x^2 - 3x > 0$ _____

3. $x^2 - 5x + 4 \leq 0$ _____

4. $x^2 + 2x - 8 \geq 0$ _____

5. $x^2 + 6x + 9 > 0$ _____

6. $t^2 \leq 12 + t$ _____

7. $16x^2 < 1$ _____

8. $u^2 \geq 4$ _____

B. Solve each inequality.

9. $\frac{2}{x} > 1$ _____

SOLUTION.

Multiply both sides by x^2, which is positive (because $x \neq 0$). This preserves the sense of inequality.

$$\frac{2}{x} \cdot x^2 \geq 3x^2$$

$$2x \geq 3x^2$$

$$0 \geq 3x^2 - 2x$$

$$0 \geq x(3x - 2)$$

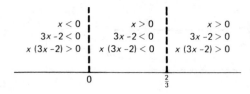

Figure 14.4

Note that $x(3x - 2) = 0$ when $x = 0$ and when $x = \frac{2}{3}$. The solution set is

$$(-\infty, \ 0] \cup \left[\frac{2}{3}, \ \infty\right).$$

▶ 14.6   Absolute Value in Equations (text page 482)

KEY TOPICS

A.   Which numbers are 5 units from 3?

SOLUTION.

3 + 5 and 3 - 5 are 5 units from 3.   Thus
8 and -2 are 5 units from 3.

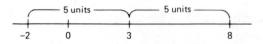

Figure 14.5

129 LEFT

10. $\dfrac{3}{t} < -2$ _____

11. $\dfrac{1}{x - 2} \le 2$ _____

12. $\dfrac{2}{x + 1} \ge 1$ _____

13. $\dfrac{x}{x + 2} < 1$ _____

14. $\dfrac{x}{x - 1} \le -1$ _____

15. $\dfrac{x + 4}{x + 2} > 2$ _____

16. $(x + 1)^2 + 3 \ge 0$ _____

KEY EXERCISES

A.

1. Which numbers are 2 units from 6? _____

2. Which numbers are 3 units from 1? _____

3. Which numbers are 10 units from −2? _____

4. Which numbers are $\dfrac{1}{2}$ unit from −5? _____

B.   Solve the equation

$$|x + 2| = 8.$$

Check the roots.

SOLUTION.

$$|x - (-2)| = 8$$

$$x - (-2) = \pm 8$$

$$x = -2 \pm 8$$

$x = -2 + 8$	$x = -2 - 8$
$x = 6$	$x = -10$

CHECK:

$\|6 - (-2)\| \overset{?}{=} 8$	$\|-10 + 2\| \overset{?}{=} 8$
$\|8\| \overset{?}{=} 8$	$\|-8\| \overset{?}{=} 8$
$8 \overset{\checkmark}{=} 8$	$8 \overset{\checkmark}{=} 8$

C.   Solve the equation

$$|x - 3| = 2x.$$

Check the (supposed) roots.

SOLUTION.

$$x - 3 = \pm 2x$$

$x - 3 = 2x$	$x - 3 = -2x$
$-3 = x$	$3x = 3$
$\left(\text{False, because } x = \dfrac{\|x - 3\|}{2} \geq 0\right)$	$x = 1$

B.   Solve each equation. Check the ones so indicated.

5. $|x| = 5$ _____

6. $|x| = -5$ _____

7. $|x - 2| = 3$ _____ (Check.)

8. $|x + 8| = 4$ _____

9. $\left|\dfrac{x}{3} - 7\right| = 1$ _____

10. $|2x - 3| = 6$ _____

11. $|2x + 1| = |3 - x|$ _____ (Check.)

12. $|x + 5| = |x + 1|$ _____

CHECKS:

7.

11.

C.   Solve each equation. Check the (supposed) roots.

13. $|x + 3| = x$ _____

14. $|5x - 2| = 2x$ _____

15. $|x - 2| = -x$ _____

16. $\left|x + \dfrac{1}{2}\right| = 4x$ _____

CHECKS:

13.

CHECK:

$$|1 - 3| \stackrel{?}{=} 2(1)$$

$$|-2| \stackrel{?}{=} 2$$

$$2 \stackrel{\checkmark}{=} 2$$

The only solution is 2.

▶ 14.7   Absolute Value in Inequalities (text page 488)

KEY TOPICS

A.   Solve the inequalities:

(a) $|2x - 5| < 1$ (b) $\left|\dfrac{x}{3} + 1\right| \geq 2$

SOLUTION.

(a) $|2x - 5| < 1$

$$-1 < 2x - 5 < 1$$

$$4 < 2x < 6$$

$$2 < x < 3$$

The solution set is (2, 3).

(b) $\left|\dfrac{x}{3} + 1\right| \geq 2$

$$\dfrac{x}{3} + 1 \leq -2 \quad \text{or} \quad \dfrac{x}{3} + 1 \geq 2$$

$$\dfrac{x}{3} \leq -3 \qquad \text{or} \quad \dfrac{x}{3} \geq 1$$

$$x \leq -9 \qquad \text{or} \quad x \geq 3$$

The solution set is $(-\infty, -9] \cup [3, \infty)$.

14.

15.

16.

KEY EXERCISES

A. Solve each inequality.

1. $|x| < 6$ _____

2. $|x| > 20$ _____

3. $|x - 5| < 5$ _____

4. $|x + 8| > 4$ _____

5. $|2x - 1| \leq 9$ _____

6. $\left|\dfrac{x}{3} + 1\right| \geq 2$ _____

7. $\left|\dfrac{x}{3} - \dfrac{2}{5}\right| < \dfrac{1}{3}$ _____

8. $|4x - 1| > 0$ _____

B.   Determine c:

$$1 \le x \le 7 \text{ means } |x - c| \le 3.$$

SOLUTION.

c = 4 because

$$1 \le 4 \le 7 \text{ means the same as } |x - 4| \le 3.$$

▶ 14.8   Properties of Absolute Value (text page 494)

KEY TOPICS

A.   Let $f(x) = |x - 4|$. Determine:

      (a) $f(-4)$ (b) $f(0)$

      (c) $f(4)$ (d) $f(6)$

      (e) $f(7.5)$

SOLUTION.

      (a) $f(-4) = |-4 - 4| = |-8| = 8$

      (b) $f(0) = |0 - 4| = |-4| = 4$

      (c) $f(4) = |4 - 4| = |0| = 0$

      (d) $f(6) = |6 - 4| = |2| = 2$

      (e) $f(7.5) = |7.5 - 4| = |3.5| = 3.5$

B.   Determine c.

9. $-3 \leq x \leq 3$ means the same as $|x| \leq c.$ _____

10. $-3 < x < 9$ means the same as $|x - 3| < c.$ _____

11. $4 < x < 10$ means the same as $|x - c| < 3.$ _____

12. x is in $(-\infty, -5) \cup (5, \infty)$ means the same as $|x| > c.$ _____

13. $x^2 > 81$ means the same as $|x| > c.$ _____

14. $x^2 < \frac{1}{9}$ means the same as $-c < x < c.$ _____

KEY EXERCISES

A.   Find the indicated function values.

1. $f(x) = |x + 6|$

(a) $f(-7)$ _____   (b) $f(-6)$ _____   (c) $f(-3)$ _____

(d) $f(0)$ _____   (e) $f(6)$ _____

2. $f(x) = |3x|$

(a) $f(-1)$ _____   (b) $f(0)$ _____   (c) $f\left(\frac{1}{3}\right)$ _____

(f) $f(3)$ _____   (e) $f\left(\frac{10}{3}\right)$ _____

3. $f(x) = |2x - 1|$

(a) $f(-4)$ _____   (b) $f(-1)$ _____   (c) $f\left(\frac{-1}{2}\right)$ _____

(d) $f\left(\frac{1}{2}\right)$ _____   (e) $f(2)$ _____

4. $f(x) = |x| - 1$

(a) $f(-1)$ _____   (b) $f(0)$ _____   (c) $f\left(\frac{1}{2}\right)$ _____

(d) $f(1)$ _____   (e) $f(10)$ _____

B.   Graph $f(x) = |x| - 2$, $-3 \leq x \leq 3$.

SOLUTION.

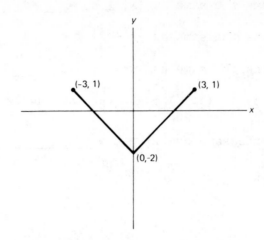

Figure 14.6   The graph of $f(x) = |x| - 2$, $-3 \leq x \leq 3$

The points $(-3, 1)$ and $(3, 1)$ are included.

C.   Answer "true" or "false".

For all a and b, $|a + b| = |a| + |b|$

SOLUTION.

False. Let $a = 2$, $b = -1$. Then $|a + b| = |2 - 1| = 1$,
whereas $|a| + |b| = |2| + |-1| = 2 + 1 = 3$

D.   Determine all roots of the equation

$$\left| \frac{4x}{x + 1} \right| = 2.$$

SOLUTION.

$$\left| \frac{4x}{x + 1} \right| = 2$$

$$\frac{|4x|}{|x + 1|} = 2$$

$$\frac{4|x|}{|x + 1|} = 2$$

B.   Graph each function. Unless indicated, assume the domain is the set of all real numbers.

5. $f(x) = |x + 2|$

6. $f(x) = |x| + 2$

7. $f(x) = \dfrac{|x|}{3}$

8. $f(x) = |x| + x,\ -3 \le x \le 3$

C.   Answer "true" or "false".

9.   For all a, $|a + 5| = |a| + 5$ _____

10.   For all a, $\dfrac{|a|}{5} = \left|\dfrac{a}{5}\right|$ _____

11.   For all a and b, $|ab| = |-a||-b|$ _____

12.   For a > 0 and b < 0, $|a + b| < |a| + |b|$ _____

D.   Determine all roots.

13. $\left|\dfrac{x}{x + 5}\right| = 1$ _____   14. $\left|\dfrac{2x - 1}{x + 1}\right| = 3$ _____

15. $\left|\dfrac{x - 2}{x + 2}\right| = \dfrac{1}{4}$ _____   16. $\left|\dfrac{2x - 7}{3x + 9}\right| = 0$ _____

$$\frac{2|x|}{|x+1|} = 1$$

$$2|x| = |x+1|$$

$$2x = \pm(x+1)$$

$2x = x + 1$	$2x = -(x+1)$
$x = 1$	$3x = -1$
	$x = \dfrac{-1}{3}$

CHAPTER 15

CONIC SECTIONS

▶ 15.1   Distance (text page 503)

KEY TOPICS

A.   Let $P_1 = (3, 4)$ and $P_2 = (5, 2)$.   Then

$$\text{dist }(P_1, P_2) = \sqrt{(5 - 3)^2 + (2 - 4)^2}$$

$$= \sqrt{2^2 + (-2)^2}$$

$$= \sqrt{8}$$

$$= 2\sqrt{2}$$

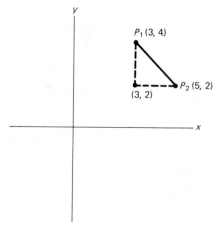

Figure 15.1 $\text{dist }(P_1, P_2) = \sqrt{2^2 + (-2)^2} = 2\sqrt{2}$

B.   Let $P = (2, 6)$ and let L be the line given by

$$y = 3 .$$

Then dist $(P, L) = 6 - 3 = 3$

KEY EXERCISES

A.   Determine dist (P_1, P_2).

1. $P_1 = (3, 4)$, $P_2 = (3, 8)$ _____

2. $P_1 = (5, -2)$, $P_2 = (-3, -2)$ _____

3. $P_1 = (2, 4)$, $P_2 = (5, 8)$ _____

4. $P_1 = (0, -2)$, $P_2 = (5, 10)$ _____

5. $P_1 = (1, 3)$, $P_2 = (2, 2)$ _____

6. $P_1 = (-1, -1)$, $P_2 = (-2, -3)$ _____

7. $P_1 = (2, 6)$, $P_2 = (6, 2)$ _____

8. $P_1 = \left(\frac{1}{4}, \frac{1}{2}\right)$, $P_2 = \left(0, \frac{1}{4}\right)$ _____

B.   Determine dist (P, L), where the point P and the line L are
      as indicated.

9. $P = (4, 3)$, L: $x = 5$ _____

10. $P = (-1, 2)$, L: $y = 5$ _____

11. $P = \left(\frac{1}{2}, \frac{3}{4}\right)$, L: $x = 1$ _____

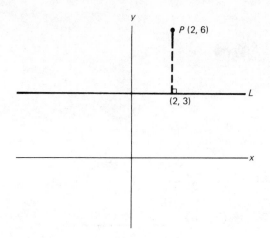

Figure 15.2   dist (P, L) = 6 − 3 = 3

▶ 15.2   Circles (text page 510)

KEY TOPICS

A.   Determine (a) the center and (b) the radius of the circle given by

$$(x - 5)^2 + (y + 7)^2 = 81 .$$

SOLUTION.

(a)   (5, −7)   (b)   9

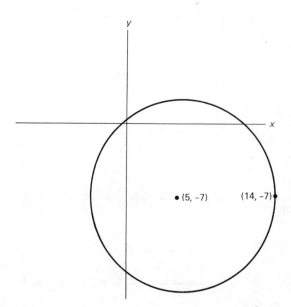

Figure 15.3   The circle given by $(x - 5)^2 + (y + 7)^2 = 81$

12. P = (-6, -5), L: the x-axis _____

13. P = (-4, 3), L: the y-axis _____

14. P = (-2, -8), L: y = $\frac{-1}{2}$ _____

KEY EXERCISES

A. Determine (a) the center and (b) the radius of the given circle.

1. $x^2 + y^2 = 100$ (a)_____ (b)_____

2. $(x - 4)^2 + (y - 2)^2 = 25$ (a)_____ (b)_____

3. $(x + 1)^2 + (y - 6)^2 = 4$ (a)_____ (b)_____

4. $\left(x - \frac{1}{2}\right)^2 + \left(y + \frac{1}{4}\right)^2 = \frac{1}{4}$ (a)_____ (b)_____

5. $(x - 8)^2 + (y + 8)^2 = 8$ (a)_____ (b)_____

B. Determine the equation of the circle consisting of all points that are 4 units from $(-2, 3)$.

SOLUTION.

$$[x - (-2)]^2 + (y - 3)^2 = 4^2$$

or

$$(x + 2)^2 + (y - 3)^2 = 16$$

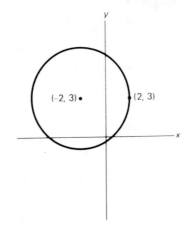

Figure 15.4   The circle given by $(x + 2)^2 + (y - 3)^2 = 16$

C. Complete the square to determine the center and radius of the corresponding circle:

$$x^2 + y^2 - 4x + 10y = 0$$

SOLUTION.

Regroup terms:

$$(x^2 - 4x) + (y^2 + 10y) = 0$$

Complete the square in each group.

$$(x - 2)^2 + (y + 5)^2 = 4 + 25$$

$$(x - 2)^2 + (y + 5)^2 = 29$$

Center $(2, -5)$, radius $\sqrt{29}$

B.

6. Determine the equation of the circle consisting of all points that are 3 units from (1, 2).

   _____

7. Determine the equation of the circle consisting of all points that are 8 units from (0, -7).

   _____

8. Determine the equation of the circle consisting of all points that are $\sqrt{3}$ units from (2, -1).

   _____

C. Complete the square to determine the center and radius of the corresponding circle.

9. $x^2 + y^2 + 8y = 0$ _____

10. $x^2 + y^2 + 2x + 12y = 0$ _____

11. $x^2 + y^2 - 4x + 2y = 4$ _____

12. $x^2 + y^2 + x - 3y = 0$ _____

▶ 15.3   Parabolas (text page 517)

KEY TOPICS

A.   Determine the vertex, axis, focus, and directrix of the
      parabola with the equation

$$x^2 = -8y .$$

SOLUTION.

Vertex (0, 0); axis: y-axis; focus (0, -2); directrix: y = 2

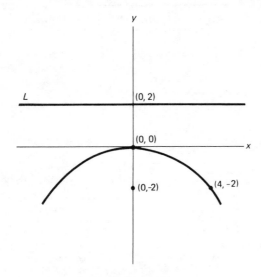

Figure 15.5

The parabola with the equation

$$x^2 = -8y$$

B.   Determine the equation of the parabola with focus (4, 0) and
      directrix: x = -4.

SOLUTION.

$$y^2 = 16x$$

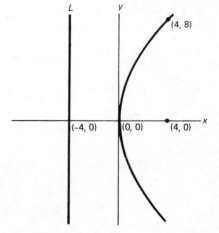

Figure 15.6

The parabola with the equation

$$y^2 = 16x$$

KEY EXERCISES

A.   Determine the vertex, axis, focus, and directrix of the
      parabola with the given equation.   Graph the ones so indicated.

1. $x^2 = 4y$ (Graph.) _____

2. $y^2 = 4x$ _____

3. $x^2 = -12y$ _____

4. $y^2 = -8x$ (Graph.) _____

5. $x^2 = 2y$ _____

6. $y^2 = x$ _____

7. $x^2 + 3y = 0$ _____

8. $6y^2 - 9x = 0$ _____

B.   Determine the equation of the parabola with focus and directrix
      as indicated.

9.   focus $(2, 0)$, directrix: $x = -2$ _____

10. focus $(0, 5)$, directrix: $y = -5$ _____

11. focus $(-5, 0)$, directrix: $x = 5$ _____

12. focus $\left(0, \frac{-1}{2}\right)$, directrix: $y = \frac{1}{2}$ _____

C.   Determine the equation of the parabola with vertex at the origin and focus (0, 8).

SOLUTION.

$$x^2 = 32y$$

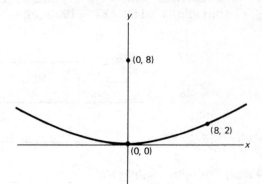

Figure 15.7

The parabola with the equation

$$x^2 = 32y$$

▶ 15.4   Ellipses and Hyperbolas (text page 525)

KEY TOPICS

A.   (a) Locate the vertices of the ellipse given by

$$\frac{x^2}{25} + \frac{y^2}{16} = 1.$$

(b) Graph the ellipse.

SOLUTION.

(a) The vertices are (5, 0), (−5, 0), (0, 4), and (0, −4).

(b)

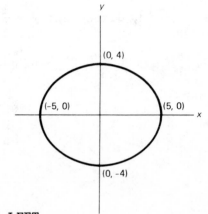

Figure 15.8

The ellipse given by

$$\frac{x^2}{25} + \frac{y^2}{16} = 1$$

C. Determine the equation of the parabola with vertex at the origin and

13. focus (6, 0). _____

14. directrix: x = 6. _____

15. focus (0, -2). _____

16. directrix: y = -2. _____

KEY EXERCISES

A. Determine the vertices of the ellipse given by each equation. Graph the ones so indicated.

1. $\dfrac{x^2}{36} + \dfrac{y^2}{9} = 1$ (Graph.) _____

2. $\dfrac{x^2}{9} + \dfrac{y^2}{25} = 1$ _____

3. $\dfrac{x^2}{16} + \dfrac{y^2}{9} = 1$ _____

4. $\dfrac{x^2}{4} + \dfrac{y^2}{25} = 1$ (Graph.) _____

5. $\dfrac{x^2}{49} + \dfrac{y^2}{36} = 1$ _____

6. $x^2 + \dfrac{y^2}{9} = 1$ _____

B.   Consider the hyperbola given by

$$\frac{x^2}{64} - \frac{y^2}{36} = 1.$$

(a) Locate the vertices.   (b) What are the asymptotes?

(c) Graph the hyperbola.

SOLUTION.

(a) $(8, 0)$, $(-8, 0)$ (b) $y = \frac{3}{4}x$, $y = \frac{-3}{4}x$

(c)

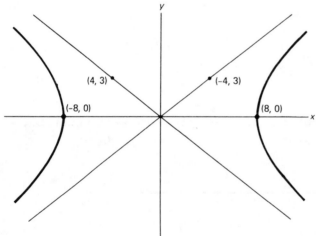

Figure 15.9

The hyperbola given by

$$\frac{x^2}{64} - \frac{y^2}{36} = 1$$

▶ 15.5   Intersecting Figures (text page 535)

KEY TOPICS

A.   Determine all intersections of the circle given by

$$x^2 + y^2 = 16$$

with the line given by

$$x + y = 4.$$

7. $4x^2 + 9y^2 = 1$ _____

8. $25x^2 + 16y^2 = 1$ _____

B.　　Consider the hyperbola given by each equation.

　　　　　　(a) Locate the vertices.
　　　　　　(b) What are the asymptotes?

9. $\dfrac{y^2}{9} - \dfrac{x^2}{25} = 1$　(Graph.) _____

10. $x^2 - \dfrac{y^2}{16} = 1$ _____

11. $\dfrac{y^2}{36} - \dfrac{x^2}{25} = 1$ _____

12. $\dfrac{x^2}{4} - \dfrac{y^2}{9} = 1$ _____

13. $16x^2 - 25y^2 = 400$ _____

14. $9y^2 - 4x^2 = 36$ _____

KEY EXERCISES

A.　　(a) Determine all intersections.

　　　(b) Indicate what figure (line, circle, parabola, ellipse,
　　　　　 hyperbola) is represented by each equation.

　　　(c) When called for, graph the figures on the same coordinate
　　　　　 system to illustrate the points of intersection.

SOLUTION.

From the equation of the line,

$$y = 4 - x.$$

Replace y by 4 - x in the equation of the circle.

$$x^2 + (4 - x)^2 = 16$$

$$x^2 + 16 - 8x + x^2 = 16$$

$$2x^2 - 8x = 0$$

$$x^2 - 4x = 0$$

$$x(x - 4) = 0$$

x = 0	x - 4 = 0
y = 4 - 0 = 4	x = 4
	y = 4 - 4 = 0

The intersection points are (0, 4) and (4, 0).

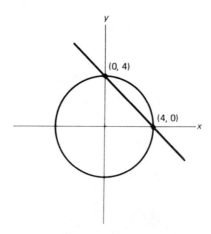

Figure 15.10

1. $x^2 + y^2 = 25$, $y = 4$ (Graph.)   (a) _____ (b) _____

2. $y = x^2$ and $y = x$ (Graph.)   (a) _____ (b) _____

3. $x^2 + y^2 = 4$ and $x + y + 2 = 0$ (a) _____ (b) _____

4. $x^2 + y^2 = 9$ and $(x - 3)^2 + y^2 = 9$ (Graph.)

(a) _____ (b) _____

5. $x^2 + y^2 = 16$ and $x^2 + y^2 = 36$ (Graph.)

(a) _____ (b) _____

6. $\dfrac{x^2}{9} + \dfrac{y^2}{16} = 1$ and $x = 1$ (a) _____ (b) _____

7. $\dfrac{x^2}{25} + y^2 = 1$ and $x^2 + y^2 = 25$ (a) _____ (b) _____

8. $x^2 - y^2 = 1$ and $x = 1$ (a) _____ (b) _____

▶ 16.1   Direct Variation (text page 543)

KEY TOPICS

A.   Assume y varies directly as x. Determine the constant of
      variation if

$$y = 8 \text{ when } x = 2.$$

SOLUTION.

$$y = kx$$

$$8 = k \cdot 2$$

$$4 = k$$

B.   Assume y varies directly as x. Suppose y = 12 when x = 8.
      Find y when x = 12.

SOLUTION.

Replace y by 12 and x by 8 in the equation.

$$y = kx$$

$$12 = k \cdot 8$$

$$\frac{3}{2} = k$$

Now replace x by 12 in the equation.

$$y = \frac{3}{2}x .$$

$$y = \frac{3}{2} \cdot 12$$

$$y = 18$$

KEY EXERCISES

A. Assume y varies directly as x. Determine the constant of
    variation.

1. y = 12 when x = 4 _____

2. y = -6 when x = 3 _____

3. y = -25 when x = -5 _____

4. y = 2 when x = 4 _____

5. y = -1 when x = $\frac{1}{2}$ _____

B. Assume y varies directly as x.

6. Suppose y = 10 when x = 5. Find y when x = 20. _____

7. Suppose y = -4 when x = 2. Find x when y = 2. _____

8. Suppose y = 12 when x = 2. Find y when x = -4. _____

9. Suppose y = 3 when x = 5. Find y when x = 3. _____

C.   Assume y varies directly as x^2. Suppose y = 18 when x = 3.
      Find y when x = 2.

SOLUTION.

$$y = kx^2$$

$$18 = k \cdot 3^2$$

$$18 = 9k$$

$$2 = k$$

$$y = 2x^2$$

Replace x by 2.

$$y = 2 \cdot 2^2$$

$$y = 8$$

▶ 16.2   Inverse Variation (text page 548)

KEY TOPICS

A.   Assume that y varies inversely as x. Determine the constant
      of variation if y = 8 when x = 2.

SOLUTION.

$$y = \frac{k}{x}$$

$$8 = \frac{k}{2}$$

$$16 = k$$

B.   Assume that y varies inversely as x. Suppose y = 4 when
      x = 3. Find x when y = 6.

SOLUTION.

$$y = \frac{k}{x}$$

$$4 = \frac{k}{3}$$

C.

10. Assume y varies directly as x^2. Suppose y = 16 when x = 2. Find the constant of variation.

_____

11. Assume y varies directly as x^2. Suppose y = 50 when x = 5. Find y when x = 10.

_____

12. Assume y varies directly as x^3. Suppose y = 24 when x = 2. Find y when x = 3.

_____

KEY EXERCISES

A. Assume that y varies inversely as x. Determine the constant of variation.

1. y = 5 when x = 2   _____

2. y = 3 when x = 3   _____

3. y = -1 when x = -4   _____

4. y = 6 when x = $\frac{1}{2}$ _____

B. Assume y varies inversely as x.

5. Suppose y = 4 when x = 2. Find y when x = 4.   _____

6. Suppose y = 6 when x = 4. Find y when x = 12.   _____

7. Suppose y = 8 when x = -3. Find y when x = 6.   _____

8. Suppose y = 10 when x = $\frac{1}{2}$. Find x when y = 100.   _____

$$12 = k$$

$$y = \frac{12}{x}$$

Replace y by 6 and solve for x.

$$6 = \frac{12}{x}$$

$$6x = 12$$

$$x = 2$$

C.   Assume that y varies inversely as x^2. Suppose y = 2 when
      x = 3. Find y when x = 2.

SOLUTION.

$$y = \frac{k}{x^2}$$

$$2 = \frac{k}{3^2}$$

$$18 = k$$

$$y = \frac{18}{x^2}$$

Replace x by 2.

$$y = \frac{18}{2^2} = \frac{18}{4} = 4.5$$

▶ 16.3   Joint Variation (text page 553)

KEY TOPICS

A.   Assume t varies jointly as x and y. Determine the constant
      of variation if t = 60 when x = 5 and y = 6.

SOLUTION.

$$t = kxy$$

$$60 = k \cdot 5 \cdot 6$$

C.

9. Assume y varies inversely as x^2. Suppose y = 3 when x = 2. Find the constant of variation.

   _____

10. Assume y varies inversely as x^2. Suppose y = 4 when x = 3. Find y when x = 6.

11. Assume y varies inversely as x^2. Suppose y = $\frac{1}{2}$ when x = 2. Find y when x = 4.

   _____

KEY EXERCISES

A.   Assume t varies jointly as x and y. Determine the constant of variation.

1. t = 40, x = 4, y = 5   _____

2. t = 30, x = 6, y = 10   _____

$$60 = 30k$$

$$2 = k$$

B. Assume t varies jointly as x and y. Suppose t = 24 when x = 2 and y = 3. Find t when x = 5 and y = 10.

SOLUTION.

$$t = kxy$$

$$24 = k \cdot 2 \cdot 3$$

$$24 = 6k$$

$$4 = k$$

$$t = 4xy$$

Replace x by 5 and y by 10.

$$t = 4 \cdot 5 \cdot 10$$

$$t = 200$$

C. Assume t varies inversely as x and y. If t = 3 when x = 2 and y = 3, find t when x = 9 and y = −2.

SOLUTION.

$$t = \frac{k}{xy}$$

$$3 = \frac{k}{2 \cdot 3}$$

$$18 = k$$

$$t = \frac{18}{xy}$$

Replace x by 9 and y by −2.

$$t = \frac{18}{9(-2)}$$

$$t = -1$$

3. $t = 12$, $x = \frac{1}{2}$, $y = \frac{3}{4}$ _____

4. $t = -16$, $x = 8$, $y = 2$ _____

B.   Assume t varies jointly as x and y.

5. Suppose $t = 54$ when $x = 2$ and $y = 9$. Find t when $x = 6$ and $y = 3$.
        _____

6. Suppose $t = 20$ when $x = 4$ and $y = -5$. Find t when $x = 10$ and $y = 10$.
        _____

7. Suppose $t = 40$ when $x = 5$ and $y = 2$. Find x when $t = 20$ and $y = -2$.
        _____

8. Suppose $t = .02$ when $x = .1$ and $y = .1$. Find t when $x = .4$ and $y = .01$.
        _____

C.   Assume t varies inversely as x and y.

9. If $t = 12$ when $x = 1$ and $y = 2$, find t when $x = 2$ and $y = 3$.

                                         _____

10. If $t = 12$ when $x = 2$ and $y = -2$, find t when $x = -1$ and $y = -3$.

                                         _____

11. If $t = \frac{1}{2}$ when $x = 6$ and $y = 3$, find x when $t = \frac{1}{4}$ and $y = 12$.

                                         _____

12. If $t = 3$ when $x = -2$ and $y = \frac{1}{6}$, find y when $t = -12$ and $x = \frac{-1}{2}$.

                                         _____

D.   Suppose t varies directly as x and inversely as y. If
      t = 100 when x = 10 and y = 2, find t when x = 5 and y = 4.

SOLUTION.

$$t = \frac{kx}{y}$$

$$100 = \frac{k \cdot 10}{2}$$

$$100 = 5k$$

$$20 = k$$

$$t = \frac{20x}{y}$$

Replace x by 5 and y by 4.

$$t = \frac{20 \cdot 5}{4}$$

$$t = 25$$

D.

13. Suppose t varies directly as x and inversely as y. If t = 120 when x = 60 and y = 3, find t when x = 30 and y = 12.

_____

14. Suppose t varies jointly as x^2 and y. If t = 90 when x = 3 and y = 5, find t when x = 4 and y = 2.

_____

15. Suppose t varies jointly as x and y and inversely as z. If t = 64 when x = 4, y = 8 and z = 2, find t when x = 3, y = -1 and z = 2.

_____

16. Suppose t varies as x^2 and inversely as y and z. If t = 6 when x = 4, y = 2 and z = 4, find t when x = 6, y = 4 and z = 3.

_____

CHAPTER 17

PROGRESSIONS

▶ 17.1 Sequences (text page 560)

KEY TOPICS

A. (a) Determine the first 8 terms of the sequence given by

$$a_i = 2i + 1 .$$

(b) Graph this sequence.

(c) Is the sequence increasing, decreasing, or neither of these?

SOLUTION.

(a) $a_1 = 2 \cdot 1 + 1 = 3$ $a_2 = 2 \cdot 2 + 1 = 5$

$a_3 = 2 \cdot 3 + 1 = 7$ $a_4 = 2 \cdot 4 + 1 = 9$

$a_5 = 2 \cdot 5 + 1 = 11$ $a_6 = 2 \cdot 6 + 1 = 13$

$a_7 = 2 \cdot 7 + 1 = 15$ $a_8 = 2 \cdot 8 + 1 = 17$

(b)

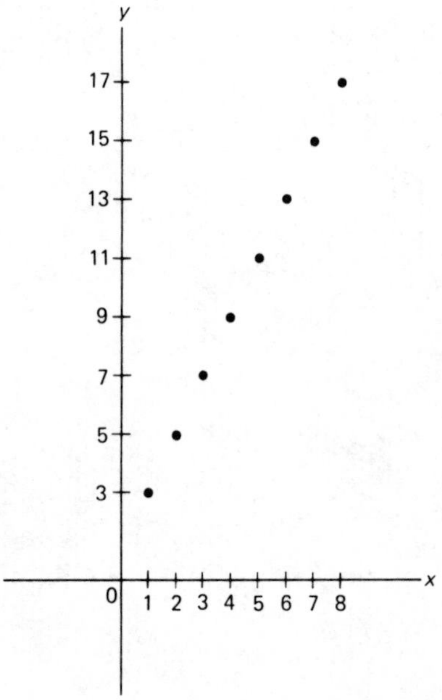

Figure 17.1

The graph of the sequence given by

$$a_i = 2i + 1$$

KEY EXERCISES

A. (a) Determine the first 8 terms of the indicated sequence.

    (b) Graph the sequence.

    (c) Is the sequence increasing, decreasing, or neither of these?

1. $a_i = i + 4$ (a) _____ (c) _____

2. $a_i = \dfrac{i}{2}$ (a) _____ (c) _____

3. $a_i = 1 - i$ (a) _____ (c) _____

4. $a_i = 4$ for all i (a) _____ (c) _____

5. $a_i = 2i - 3$ (a) _____ (c) _____

(c)   The sequence is increasing.

B.   Let $a_i = 3i - 1$. Determine:

(a) a_2 (b) a_5 (c) a_{10} (d) a_{100}

SOLUTION.

(a) $a_2 = 3 \cdot 2 - 1 = 5$ (b) $a_5 = 3 \cdot 5 - 1 = 14$

(c) $a_{10} = 3 \cdot 10 - 1 = 29$ (d) $a_{100} = 3 \cdot 100 - 1 = 299$

C.   Describe the ith term of the sequence given by

$$-4, -8, -12, -16, -20, -24, \ldots \ .$$

SOLUTION.

$$a_i = -4i$$

▶ 17.2 Sigma Notation (text page 566)

KEY TOPICS

A.   Express in $\sum$ - notation:

(a) $a_1 + a_2 + a_3 + \ldots + a_{20}$

(b) $b_{10} + b_{11} + b_{12} + b_{13}$

B. Consider the sequence given by a_i for $i = 1, 2, 3, \ldots$. Determine the indicated terms.

6. $a_i = 2i$

   (a) a_3 _____ (b) a_7 _____ (c) a_{10} _____ (d) a_{20} _____

7. $a_i = 4 - i$

   (a) a_1 _____ (b) a_4 _____ (c) a_8 _____ (d) a_{24} _____

8. $a_i = 2 + (-1)^i$

   (a) a_1 _____ (b) a_2 _____ (c) a_3 _____ (d) a_4 _____

9. $a_i = \dfrac{i}{i + 2}$

   (a) a_1 _____ (b) a_3 _____ (c) a_{10} _____ (d) a_{18} _____

C. Describe the ith term, a_i, of the suggested sequence.

10. 3, 4, 5, 6, 7, 8, . . . _____

11. -2, -4, -6, -8, -10, -12, . . . _____

12. 3, 5, 7, 9, 11, 13, . . . _____

13. -3, 6, -9, 12, -15, 18, . . . _____

14. 2, 4, 8, 16, 32, 64, . . . _____

KEY EXERCISES

A. Express in $\sum$ - notation.

1. $a_1 + a_2 + a_3 + a_4 + a_5$ _____

2. $a_1 + a_2 + a_3 + \ldots + a_{15}$ _____

SOLUTION.

(a) $$\sum_{i=1}^{20} a_i$$ (b) $$\sum_{i=10}^{13} b_i$$

B.   Find the numerical value of

$$\sum_{i=1}^{4} (2i + 1).$$

SOLUTION.

$$\sum_{i=1}^{4} (2i + 1) = 3 + 5 + 7 + 9 = 24$$

C.   Write $\frac{2}{3} + \frac{3}{4} + \frac{4}{5} + \frac{5}{6} + \frac{6}{7}$ in $\sum$ - notation.

SOLUTION.

Let $a_1 = \frac{2}{3}$. Observe that $a_1 = \frac{1 + 1}{1 + 2}$. Similarly,

$a_2 = \frac{2 + 1}{2 + 2}$ and $a_3 = \frac{3 + 1}{3 + 2}$. In general, $a_i = \frac{i + 1}{i + 2}$. Thus

$$\frac{2}{3} + \frac{3}{4} + \frac{4}{5} + \frac{5}{6} + \frac{6}{7} = \sum_{i=1}^{5} \frac{i + 1}{i + 2}$$

D.   If $$\sum_{i=1}^{50} a_i - \sum_{i=1}^{30} a_i = \sum_{i=m}^{50} a_i,$$ find m.

3. $b_4 + b_5 + b_6$ _____

4. $c_{101} + c_{102} + c_{103} + \ldots + c_{150}$ _____

B. Find the numerical value of each sum.

5. $\sum_{i=1}^{5} i$ _____

6. $\sum_{i=1}^{4} (i + 3)$ _____

7. $\sum_{i=1}^{3} \frac{1}{2i}$ _____

8. $\sum_{i=1}^{4} i^2$ _____

C. Write in $\sum$ - notation.

9. $5 + 6 + 7 + 8 + 9 + 10$ _____

10. $1^2 + 2^2 + 3^2 + \ldots + 50^2$ _____

11. $\frac{1}{3} + \frac{1}{4} + \frac{1}{5} + \ldots + \frac{1}{22}$ _____

12. $-3 - 6 - 9 - 12 - \ldots - 30$ _____

D. Determine the indicated numbers.

13. $5 \sum_{i=1}^{100} a_i = \sum_{i=1}^{100} ca_i$. Find c. _____

SOLUTION.

On the left, the first 30 terms of the sequence are
discarded. Begin with the 31st term on the right.
Let m = 31.

$$\sum_{i=1}^{50} a_i - \sum_{i=1}^{30} a_i = \sum_{i=31}^{50} a_i$$

▶ 17.3 Arithmetic Progressions (text page 573)

KEY TOPICS

A.   The sequence indicated by

$$1, 4, 7, 10, 13, 16, \ldots$$

is an arithmetic progression with common difference 3.

B.   Determine the 12th term of the arithmetic progression

$$3, 8, 13, 18, 23, \ldots$$

SOLUTION.

$$a_i = 3 + 5(i - 1)$$

$$a_{12} = 3 + 11 \cdot 5 = 58$$

14. $$\sum_{i=1}^{10} a_i + \sum_{i=11}^{20} a_i = \sum_{i=1}^{n} a_i .$$ Find n. _____

15. $$\sum_{i=1}^{8} a_i = \sum_{i=1}^{n} a_i + a_8 .$$ Find n. _____

KEY EXERCISES

A.   Consider the sequence indicated by means of its first few
     terms. (Assume a regular pattern, as suggested.) Determine
     whether the sequence is an arithmetic progression. If so,
     find the common difference.

1.   3, 6, 9, 12, 15, . . .   _____

2.   4, 8, 16, 32, 64, . . .   _____

3.   -9, -11, -13, -15, -17, . . .   _____

4.   2, 0, -2, 0, 2, 0, -2, . . .   _____

5. $\frac{1}{4}$, $\frac{1}{2}$, $\frac{3}{4}$, 1, $\frac{5}{4}$, . . .   _____

B.

6.   Determine the 10th term of the arithmetic progression
     5, 8, 11, 14, 17, ...

                    _____

7.   Determine the 15th term of the arithmetic progression
     -1, 4, 9, 14, 19, ...

                    _____

8.   Determine the 20th term of the arithmetic progression
     3, 3 + 2π, 3 + 4π, 3 + 6π, 3 + 8π, ...

                         _____

9.   Determine the 20th term of the arithmetic progression with
     2nd term 4 and common difference 3.

                         _____

C. Determine the sum of the first 20 terms of the arithmetic
    progression

$$4, \ 6, \ 8, \ 10, \ 12, \ 14, \ \ldots \ .$$

SOLUTION.

$$\sum_{i=1}^{n} a_i = \frac{n}{2} \left[2a_1 + (n - 1)d \right]$$

$$\sum_{i=1}^{20} a_i = 10[8 + 19 \cdot 2]$$

$$= 460$$

D. Let $a_i = 7 + 4i$, $i = 1, 2, 3, \ldots$.

    Evaluate $\displaystyle\sum_{i=5}^{20} a_i$.

SOLUTION.

$$\sum_{i=5}^{20} a_i = \sum_{i=1}^{16} a_{i+4}$$

$$= \frac{16}{2} (a_5 + a_{20})$$

$$= 8(27 + 87)$$

$$= 912$$

C. Determine the sum of the first 20 terms of the indicated arithmetic progression.

10. 3, 5, 7, 9, 11, . . . _____

11. -1, -3, -5, -7, -9, . . . _____

12. -1, 3, 7, 11, 15, . . . _____

13. $a_1 = 6$, $d = 3$ _____

D. Evaluate $\sum_{i=11}^{50} a_i$ for the arithmetic progression

$a_1, a_2, \ldots a_i, \ldots$ in each example.

14. $a_i = 2 + 3i$ _____

15. $a_1 = 6$, $d = 4$ _____

16. $a_1 = 7$, $a_2 = 4$ _____

17. $a_1 = 3$, $a_{10} = 48$ _____

▶ 17.4   Geometric Progressions (text page 579)

KEY TOPICS

A.   The sequence

$$2, 6, 18, 54, 162, \ldots$$

is a geometric sequence with common ratio 3.

B.   Determine the 5th term of the geometric sequence with first term 10 and common ratio 3.

SOLUTION.

$$a_5 = 10 \cdot 3^4 = 10 \cdot 81 = 810$$

C.   Evaluate $\displaystyle\sum_{i=1}^{6} 4^i$.

SOLUTION.

$$\sum_{i=1}^{n} a^i = \frac{a_1(1 - r^n)}{1 - r}, \quad \text{where } a_1 = 4 \text{ and } r = 4$$

Thus

$$\sum_{i=1}^{6} a_i = \frac{4(1 - 4^6)}{1 - 4} = \frac{4(-4095)}{-3} = 5460$$

KEY EXERCISES

A. Consider the sequence indicated by means of its first few
    terms. (Assume a regular pattern, as suggested.) Determine
    whether the sequence is a geometric progression. If so,
    find the common ratio. Also, determine whether the sequence
    is an arithmetic progression.

1. 3, 6, 12, 24, 48, . . . _____

2. 10, 20, 30, 40, 50, . . . _____

3. -5, 10, -20, 40, -80, . . . _____

4. 6, -6, 6, -6, 6, . . . _____

5. $\frac{1}{3}$, $\frac{1}{9}$, $\frac{1}{27}$, $\frac{1}{81}$, $\frac{1}{243}$, . . . _____

B.

6. Determine the 5th term of the geometric progression with
    first term 6 and common ratio 2.

    _____

7. Determine the 32nd term of the geometric progression with
    first term 13 and 94th term -13.

    _____

8. Determine the first term of the geometric progression with
    4th term 5 and 5th term 25.

    _____

C. Evaluate the indicated sum.

9. $\sum\limits_{i=1}^{6} 2^i$ _____

10. $\sum\limits_{i=1}^{5} 3^i$ _____

11. $\sum\limits_{i=1}^{8} \frac{1}{2^i}$ _____

12. $\sum\limits_{i=1}^{19} (-1)^i$ _____

152 RIGHT

▶ 17.5 Binomial Expansion (text page 585)

KEY TOPICS

A. $\dfrac{14!}{9!5!} = \dfrac{14 \cdot 13 \cdot 12 \ldots 3 \cdot 2 \cdot 1}{(9 \cdot 8 \cdot 7 \ldots 3 \cdot 2 \cdot 1)(5 \cdot 4 \cdot 3 \cdot 2 \cdot 1)}$

$= \dfrac{14 \cdot 13 \cdot \cancel{12} \cdot 11 \cdot \cancel{10}}{\cancel{5} \cdot \cancel{4} \cdot \cancel{3} \cdot \cancel{2} \cdot 1}$

$= 2002$

B. $\dbinom{16}{3} = \dfrac{16!}{3!(16-3)!}$

$= \dfrac{16 \cdot 15 \cdot 14 \ldots 3 \cdot 2 \cdot 1}{(3 \cdot 2 \cdot 1)(13 \cdot 12 \cdot 11 \ldots 3 \cdot 2 \cdot 1)}$

$= \dfrac{\overset{8}{\cancel{16}} \cdot \overset{5}{\cancel{15}} \cdot 14}{\cancel{3} \cdot \cancel{2} \cdot 1}$

$= 560$

C. Use the binomial expansion to expand

$$(x - 1)^4.$$

SOLUTION.

$$(x - 1)^4 = \sum_{i=0}^{4} \binom{4}{i} x^{4-i} (-1)^i$$

$$= \sum_{i=0}^{4} (-1)^i \binom{4}{i} x^{4-i}$$

$$= x^4 - 4x^3 + 6x^2 - 4x + 1$$

D. (a) Express $(xy + 1)^{10}$ in $\sum$ – notation.

KEY EXERCISES

A.   Evaluate each expression.

1. 6! _____   2. 4! · 3! _____

3. $\frac{12!}{8!}$ _____   4. $\frac{20!}{17!\ 3!}$ _____

5. $(4!)^2$ _____

B.   Evaluate each binomial coefficient.

6. $\binom{4}{3}$ _____   7. $\binom{5}{5}$ _____

8. $\binom{10}{8}$ _____   9. $\binom{7}{5}$ _____

10. $\binom{11}{3}$ _____

C.   Use the binomial expansion to expand each power.

11. $(x + 1)^4$ _____

12. $(x - a)^4$ _____

13. $\left(x + \frac{1}{2}\right)^5$ _____

14. $(x^2 y - 1)^4$ _____

D.   (a) Express each power in $\sum$ - notation.

(b) Determine the sum of the first 4 terms of this expansion.

SOLUTION.

$$(a) \quad (xy + 1)^{10} = \sum_{i=0}^{10} \binom{10}{i} (xy)^{10-i} 1^i$$

$$= \sum_{i=0}^{10} \binom{10}{i} x^{10-i} y^{10-i}$$

$$(b) \quad x^{10} y^{10} + 10 x^9 y^9 + 45 x^8 y^8 + 120 \, x^7 y^7$$

E. Use the binomial expansion to determine $(2.1)^4$ to 4 decimal places.

SOLUTION.

$$(2.1)^4 = [2 + (.1)]^4 = \sum_{i=0}^{4} \binom{4}{i} 2^{4-i} (.1)^i$$

$$= \binom{4}{0} 2^4 + \binom{4}{1} 2^3 (.1) + \binom{4}{2} 2^2 (.1)^2 + \binom{4}{3} 2 (.1)^3 + \binom{4}{4} (.1)^4$$

$$= 2^4 + 4(8)(.1) + 6(4)(.01) + 4(2)(.001) + .0001$$

$$= 16 + 3.2 + .24 + .008 + .0001$$

$$= 19.4481$$

(b) Determine the sum of the first 4 terms of this expansion.

15. $(x + y)^9$ (a) _____ (b) _____

16. $(x + 1)^{10}$ (a) _____ (b) _____

17. $(x^2 - 1)^8$ (a) _____ (b) _____

18. $(x^3 y^2 + 2)^8$ (a) _____ (b) _____

E.   Use the binomial expansion to determine each power to 4 decimal places.

19. $(1.1)^8$ _____   20. $(.9)^{10}$ _____

21. $(1.01)^6$ _____

ANSWERS

▶ CHAPTER 1

Section 1.1 (page 1)

1.

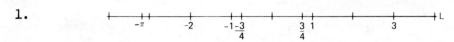

Figure 1 A

2. $P = -2.1$, $\quad Q = -1.9$, $\quad R = \frac{-3}{2}$, $\quad S = 1.9$, $\quad T = 2.1$, $\quad U = \frac{5}{2}$

3. <   4. >   5. <   6. >   7. >   8. <

9. left   10. right   11. left   12. right   13. left

14. left

Section 1.2 (page 2)

1. -20   2. -.34   3. $\frac{1}{3}$ 4. $-\pi$ 5. 0   6. -1.6

7. 12   8. 0   9. $\frac{7}{5}$ 10. .05   11. =   12. >

13. <   14. <   15. =   16. >   17. 2 and -2

18. $\frac{1}{2}$ 19. -1.4

Section 1.3 (page 3)

1. 668   2. -7151   3. -388 961

4. 900 759   5. -2094   6. 111

7. -15   8. 28   9. 137

10. -129   11. 204   12. -91

13. -23   14. 446   15. -3163

16. -71   17. 31   18. 92

Section 1.4 (page 4)

1. 156   2. -264   3. 1185   4. -335

5. 2607   6. 5   7. 257   8. -186

9. -2   10. 10   11. 2   12. 4

13. 5   14. 9   15. 1   16. 29

17. -1   18. 22   19. 32   20. 8

21. 691   22. -23

Section 1.5 (page 5)

1. -154   2. 154   3. 72   4. -40   5. 48

6. 38 916   7. 276   8. 122 480   9. 4 068 102   10. -4

11. 3   12. -4   13. 0   14. not defined

15. 5   16. 4   17. 60   18. 16 000   19. 1

20. -1   21. $\dfrac{-3}{10}$ 22. $\dfrac{14}{3}$

Section 1.6 (page 6)

1. 18   2. 30   3. 42   4. 24   5. 33   6. 9

7. 7   8. 3   9. 4   10. 4   11. $\dfrac{1}{2}$ 12. -1

13. -5   14. -6   15. 13   16. 91   17. 17   18. -10

19. 4

Section 1.7 (page 7)

1. 25   2. 16   3. 9   4. 100   5. 400

6. 27   7. 16   8. 125   9. 32   10. 10 000

11. 9   12. 3   13. 5   14. 36   15. 12

16. 36   17. 12   18. 17   19. 16

Section 2.1 (page 9)

1, 2, 3, and 5 are terms; 4 and 6 are not.

7. 7   8. $\frac{5}{3}$ 9. 6   10. −6   11. 0

12. 15xy   13. $2x^2y$ 14. $\frac{3}{5}x^2y$ 15. 10xyt

16, 17, 18, and 20 are polynomials; 19 is not.

Section 2.2 (page 10)

1. 3   2. 8   3. 1   4. 13

5. 31   6. (a) 3, (b) 19   7. (a) −1, (b) −5

8. (a) 10, (b) −2   9. (a) 7, (b) 142   10. 3   11. 0

12. 30   13. 11   14. −66

Section 2.3 (page 11)

1. similar   2. not similar   3. similar

4. not similar   5. similar   6. 15a

7. 6xy   8. m + 10n

9. 3x − 2y − 5z   10. a − 2b + 4c − 2   11. 14x + 10y

12. 10r + 6s − 2t   13. 6w + 3x + 2y − 5z

14. $5x^2 + y^2 + x + 3y$ 15. a + 2b   16. x + 7y

17. −x + 2y − 2z   18. 6r − 3u   19. 4b − 2c

20. 3x − 2z   21. $-2x^2 + 3x + y$ 22. 3 + 2b

Section 2.4 (page 12)

1. x^8 2. y^9 3. m^{17}

4. a^{15} 5. $10x^3y^2$ 6. $-12a^5b^2$

7. $60u^8v^4$ 8. $-40a^3b^4c^8d^6$ 9. $m^2 + 3m + 2$

10. $x^2 + 2x - 15$ 11. $x^2 + 2xy + x + y^2 + y$

12. $x^2 + 2xy + y^2 - z^2$

13. $ax + bx + cx + ay + by + cy$

14. $x^2 + 2x + 1$ 15. $x^2 - 2x + 1$ 16. $y^2 + 8y + 16$

17. $a^2 - 4a + 4$ 18. $x^2 - 25$ 19. $z^2 - 100$

20. $8x + 20$ 21. $2x^2 - 36$ 22. $4xy$

23. $-2x - y$ 24. $3x^2 - 2y + 2xy$

Section 2.5 (page 14)

1. x^2 2. a^4 3. x^4 4. y^5 5. z 6. $3x$

7. a^2 8. $3m^3$ 9. $7r^5$ 10. $-3x^4$ 11. 1   12. -1

13. $\dfrac{a}{3}$ 14. $\dfrac{1}{2}$

Section 2.6 (page 14)

1. 0   2. 4

3. 4   4. 4

5. 10   6. $x^3 + x^2 - x + 1$

7. $5y^4 - 4y^3 + 3y^2 - 2y + 1$ 8. $-m^{12} + m^{10} + m^9 - 7m^4 + m^2 - 7$

9. $2x^4$ 10. $x^6 - 4x^5 + 2x^3 + 1$

11. 5   12. 4   13. 4   14. 1   15. 4

Section 2.7 (page 16)

(The checks are given below.)

1. $2x + 1$ 2. $5x - 1$ 3. $-y^2 + y - 2$

4. $9a^2 - 2a + 4$ 5. $x + 5$ 6. $a - 3$

7. $2x - 3$ 8. $y^2 + 2y + 1$ 9. $m + 2$

10. $x - 4$ 11. $x^3 + 1$ 12. $2a^3 + 2$

13. $m^4 + 3m^2 + 2$ 14. $x + 1 + \dfrac{2}{x + 4}$. The remainder is 2.

15. $x^2 + 2 + \dfrac{4}{2x + 3}$. The remainder is 4.

16. $y^2 - y + 1 + \dfrac{1}{y^2 + 3y}$. The remainder is 1.

17. $a^2 - 2a - 2 + \dfrac{2a + 2}{a^2 + 1}$. The remainder is $2a + 2$.

18. $x^2 - 2x + \dfrac{-4x - 2}{x^2 + 2x + 1}$. The remainder is $-4x - 2$.

CHECKS:

1. $2x + 1$ quotient
$\underline{\times \quad x}$ divisor
$2x^2 + x$ dividend

3. $-y^2 + y - 2$ quotient
$\underline{\times \quad -2y}$ divisor
$2y^3 - 2y^2 + 4y$ dividend

5. $x + 5$ quotient
$\underline{\times \quad x + 4}$ divisor
$x^2 + 5x$
$\underline{\qquad 4x + 20}$
$x^2 + 9x + 20$ dividend

8. $y^2 + 2y + 1$ quotient
$\underline{\times \quad y + 1}$ divisor
$y^3 + 2y^2 + y$
$\underline{\qquad y^2 + 2y + 1}$
$y^3 + 3y^2 + 3y + 1$ dividend

A5

14.
$$x + 1 \quad \text{quotient}$$
$$\underline{\times\ x + 4} \quad \text{divisor}$$
$$x^2 + x$$
$$\underline{\quad\quad 4x + 4}$$
$$x^2 + 5x + 4$$
$$\underline{+\quad\quad\quad\quad 2} \quad \text{remainder}$$
$$x^2 + 5x + 6 \quad \text{dividend}$$

17.
$$a^2 - 2a - 2 \quad \text{quotient}$$
$$\underline{\times\ a^2 + 1} \quad \text{divisor}$$
$$a^4 - 2a^3 - 2a^2$$
$$\underline{\quad\quad\quad\quad\quad\quad a^2 - 2a - 2}$$
$$a^4 - 2a^3 - a^2 - 2a - 2$$
$$\underline{+\quad\quad\quad\quad\quad\quad\quad 2a + 2} \quad \text{remainder}$$
$$a^4 - 2a^3 - a^2 \quad \text{dividend}$$

Section 2.8 (page 18)

1. $\underline{-1}\,|\ 1\ 6\ 5$

2. $\underline{1}\,|\ 1\ 1\ -5\ 3$

3. $\underline{2}\,|\ 1\ -1\ 0\ -4$

4. $\underline{4}\,|\ 1\ 0\ -18\ 9\ -4$

5. $x + 3$ (no remainder)

6. $2x^2 + 3x + 1$ (remainder 1)

7. $x^2 + 4$ (no remainder)

8. $2x^4 + 3x^2 + 2x$ (remainder -1)

9. $x + 9$

10. $t^2 + 4t + 5$

11. $x^2 + 2x + 1$

12. $x^3 - 2x + 5$

13. $y^3 - 3y^2 + 3y + 1$

14. $x + 3$ (remainder -2)

15. $y^2 + y + 1$ (remainder 1)

16. $x^3 + 2x^2 + 4x + 2$ (remainder 4)

▶ CHAPTER 3

Section 3.1 (page 20)

1. prime

2. not prime

3. prime

4. prime

5. not prime

6. prime

7. $28 = 2^2 \cdot 7$

8. $32 = 2^5$

9. $-48 = -(2^4 \cdot 3)$

10. $98 = 2 \cdot 7^2$

11. $990 = 2 \cdot 3^2 \cdot 5 \cdot 11$ 12. $14\,400 = 2^6 \cdot 3^2 \cdot 5^2$

13. 10   14. 6   15. 32   16. 72   17. 2   18. 1

19. 5   20. 6

Section 3.2 (page 21)

1. $2(a + 3b)$ 2. $5(x - 2y)$ 3. $x(3x + 5)$

4. $ab(a - b)$ 5. $3(3x + 4)$ 6. $4x(x - 2)$

7. $4ab(2a + 3)$ 8. $10x(2x^2 + 1)$ 9. $mn(mn + n^2 - m)$

10. $xy^9(x^7 + x^3y - y^3)$

11. $2(15x^2 - 9x + 50)$

12. $3abc(6abc - 9b + 10ac)$

Section 3.4 (page 21)

1. $(a + 4)(a - 4)$ 2. $(x + 9)(x - 9)$

3. $(1 + y)(1 - y)$ 4. $(a + b)(a - b)$

5. $(3x + 10y)(3x - 10y)$ 6. $4(4a + 3c)(4a - 3c)$

7. $5(x + 3z)(x - 3z)$ 8. $a(a + 1)(a - 1)$

9. $(x^2 + y^2)(x + y)(x - y)$ 10. $(a^3 + b^4)(a^3 - b^4)$

11. $(4x^2 + 1)(2x + 1)(2x - 1)$ 12. $(a - b + 7)(a - b - 7)$

13. $(a + b)^3(a - b)^3$ 14. $6a(x + 3)(x - 3)$

Section 3.5 (page 22)

1. $(x + 5)(x + 1)$ 2. $(x - 5)(x - 1)$ 3. $(x + 5)(x - 1)$

4. $(x - 5)(x + 1)$ 5. $(a + 2)(a + 3)$ 6. $(b + 7)(b + 2)$

7. $(z - 4)(z - 2)$ 8. $(m - 5)(m - 2)$ 9. $(t + 2)(t - 6)$

10. $(t - 4)^2$ 11. $a^2(x - 4)(x - 1)$ 12. $5(z + 1)(z - 7)$

13. $x(x - 6)(x - 3)$ 14. $-(a + 1)(a - 4)$

Section 3.6 (page 23)

1. $(2x + 1)(x + 3)$ 2. $(3y + 1)(y + 2)$ 3. $(2x + 5)(x + 1)$

4. $(2a + 3)(2a + 5)$ 5. $(2x + 1)(2x - 3)$ 6. $(3y - 2)(y - 1)$

7. $(7b + 1)(b + 1)$ 8. $(5a - 1)(a - 2)$ 9. $2(2z + 1)(3z + 1)$

10. $a(2a + 5)(a - 3)$ 11. $(2x + y)(x + 2y)$ 12. $(3a + b)(a - 2b)$

13. $(2m + n)(5m - n)$ 14. $(2y - 3z)(3y - 4z)$

Section 3.7 (page 24)

1. $(c + d)(x + y)$ 2. $(a - b)(m - n)$ 3. $(a + 3)(x - y)$

4. $(a + b)(c + d)$ 5. $(a - b)(x - 2y)$ 6. $(a + 5b)(s + t)$

7. $(x + y)(y + 1)$ 8. $(m^2 + n)(m + 1)$ 9. $(a + b)(x + 1)(x - 1)$

10. $(a + 3)(a - 3)(x + 1)(x - 1)$

11. $(t + 3)(t - 3)(s + 2)(s - 2)$

12. $(a^2 + 1)(x - 1)(x - 2)$

13. $(a + b)(a - b)(m + 4)^2$

14. $(y + z)(y - z)(x - 3)(x + 2)$

Section 3.8 (page 26)

1. $(a - 1)(a^2 + a + 1)$ 2. $(b + 4)(b^2 - 4b + 16)$

3. $(x + 5)(x^2 - 5x + 25)$ 4. $(ab - 10)(a^2b^2 + 10ab + 100)$

5. $(xy - 2)(x^2y^2 + 2xy + 4)$ 6. $(10x - 3a)(100x^2 + 30ax + 9a^2)$

7. $(a^2 - b)(a^4 + a^2b + b^2)$ 8. $(c^3 + d)(c^6 - c^3d + d^2)$

9. $a^3(b + c)(b^2 - bc + c^2)$ 10. $a^3b^3(c - 1)(c^2 + c + 1)$

11. $a^2(x - 5)(x^2 + 5x + 25)$

12. $(x + a + 3)[(x + 1)^2 - (x + 1)(a + 2) + (a + 2)^2]$

13. $(a - 1)(a^2 + a + 1)(x + 2)(x - 2)$

14. $(a + 1)(a^2 - a + 1)(b + c)(b - c)$

▶ CHAPTER 4

Section 4.1 (page 27)

1. $\dfrac{-3}{5}$ 2. $\dfrac{3}{5}$ 3. $\dfrac{5}{8}$ 4. $\dfrac{-2}{\pi}$ 5. $\dfrac{-3}{4}$ 6. $\dfrac{2}{9}$

7. $\dfrac{1}{2}$ 8. $\dfrac{1}{5}$ 9. $\dfrac{1}{3}$ 10. $\dfrac{-7}{10}$ 11. $\dfrac{-2}{5}$ 12. $\dfrac{2}{9}$

13. $\dfrac{3}{4}$ 14. $\dfrac{-5}{9}$ 15. $\dfrac{9}{10}$ 16. 4   17. 1   18. $\dfrac{-1}{9}$

19. $\dfrac{5}{7}$ 20. $\dfrac{2}{7}$ 21. $\dfrac{5}{27}$ 22. $\dfrac{25}{121}$ 23. $\dfrac{-21}{4}$ 24. $\dfrac{25}{13}$

Section 4.2 (page 28)

1. 1   2. $\dfrac{1}{6}$ 3. $\dfrac{-9}{100}$

4. $\dfrac{7}{10}$ 5. $\dfrac{5}{4}$ 6. (a) -3, (b) 5

7. (a) $\dfrac{4}{5}$, (b) $\dfrac{1}{2}$ 8. (a) $\dfrac{1}{10}$, (b) 1   9. (a) $\dfrac{-1}{3}$, (b) $\dfrac{-5}{3}$

10. (a) $\dfrac{5}{3}$, (b) $\dfrac{29}{7}$ 11. $\dfrac{2}{3}$ 12. $\dfrac{7}{6}$

13. $\dfrac{4}{9}$ 14. $\dfrac{1}{41}$ 15. $\dfrac{-7}{11}$

16. (a) $\frac{2}{3}$, (b) $\frac{-1}{3}$ 17. (a) $\frac{-1}{3}$, (b) $\frac{9}{2}$ 18. (a) 0, (b) $\frac{99}{12}$

19. (a) 1, (b) $\frac{-5}{8}$ 20. (a) $\frac{-2}{5}$, (b) $\frac{2}{5}$

Section 4.3 (page 29)

1. $3a$

2. $3x^2$

3. $6xy$

4. $\frac{-5ab^3}{2}$

5. b

6. $\frac{1}{y}$

7. $\frac{-n}{m}$

8. $a^2 d$

9. $\frac{y^2 z^6}{x}$

10. $2a$

11. $4ab$

12. $\frac{2y^3}{3z}$

13. $\frac{4ax}{5y}$

14. $\frac{2xyz}{3}$

15. $\frac{4ab^3}{7c^2}$

16. $\frac{-3np^6}{4m^2}$

17. $\frac{1}{x + y}$

18. $x - y$

19. $\frac{(x + y)^2}{2}$

20. $\frac{y + z}{a + b}$

21. $\frac{1}{a}$

22. $\frac{m(m + n)}{m - n}$

23. $\frac{(a + b)(x + y)}{x - y}$

24. $\frac{7(c - d)}{4c(a + b)^3(c + d)^4}$

Section 4.4 (page 31)

1. $ab(a + b)$

2. $x(y^2 - x)$

3. $ab^2(a + b)(a - b)$

4. $xy(xz - 1)$

5. $x(2y + 3)$

6. $ab(3c + 5)$

7. $\frac{mn^2(3mn - 4)}{2}$

8. $b + a$

9. $z + x$

10. $\frac{c(c^2 + a^2)}{a}$

11. $\frac{x(y^3 - xz^4)}{y}$

12. $2c + 5a$

13. $\dfrac{n(2m - 3n^2)}{4m}$

14. $\dfrac{3x^3z + 4y^2}{x}$

15. $\dfrac{3ab + 4a^2 - 6b}{ab}$

16. $\dfrac{2xy - x + 4}{x}$

17. $3xz + 4xy + 2y$

18. $\dfrac{5c^2 - 10a^3 + 4b^2c}{2b}$

19. $\dfrac{7x^2y^2z^3 + 2x^4 + 5yz^3}{2}$

20. $\dfrac{-6ab^3c^7d^3 + 15ab^3c^4d^4 - 4d + 8}{2bc}$

21. $\dfrac{1}{y^2 + 1}$

22. $\dfrac{2}{ab + 2}$

23. $\dfrac{5}{y(x - 1)}$

24. $\dfrac{1}{3m^2n^3 - 2mn + 6}$

Section 4.5 (page 32)

1. 2

2. $\dfrac{3(x - y)}{x + y}$

3. $\dfrac{6x - 1}{2x + 1}$

4. $\dfrac{a - b}{2(a + b)}$

5. $x - y$

6. $\dfrac{1}{2(u - v)}$

7. cannot be simplified (by present methods)

8. $\dfrac{1}{a + b}$

9. $c + 5$

10. $\dfrac{-(a + 6)}{3}$

11. $\dfrac{a + 2}{a + 1}$

12. $\dfrac{x - 2}{x + 2}$

13. $\dfrac{u + 10}{u^2}$

14. $\dfrac{z}{1 - z}$

15. $\dfrac{(a - 3)(a - 2)}{(a + 3)(a + 2)}$

16. $\dfrac{m + 4}{m - 4}$

17. $\dfrac{a}{b - 1}$

18. $\dfrac{x}{x - 3}$

19. $(1 + u)(1 - u)$

20. $\dfrac{x^2 + xy + y^2}{4}$

CHAPTER 5

Section 5.1 (page 34)

1. $\dfrac{1}{8}$

2. $\dfrac{-2}{21}$

3. $\dfrac{1}{6}$

4. $\dfrac{1}{12}$

5. $\dfrac{-11}{42}$

6. $\dfrac{7}{4}$

7. $\dfrac{3}{xy}$

8. $\dfrac{1}{x}$

9. $\dfrac{1}{y^2 b}$

10. $\dfrac{x - a}{4}$

11. $\dfrac{(x - a)(x + y)}{6}$

12. $\dfrac{5(a + 4)}{(a + b)(a - 3)}$

13. $\dfrac{3}{2}$

14. $\dfrac{1}{2}$

15. $\dfrac{4}{3}$

16. $\dfrac{14}{15}$

17. $\dfrac{22}{21}$

18. $\dfrac{3}{5}$

19. $\dfrac{4a}{3b}$

20. $\dfrac{xd}{yc}$

21. $\dfrac{3(x - y)}{x + y}$

22. $\dfrac{1}{(a + b)(x - y)}$

23. $\dfrac{(a - 4)(x + 1)}{(x - 1)(a + 2)}$

24. $\dfrac{(y + 3)(x - z)}{(x^2 + xz + z^2)(y + 5)}$

25. $(m - n)(m - 5)$

26. $x - 5$

27. $x + 4$

28. $\dfrac{(x + 1)^4}{(x + 3)^2}$

Section 5.2 (page 36)

1. 42

2. 150

3. 288

4. 24

5. 840

6. $x^2 y^2 z^3$

7. $(x + a)(x - a)$

8. $(x + 2)(x - 2)(x - 3)$

9. $a^4 b^3 c^3$

10. $(x + 3)^2 (x - 3)(x + 4)$

11. (a) 24 (b) $\dfrac{1}{8} = \dfrac{3}{24}$, $\dfrac{1}{12} = \dfrac{2}{24}$

12. (a) 80   (b) $\frac{5}{16} = \frac{25}{80}$, $\frac{3}{40} = \frac{6}{80}$

13. (a) 90   (b) $\frac{-5}{18} = \frac{-25}{90}$, $\frac{2}{45} = \frac{4}{90}$

14. (a) 300   (b) $\frac{3}{20} = \frac{45}{300}$, $\frac{1}{25} = \frac{12}{300}$, $\frac{7}{30} = \frac{70}{300}$

15. (a) 432   (b) $\frac{5}{54} = \frac{40}{432}$, $\frac{-1}{72} = \frac{-6}{432}$, $\frac{11}{144} = \frac{33}{432}$

16. (a) xy   (b) $\frac{a}{x} = \frac{ay}{xy}$, $\frac{b}{y} = \frac{bx}{xy}$

17. (a) $(x - 2)(x - 3)$

  (b) $\dfrac{1}{x - 2} = \dfrac{x - 3}{(x - 2)(x - 3)}$, $\dfrac{2}{x - 3} = \dfrac{2x - 4}{(x - 2)(x - 3)}$

18. (a) $(x + 2)^2(x - 2)$

  (b) $\dfrac{2}{x^2 - 4} = \dfrac{2x + 4}{(x + 2)^2(x - 2)}$, $\dfrac{x}{x^2 + 4x + 4} = \dfrac{x^2 - 2x}{(x + 2)^2(x - 2)}$

19. (a) $x^2 y^2$

  (b) $\dfrac{a}{xy^2} = \dfrac{ax}{x^2 y^2}$, $\dfrac{-b}{x^2} = \dfrac{-by}{x^2 y^2}$, $\dfrac{ab}{x^2 y^2} = \dfrac{ab}{x^2 y^2}$

20. (a) $(x + 2)(x + 4)(x - 4)$

  (b) $\dfrac{2}{x^2 + 6x + 8} = \dfrac{2x - 8}{(x + 2)(x + 4)(x - 4)}$, $\dfrac{x}{x^2 - 16} = \dfrac{x^2 + 2x}{(x + 2)(x + 4)(x - 4)}$,

  $\dfrac{-3x}{x^2 - 2x - 8} = \dfrac{-3x^2 - 12x}{(x + 2)(x + 4)(x - 4)}$

Section 5.3 (page 38)

1. 1   2. $\frac{4}{5}$ 3. $\frac{3}{7}$

4. $\frac{11}{6}$ 5. $\frac{3}{4}$ 6. $\frac{1}{8}$

7. $\dfrac{6}{5}$ 8. $\dfrac{29}{54}$ 9. $\dfrac{-7}{192}$

10. $\dfrac{29}{100}$ 11. $\dfrac{3}{x}$ 12. $\dfrac{1}{a}$

13. $\dfrac{a + b}{y}$ 14. $\dfrac{a + bc - 1}{xy}$ 15. $\dfrac{y + x}{xy}$

16. $\dfrac{a - 2}{a^2}$ 17. $\dfrac{ay + bx}{x^2 y^2}$ 18. $\dfrac{3x - a}{(x - a)(x + a)}$

19. $\dfrac{-3}{(x + 2)(x - 2)}$ 20. $\dfrac{5x^2 + 12x + 27}{(x + 3)^2 (x - 3)^2}$ 21. $\dfrac{x - 14}{(x + 5)(x - 5)(x - 4)}$

22. $\dfrac{x^2 - (a + 1)x}{x(x + a)(x - a)}$

Section 5.4 (page 40)

1. $\dfrac{1}{8}$ 2. 18   3. 3   4. -9 5. 6   6. -10

7. -5 8. $\dfrac{2}{15}$ 9. $\dfrac{xz}{y}$ 10. $\dfrac{-a}{bc}$ 11. $\dfrac{y}{x}$ 12. $\dfrac{a}{bx}$

13. $\dfrac{y}{2ax}$ 14. $\dfrac{-1}{a + b}$ 15. $2x$ 16. $\dfrac{x - 1}{4}$

Section 5.5 (page 42)

1. 1.5   2. 1.029   3. 2.983   4. 1.23x

5. .22   6. $-.73$ 7. -1.16 8. $-.55xy$

9. 82.5   10. .005 75   11. .037 26x^3 12. .04

13. .0001   14. .000 125   15. .0401   16. .009

17. 3   18. .11   19. .08   20. $-.0159$

21. 22.4   22. 2 424 000   23. .02   24. .05

▶ CHAPTER 6

Section 6.1 (page 44)

1. Yes; i. true   2. No; ii. yes   3. Yes; i. false

4. No; ii. no   5. No; ii. no   6. root

7. root   8. not a root   9. root

10. root   11. root   12. not a root

13. root   14. not a root   15. not a root

Section 6.2 (page 45)

1. 8   2. 5   3. 1   4. 12   5. 2   6. 12

7. -5   8. -3   9. 3   10. $\frac{-1}{3}$ 11. 2   12. $\frac{-10}{9}$

13. 4   14. -20

Check: $2(4) + 9 \overset{?}{=} 17$ Check: $\frac{-20}{5} \overset{?}{=} -4$

$\quad\quad\quad 17 \overset{\checkmark}{=} 17$ $\quad\quad\quad -4 \overset{\checkmark}{=} -4$

15. -3   16. -1

Check: $3(-3) - 2 \overset{?}{=} 5(-3) + 4$ Check: $\frac{-1 + 3}{6} \overset{?}{=} \frac{1}{3}$

$\quad\quad\quad -11 \overset{\checkmark}{=} -11$

$\quad\quad\quad\quad\quad\quad\quad\quad \frac{2}{6} \overset{?}{=} \frac{1}{3}$

$\quad\quad\quad\quad\quad\quad\quad\quad \frac{1}{3} \overset{\checkmark}{=} \frac{1}{3}$

Section 6.3 (page 46)

1. 3   2. $\frac{3}{2}$ 3. 9   4. 7   5. 0   6. 7

7. -8   8. -5   9. 4   10. 4   11. 12   12. 2

13. 10

Check: $\frac{10 + 2}{3} \overset{?}{=} \frac{10 - 2}{2}$

$\quad\quad\quad 4 \overset{\checkmark}{=} 4$

14. $\dfrac{-2}{3}$

Check: $\dfrac{1}{\dfrac{-2}{3} + 2} \overset{?}{=} \dfrac{3}{4}$

$\dfrac{1}{\dfrac{4}{3}} \overset{?}{=} \dfrac{3}{4}$

$\dfrac{3}{4} \overset{\checkmark}{=} \dfrac{3}{4}$

15. 4

Check: $\dfrac{4}{4 + 2} \overset{?}{=} \dfrac{2}{3}$

$\dfrac{4}{6} \overset{?}{=} \dfrac{2}{3}$

$\dfrac{2}{3} \overset{\checkmark}{=} \dfrac{2}{3}$

16. $\dfrac{1}{2}$

Check: $\dfrac{1}{\dfrac{1}{2}} + \dfrac{1}{2 \cdot \dfrac{1}{2}} \overset{?}{=} 3$

$2 + 1 \overset{?}{=} 3$

$3 \overset{\checkmark}{=} 3$

Section 6.4 (page 48)

1. $\dfrac{3a}{10}$

Check: $10 \cdot \dfrac{3a}{10} \overset{?}{=} 3a$

$3a \overset{\checkmark}{=} 3a$

2. $2b + 1$

Check: $5(2b + 1) - 2b \overset{?}{=} 4(2b + 1) + 1$

$10b + 5 - 2b \overset{?}{=} 8b + 4 + 1$

$8b + 5 \overset{\checkmark}{=} 8b + 5$

3. $4bc - 1 + a$

Check: $\dfrac{(4bc - 1 + a) + 1 - a}{b} \overset{?}{=} 4c$

$$\frac{4bc}{b} \overset{?}{=} 4c$$

$$4c \overset{\checkmark}{=} 4c$$

4. $\dfrac{4a - b}{2}$

Check: $4\left(\dfrac{4a - b}{2}\right) - \left[2\left(\dfrac{4a - b}{2}\right) + a\right] \overset{?}{=} 3a - b$

$$8a - 2b - [4a - b + a] \overset{?}{=} 3a - b$$

$$3a - b \overset{\checkmark}{=} 3a - b$$

5. $\dfrac{5 - a}{2c}$

Check: $\dfrac{5 - a}{2\left[\dfrac{5 - a}{2c}\right]} \overset{?}{=} c$

$$\frac{2c(5 - a)}{2(5 - a)} \overset{?}{=} c$$

$$c \overset{\checkmark}{=} c$$

6. $\dfrac{3}{2 - ab - 2b}$

Check: $\dfrac{2\left(\dfrac{3}{2 - ab - 2b}\right) - 3}{a + 2} \overset{?}{=} b\left(\dfrac{3}{2 - ab - 2b}\right)$

Cross-multiply.

$$\left(\frac{6}{2 - ab - 2b} - 3\right)(2 - ab - 2b) \overset{?}{=} 3b(a + 2)$$

On each side use the Distributive Laws.

$$6 - 3(2 - ab - 2b) \overset{?}{=} 3ab + 6b$$

$$6 - 6 + 3ab + 6b \overset{?}{=} 3ab + 6b$$

$$3ab + 6b \overset{\checkmark}{=} 3ab + 6b$$

7. (a) $\dfrac{1 + 3t}{2}$ (b) $\dfrac{2x - 1}{3}$

8. (a) $\dfrac{10 + 3y - 4z}{5}$ (b) $\dfrac{5x + 4z - 10}{3}$

9. (a) $\dfrac{2xt - 4}{5t}$ (b) $\dfrac{4}{2x - 5y}$

10. (a) $\dfrac{y + b - at + ac}{t - c}$ (b) $\dfrac{y + b + cx + ca}{x + a}$

11. (a) $\dfrac{3cy - a}{2 + y}$ (b) $\dfrac{2x + a}{3c - x}$

12. (a) $\dfrac{3z - 2}{2 + z}$ (b) $\dfrac{2(y + 1)}{3 - y}$

13. $\dfrac{4 - a}{4}$ 14. $-(a + 1)$ 15. $\dfrac{2}{1 - a}$ 16. $\dfrac{ab}{a - b}$

Section 6.5 (page 49)

1. 1   2. 2   3. 0   4. 1   5. 2   6. 0   7. 1   8. 4

9. $5x - 3 \overset{?}{=} 5x + 3$ 10. $t(t - 2) \overset{?}{=} (t - 1)^2$

       $-3 \overset{\times}{=} 3$ $t^2 - 2t \overset{?}{=} t^2 - 2t + 1$

                                     $0 \overset{\times}{=} 1$

11. $4u - [3 - (2u + 5)] \overset{?}{=} 3u - (7 - 3u)$

       $4u - 3 + 2u + 5 \overset{?}{=} 3u - 7 + 3u$

            $6u + 2 \overset{?}{=} 6u - 7$

                 $2 \overset{\times}{=} -7$

12. $5u + 5(u - 3) \overset{?}{=} 7(u - 2) + 3u - 1$

       $5u + 5u - 15 \overset{?}{=} 7u - 14 + 3u - 1$

           $10u - 15 \overset{?}{=} 10u - 15$

               $-15 \overset{\checkmark}{=} -15$

13. $(y + 2)(y + 3) - 3 \overset{?}{=} y(y + 5) + 3$

       $y^2 + 5y + 6 - 3 \overset{?}{=} y^2 + 5y + 3$

$$y^2 + 5y + 3 \overset{?}{=} y^2 + 5y + 3$$

$$3 \overset{\checkmark}{=} 3$$

14. $(x + 1)^2 - (x - 1)^2 \overset{?}{=} 4x$

$$x^2 + 2x + 1 - (x^2 - 2x + 1) \overset{?}{=} 4x$$

$$x^2 + 2x + 1 - x^2 + 2x - 1 \overset{?}{=} 4x$$

$$4x \overset{?}{=} 4x$$

$$0 \overset{\checkmark}{=} 0$$

15. (a)   16. (c)   17. (b)   18. (b)

▶ CHAPTER 7

Section 7.1 (page 52)

1. $x + 1$, $x + 2$, $x + 3$

2. $y + 2$, $y + 4$

3. $2t + 3$

4. $3(n + 2)$

5. $s + (s + 2) + (s + 4)$

6. 10, 11, 12

7. 9, 11, 13

8. 6

9. 9, 10

10. 20, 28

11. $x + 5$

12. $x - 10$

13. $\dfrac{x}{2}$

14. $\dfrac{x - 4}{3} + 4$ or $\dfrac{x + 8}{3}$

15. 30

16. 28

17. 5

Section 7.2 (page 54)

1. \$1.20

2. $(15x + 20)$ cents

3. $45x$ cents

4. 10

A19

5. 22   6. 6

7. (a) $1.68   (b) 28x cents   8. (5x + 240) cents

9. 21   10. 15

11. 96 cents

Section 7.3 (page 56)

1. $3\frac{1}{2}$ miles per hour   2. 4

3. (a) 60t   (b) 70(t − 2)   4. 295 miles

5. $1\frac{1}{2}$ miles   6. 90 miles

7. 24 miles

Section 7.4 (page 57)

1. (a) .14   (b) .09   (c) .4   2. (a) .005   (b) .055   (c) .0525

3. (a) 7%   (b) 19%   (c) $6\frac{1}{2}$%   4. $40

5. $65.10   6. $30

7. (320 + .01x) dollars   8. 7%

9. $593.28   10. $5 000

11. $3 000   12. $1 000

Section 7.5 (page 59)

1. 12 pounds   2. $\frac{x}{4}$ gallons

3. 1.6   4. 10

5. 6 gallons   6. 8

7. 60 tons of alloy A and 40 tons of alloy B

Section 7.6 (page 60)

1. $\dfrac{3}{8}$
2. $\dfrac{x}{6}$
3. $\dfrac{2}{x}$

4. $2\dfrac{2}{3}$ days
5. 18 hours
6. $1\dfrac{1}{3}$ days

7. 6 minutes

▶ CHAPTER 8

Section 8.1 (page 62)

1. {Joe, Barry, Alex}

2. {Greenland, Alaska, Canada, Mexico}

3. {1, 3, 5, 7, 9}

4. {2, 4, 6, 8, 10, 12, 14, 16, 18, 20}

5. function
6. function

7. function
8. not a function

9. function
10. not a function

11. (a) {1, 2, 3}   (b) {2, 4, 6}

12. (a) {-1, -2, -3, -4}   (b) {1, 2, 3, 4}

13. (a) {1, 2, 3, 4}   (b) {2}

14. (a) {1, 2, 3, 4, 5, 6}   (b) {5, 6}

15. (a) {10, 20, 30, 40}   (b) {1, 2, 3, 4}

16. (a) {10, 20, 30, 40, 50, 60}   (b) {1}

Section 8.2 (page 64)

1. (a) 1, 2, 3, 4   (b) 4   (c) 2

2. (a) 1, 2, 3, 4, 5   (b) 10   (c) 10

3. (a) 5   (b) 10   (c) 15   (d) 20

4. (a) 8   (b) 10   (c) 7   (d) 2

5. (a) −1   (b) 5   (c) −3   (d) −5

6. (a) 1   (b) −5   (c) 3   (d) 5

7. (a) 10   (b) 10   (c) 10   (d) 10

8. (a) 5   (b) 5   (c) 8   (d) 13

9. (a) $f(t) = 200t$ (b) 2400

10. (a) $f(x) = 3x - 900$ (b) 300

11. (a) $f(x) = 15x$ (b) $12.00

12. All x except 5

13. All x except −4

14. All x

15. All x

Section 8.3 (page 66)

1. P = (2, 1)   Q = (1, 3)   R = (−1, −3)

    S = (−4, 0)   T = (2, −5)

2.−9.

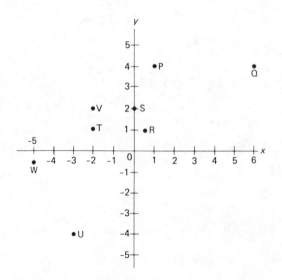

Figure 8A

10. I   11. II   12. IV

13. coordinate axis   14. III   15. IV

16. coordinate axis   17. (both) coordinate axes

Section 8.4 (page 67)

1. See Figure 8B (a).   2. See Figure 8B (b).

3. See Figure 8B (c).   4. See Figure 8B (d).

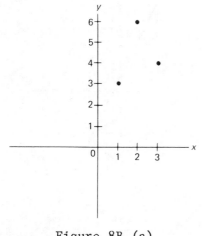

Figure 8B (a)

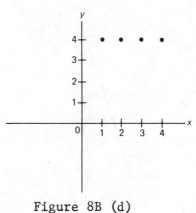

Figure 8B (b)

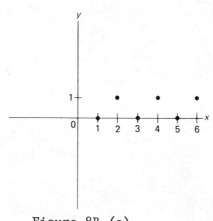

Figure 8B (c)

Figure 8B (d)

5. function   6. not a function   7. function

8. not a function   9. function   10. not a function

A23

11. See Figure 8C (a).   12. See Figure 8C (b).

13. See Figure 8C (c).   14. See Figure 8C (d).

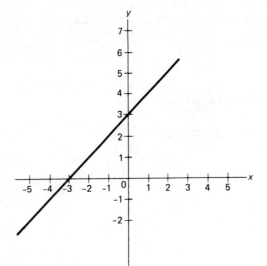

Figure 8C (a)

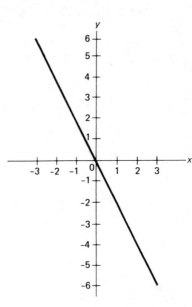

Figure 8C (b)

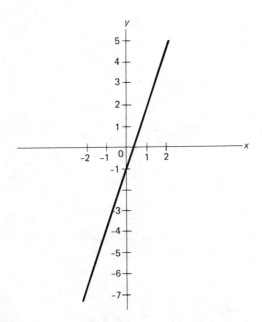

Figure 8C (c)

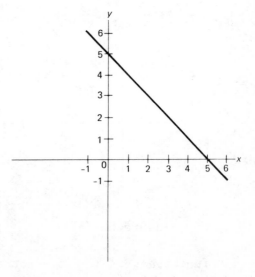

Figure 8C (d)

A24

15. See Figure 8D (a).   16. See Figure 8D (b).

17. See Figure 8D (c).   18. See Figure 8D (d).

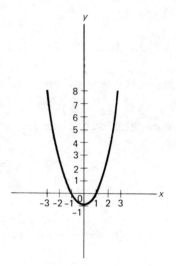

Figure 8D (a)

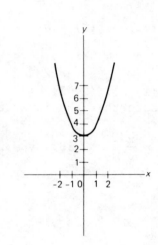

Figure 8D (b)

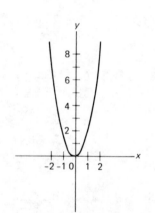

Figure 8D (c)

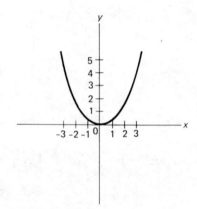

Figure 8D (d)

Section 8.5 (page 71)

1. one-one

2. one-one

3. not one-one and
   not a function

4. not one-one

5. not one-one and
   not a function

6. one-one

A25

7. one-one   8. not one-one

9. not one-one   10. one-one

11. $f(1) = f(2) = 10$ 12. $f(-1) = f(1) = 5$

13. $f(-1) = f(1) = 0$ 14. $\{(6, 1), (3, 2), (1, 3)\}$

15. $\{(10, 1), (1, 2), (8, 3), (3, 4)\}$

16. $\{(1, 1), (2, 2), (6, 3), (5, 4), (4, 5), (3, 6)\}$
     (Note that the inverse is the same as the original function.)

17. $y = \dfrac{x}{3}$ 18. $y = x - 5$ 19. $y = 1 - x$ 20. $y = \dfrac{x - 5}{6}$

▶ CHAPTER 9

Section 9.1 (page 75)

1. 4   2. $\dfrac{1}{5}$ 3. $\dfrac{2}{7}$

4. $\dfrac{-1}{3}$ 5. 9   6. -8

7. 25   8. 21   9. $\dfrac{1}{2}$

10. 6 and -6   11. 9   12. 90

13. 24   14. $b = 8$, $c = 10$ 15. $a = 12$, $c = 20$

16. $a = b = 6$

Section 9.2 (page 76)

1. 1   2. -3   3. -1   4. 2   5. 2   6. 3   7. 9

8. 3   9. $y - 4 = 2(x - 4)$

10. $y - 3 = -x$ 11. $y + 2 = 5(x + 1)$

12. $y - 6 = \dfrac{1}{2}(x - 1)$ 13. $x = 1$

14. $y = 2$ 15. $x = -1$ 16. $y = \dfrac{1}{4}$

A26

Section 9.3 (page 79)

1. (a) $\frac{-1}{4}$ (b) 1   2. (a) 6   (b) –12

3. (a) $\frac{-3}{5}$ (b) 3   4. (a) –4   (b) $\frac{-4}{3}$

5. $y = 2x - 11$ 6. $y = -x - 1$

7. $y = \frac{3}{2}x - 3$ 8. $y = 2x + 2$

9. $y - 6 = -4(x - 1)$ 10. $y - 3 = \frac{7}{2}x$

11. $y = \frac{1}{2}(x - 4)$ 12. $y + 3 = \frac{1}{2}(x - 4)$

13. $2x - y + 4 = 0$ 14. $-15x + y + 20 = 0$

15. $x - 3 = 0$ 16. $y + 2 = 0$

Section 9.4 (page 83)

1. (a)   2. (b)   3. (c)   4. (b)   5. (a)   6. (c)   7. (b)   8. (a)

9. (a) $y - 2 = 3(x - 1)$ (b) $y - 2 = \frac{-1}{3}(x - 1)$

10. (a) $y - 3 = x$ (b) $y - 3 = -x$

11. (a) $y + 1 = 4(x - 4)$ (b) $y + 1 = \frac{-1}{4}(x - 4)$

12. (a) $y = -2x$ (b) $y = \frac{x}{2}$

13. (a) $L_1 \parallel L_2$, $L_3 \parallel L_4$

     (b) $L_1 \perp L_3$, $L_1 \perp L_4$, $L_2 \perp L_3$, $L_2 \perp L_4$

14. (a) $L_1 \parallel L_3$

     (b) $L_1 \perp L_4$, $L_3 \perp L_4$, $L_2 \perp L_5$

CHAPTER 10

Section 10.1 (page 87)

1. See Figure 10A (a).   2. See Figure 10A (b).

3. See Figure 10A (c).   4. See Figure 10A (d).

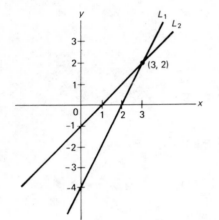

Figure 10A (a)

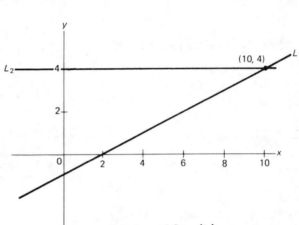

Figure 10A (b)

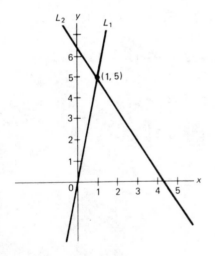

Figure 10A (c)

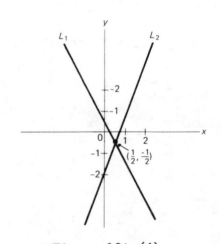

Figure 10A (d)

5. (6, 2)   6. (5, −2)   7. (1, 0)   8. (−3, 6)

9. (−2, −1)   10. (6, 4)   11. (3, 5)   12. (1, 7)

13. $\left(6, \frac{1}{2}\right)$ 14. (2, −2)

Section 10.2 (page 89)

1.   (1, 4, 2)   2.   (6, 3, 1)

3.   (10, 4, 8)   4.   (7, -1, -2)

5.   (-2, -5, 8)   6.   (4, -1, 6)

7.   (-1, 3, -5)   8. $\left(\frac{1}{2}, \ \frac{-1}{2}, \ \frac{1}{4}\right)$

Section 10.3 (page 90)

1. -6   2. 10   3. 10   4. -1   5. 0   6. 4   7. 1   8. $\frac{1}{5}$

9. (a) Cramer's Rule applies.   (b) (2, 3)

10. (a) Cramer's Rule applies.   (b) (-2, 5)

11. (a) Cramer's Rule applies.   (b) (-3, 8)

12. (a) Cramer's Rule does not apply.

13. (a) Cramer's Rule applies.   (b) (4, 0)

14. (a) Cramer's Rule does not apply.

Section 10.4 (page 92)

1. -3   2. 15   3. -4   4. -8   5. 2   6. 2

7. (a) Cramer's Rule applies.   (b) (3, 2, 1)

8. (a) Cramer's Rule does not apply.

9. (a) Cramer's Rule applies.   (b) (7, 2, -1)

10. (a) Cramer's Rule does not apply.

▶ CHAPTER 11

Section 11.1 (page 95)

1. $\frac{1}{6}$ 2. 1   3. $\frac{1}{16}$

4. $\dfrac{25}{9}$ 5. 8   6. -2

7. -2 8. 0   9. -3

10. b^{-3} 11. $a^{-2}x^{-3}y^{-1}$ 12. $4x^{-6}y^{-4}$

13. x^3 14. $(a - b)^2$

Section 11.2 (page 96)

1. a^{10} 2. a^2 3. $\dfrac{1}{a^2}$ 4. $\dfrac{1}{a^2}$

5. a^{10} 6. a^4b^4 7. a^6b^9 8. $\dfrac{a^5}{b^5}$

9. $\dfrac{a^4}{b^6}$ 10. $\dfrac{xy}{ab^2}$ 11. $4a^2x^6$ 12. $\dfrac{b}{a}$

13. $\dfrac{20x}{a^2}$ 14. $a + b$ 15. $\dfrac{(x + y)^2}{xy}$

Section 11.3 (page 97)

1. 3.2×10^1 2. 9.847×10^3 3. 7×10^{-2}

4. 8.11×10^6 5. 4.3×10^{-4} 6. 246

7. 83 500 000   8. .0101   9. .000 004 13

10. .7171   11. 10^4 12. 3×10^{11}

13. 4×10^1 14. 2.5   15. 1.75×10^{-1}

Section 11.4 (page 98)

1. 5   2. 4   3. 8   4. $\dfrac{1}{10}$ 5. 12   6. $\dfrac{6}{7}$

7. 32   8. $\dfrac{1}{81}$ 9. 100   10. $\dfrac{1}{27}$ 11. 15   12. 13

Section 11.5 (page 99)

1. a^2

2. a

3. $a^{5/4}$

4. $a^{1/4}$

5. $x^{3/8}$

6. $a^{1/8}b^{1/2}$

7. $\dfrac{a^{1/2}}{b^{1/4}x^{1/2}y^{1/6}}$

8. $\dfrac{2a^{1/8}}{x^{1/2}y^{3/8}}$

9. $\dfrac{b^{1/2}}{c^{1/4}}$

10. $\dfrac{1}{5a^{1/4}b^{2/3}}$

11. $\dfrac{2}{3}$

12. $\dfrac{64}{125}$

13. $\dfrac{7}{10}$

14. 40

15. $\dfrac{100}{9}$

Section 11.6 (page 100)

1. 12

2. -2

3. 125

4. 10

5. -1

6. $\sqrt[4]{a^3}$

7. $\sqrt{b}\sqrt[4]{c}$

8. $2\sqrt{ab}$

9. $\sqrt{a-b}$

10. $a - \sqrt{b}$

11. $(xy)^{1/2}$

12. $2x^{1/2}yz^{3/2}$

13. $(a+b)^{1/2}$

14. $a^{1/2} + b^{1/2}$

15. $5(xy)^{-1/2}$

16. $6a^2$

17. $\dfrac{a^4 b^3}{c^2}$

18. $2ab^2$

19. $x + y$

20. $\dfrac{1}{ab}$

Section 11.7 (page 101)

1. $5\sqrt{3}$

2. $\dfrac{\sqrt{5}}{4}$

3. $9\sqrt{x}$

4. $\dfrac{3\sqrt{3}}{8}$

5. $\dfrac{-2(ab)^{1/2}}{15}$

6. $\sqrt{10} + 2$

7. $y + y^{3/4}$

8. $x - x^{1/4}$

9. $a^{5/4} + a$

10. $x - x^{1/2}$

11. $-\sqrt{3}$

12. $\sqrt{2}(\sqrt{5} + \sqrt{3})$

13. $a^2\sqrt{b}(c + 2)$

14. $x^{1/2}y^{1/2}(y - x)$

15. $y\sqrt{2xy}(2xy + 1 - 3x^3y^3)$

16. $2 - \sqrt{2}$

17. $3x + 2y$

18. $\dfrac{-1}{3}$

19. $\dfrac{xy - 1}{x^2y^3}$

20. $y(2x + y)$

Section 11.8 (page 103)

1. $\dfrac{5\sqrt{3}}{3}$

2. $\dfrac{3 \cdot 2^{1/2}}{2}$

3. $\dfrac{2\sqrt{2}}{3}$

4. $\dfrac{5\sqrt{2x}}{3x}$

5. $\dfrac{-2\sqrt{ab}}{ab}$

6. $\dfrac{\sqrt{xy}}{x^2y^2}$

7. $\dfrac{2a^{2/3}}{a}$

8. $\dfrac{-1 + \sqrt{3}}{2}$

9. $-5(1 + \sqrt{2})$

10. $\dfrac{-2(\sqrt{a} - \sqrt{b})}{a - b}$

11. $\dfrac{5(2 + 3\sqrt{x})}{4 - 9x}$

12. $\dfrac{-(2\sqrt{3} + 5\sqrt{2})}{38}$

Section 11.9 (page 104)

1. $5i$

2. $\sqrt{6}\,i$

3. $\dfrac{1}{2}i$

4. $\dfrac{3}{4}i$

5. (a) 6, (b) 5, (c) $6 - 5i$

6. (a) $\dfrac{3}{2}$, (b) -8, (c) $\dfrac{3}{2} + 8i$

7. (a) -9, (b) 0, (c) -9

8. (a) 0, (b) 4, (c) $-4i$

9. $11 + 4i$

10. $-1 - 3i$

11. $9 - 3i$

12. -25

13. $\dfrac{11}{10} + \dfrac{13}{10}i$

14. $\dfrac{2}{5} - \dfrac{1}{5}i$

15. $-i$

16. i

CHAPTER 12

Section 12.1 (page 106)

1. $\log_9 81 = 2$

2. $\log_5 125 = 3$

3. $\log_{1/2} \frac{1}{4} = 2$

4. $\log_6 \frac{1}{6} = -1$

5. $\log_{16} 2 = \frac{1}{4}$

6. 2

7. 5

8. 3

9. $\frac{1}{2}$

10. -2

11. 2

12. 6

13. 27

14. $.2$

15. 6

Section 12.2 (page 107)

1. (a) $7 = 5 + 2$

   (b) $\log_b n_1 n_2 = \log_b n_1 + \log_b n_2$. Here $b = 2$, $n_1 = 32$, $n_2 = 4$

2. (a) $2 = 3 - 1$

   (b) $\log_b \frac{n_1}{n_2} = \log_b n_1 - \log_b n_2$. Here $b = 5$, $n_1 = 125$, $n_2 = 5$

3. (a) $3 = 3 \cdot 1$

   (b) $\log_b n^r = r \log_b n$. Here $b = 10$, $n = 10$, $r = 3$

4. (a) $6 = 3 \cdot 2$

   (b) $\log_b n^r = r \log_b n$. Here $b = 2$, $n = 4$, $r = 3$

5. (a) $-4 = -2(2)$

   (b) $\log_b n^r = r \log_b n$. Here $b = 2$, $n = 4$, $r = -2$

6. $\log_{10} a + \log_{10} b$

7. $\log_5 a + \log_5 b - \log_5 c$

8. $\frac{1}{2} (\log_2 x - \log_2 y)$

9. $\frac{1}{2} \log_3 x - \log_3 y$

10. $\log_3 5 + \log_3 a + \log_3 b - \log_3 7$

11. $\log_b 2 + \log_b 5$ 12. $\log_b 3 - \log_b 5$

13. $3\log_b 3 - \log_b 2 - \log_b 5$ 14. $4\log_b 2 + \log_b 3$

15. $-(\log_b 2 + \log_b 3 + \log_b 5)$ 16. $\log_{10} abc$

17. $\log_{10} \dfrac{ac}{b}$ 18. $\log_5 a^2 b^3$ 19. $\log_2 \sqrt[10]{15}$

Section 12.3 (page 108)

1. .3139	2. .6730	3. .9763	4. .7059
5. .4955	6. 1	7. 0	8. 3
9. −1	10. −4	11. 1.5065	12. 4.6064
13. .9643 − 1	14. 5.5490	15. .8609 − 3	

Section 12.4 (page 110)

1. 4.97	2. 8.55	3. 40.4	4. 8730
5. .780	6. .0351	7. .000 010 6	
8. 4 590 000	9. 7.02	10. .000 142	

Section 12.5 (page 111)

1. .1351	2. 3.3815	3. 1.6829	
4. .9092 − 2	5. .3931 − 4	6. 4.471	7. 538.3
8. .054 58	9. 98 020	10. .001 033	

Section 12.6 (page 113)

1. 31.72	2. 18.67	3. .5041
4. 5.709	5. 93.98	6. .000 000 203 1
7. 7.432	8. 198 900	

Section 12.8 (page 114)

1. 3.10

2. 2.51

3. 3.64

4. −.94

5. −1.21

6. 50 000

7. −2.9

8. −250 000

9. 4998.5

10. .0025

11. 3.17

12. 1.68

13. 1.07

14. −5.78

15. $\dfrac{\log_5 8}{\log_5 3}$

16. $\dfrac{\log_4 12}{\log_4 5}$

17. $\dfrac{1}{3}\log_2 92$

18. $\dfrac{\log_3 242\ 000}{\log_3 4}$

▶ CHAPTER 13

Section 13.1 (page 116)

1. 5, −8

2. $\dfrac{5}{3}, \dfrac{-9}{2}$

3. 0, 4

4. 4, 5

5. 1, −8

6. 6, −3

7. −4

8. −1, −2

9. $x^2 - 7x + 6 = 0$

10. $x^2 - 11x + 24 = 0$

11. $x^2 + 6x + 8 = 0$

12. $x^2 - 2x - 15 = 0$

13. $x^2 - 12x + 36 = 0$

Section 13.2 (page 117)

1. ±4

2. $\pm\sqrt{7}$

3. $\pm 2\sqrt{2}$

4. $\pm 3\sqrt{5}$

5. ±2i

6. $\pm 3\sqrt{2}\,i$

7. $\dfrac{\pm 7}{3}$

8. ±6A

9. $\dfrac{7}{3}, \dfrac{5}{3}$

10. $\dfrac{\pm 9}{A}$

11. $-3 \pm \dfrac{2}{A}$

12. $-5 \pm \dfrac{i}{A}$

A35

Section 13.3 (page 118)

1. $2 \pm \sqrt{5}$ 2. $-1 \pm \sqrt{6}$ 3. $3 \pm \sqrt{2}$

4. $3, 7$ 5. $\dfrac{3 \pm \sqrt{5}}{2}$ 6. $-6 \pm \sqrt{3}$

7. $-2 \pm 2i$ 8. $\dfrac{-4 \pm \sqrt{10}}{2}$ 9. $\dfrac{-1 \pm \sqrt{3}}{2}$

10. $\dfrac{-1}{2} \pm \dfrac{\sqrt{3}}{2} i$

Section 13.4 (page 119)

1. (a) 0,   (b) exactly 1 real root

2. (a) -3,   (b) 2 complex conjugate roots

3. (a) 5,   (b) 2 distinct real roots

4. (a) 0,   (b) exactly 1 real root

5. (a) 2 seconds   (b) 10 seconds

6. $-2 \pm \sqrt{2}$ 7. -3 8. $\dfrac{-3 \pm \sqrt{5}}{2}$

9. $-1 \pm 2i$ 10. $-4 \pm \sqrt{11}$ 11. $\dfrac{-1}{2}, -2$

12. $\dfrac{-2 \pm \sqrt{7}}{3}$ 13. $\dfrac{-5}{2}$

Section 13.5 (page 120)

1. 6 and 11   2. $1 + \sqrt{11}$ 3. $-10, -9$

4. 10 inches by 4 inches   5. 2 seconds, 10 seconds

Section 13.6 (page 121)

1. 7   2. 15

Check: $\sqrt{7 + 2} \overset{?}{=} 3$ Check: $\sqrt{15 + 10} \overset{?}{=} 5$

$\sqrt{9} \overset{?}{=} 3$ $\sqrt{25} \overset{?}{=} 5$

$3 \overset{\checkmark}{=} 3$ $5 \overset{\checkmark}{=} 5$

3. 8

Check: $\sqrt{2 \cdot 8} - 4 \overset{?}{=} 0$

$\sqrt{16} - 4 \overset{?}{=} 0$

$4 - 4 \overset{\checkmark}{=} 0$

4. no roots
 (4 is not a root.)

Check: $\sqrt{2(4) + 1} + 3 \overset{?}{=} 0$

$\sqrt{9} + 3 \overset{?}{=} 0$

$3 + 3 \overset{\times}{=} 0$

5. 6

Check: $6 + \sqrt{6 + 3} \overset{?}{=} 9$

$6 + \sqrt{9} \overset{?}{=} 9$

$6 + 3 \overset{\checkmark}{=} 9$

(13 is not a root.)

$13 + \sqrt{13 + 3} \overset{?}{=} 9$

$13 + \sqrt{16} \overset{?}{=} 9$

$13 + 4 \overset{\times}{=} 9$

6. 10

Check: $10 - \sqrt{10 - 6} \overset{?}{=} 8$

$10 - \sqrt{4} \overset{?}{=} 8$

$10 - 2 \overset{\checkmark}{=} 8$

(7 is not a root.)

$7 - \sqrt{7 - 6} \overset{?}{=} 8$

$7 - \sqrt{1} \overset{?}{=} 8$

$7 - 1 \overset{\times}{=} 8$

7. 1

Check: $1 + \sqrt{1 + 3} \overset{?}{=} 3$

$1 + 2 \overset{\checkmark}{=} 3$

8. 8

Check: $\sqrt{8 + 1} - \sqrt{8 - 4} \overset{?}{=} 1$

$3 - 2 \overset{\checkmark}{=} 1$

9. −2

Check: $\sqrt{-2 + 3} + \sqrt{-2 + 2} \overset{?}{=} 1$

$1 + 0 \overset{\checkmark}{=} 1$

10. 1

Check: $\sqrt{1}\sqrt{1 + 8} \overset{?}{=} 3$

$1 \cdot 3 \overset{\checkmark}{=} 3$

(−9 is not a root.)

$\sqrt{-9}\sqrt{-9 + 8} \overset{?}{=} 3$

$3i \cdot i \overset{?}{=} 3$

$3(-1) \overset{\times}{=} 3$

A37

11. 6

Check: $\sqrt{6 - 2}\sqrt{6 + 3} \overset{?}{=} 6$

$\qquad\qquad 2 \cdot 3 \overset{\checkmark}{=} 6$

(−7 is not a root.)

$\sqrt{-7 - 2}\sqrt{-7 + 3} \overset{?}{=} 6$

$\qquad 3i \cdot 2i \overset{?}{=} 6$

$\qquad 6(-1) \overset{\times}{\cong} 6$

12. 2

Check: $\sqrt{4(2) + 1}\sqrt{2 - 1} \overset{?}{=} 3$

$\qquad\qquad 3 \cdot 1 \overset{\checkmark}{=} 3$

$\left(\dfrac{-5}{4} \text{ is not a root.}\right)$

$\sqrt{4\left(\dfrac{-5}{4}\right) + 1}\sqrt{\dfrac{-5}{4} - 1} \overset{?}{=} 3$

$\sqrt{-5 + 1}\sqrt{\dfrac{-9}{4}} \overset{?}{=} 3$

$2i \cdot \dfrac{3}{2}i \overset{?}{=} 3$

$3(-1) \overset{\times}{\cong} 3$

▶ CHAPTER 14

Section 14.1 (page 124)

1. (a)   2. (c)   3. (e)   4. (b)   5. (d)

6. false   7. true   8. true   9. false   10. false

11. (4, 12)   12. [2, 8]   13. (−∞, −12)

14. $\left(\dfrac{1}{2}, \ \infty\right)$ 15. [5, ∞)

16. (a) See Figure 14A (a).
     (b) [0, 5]

17. (a) See Figure 14A (b).
     (b) [1, 3]

18. (a) See Figure 14A (c).
     (b) (1, 4)

19. (a) See Figure 14A (d).
     (b) [−2, 1]

20. (a) See Figure 14A (e).
     (b) [1, ∞)

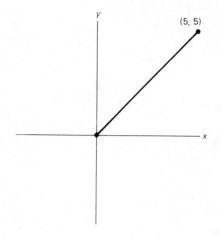

Figure 14A (a)

The function given by

$$y = x, \ 0 \le x \le 5$$

The points (0, 0) and (5, 5) are included.

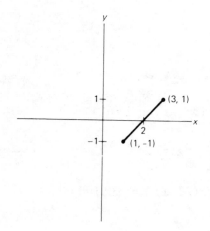

Figure 14A (b)

The function given by

$$y = x - 2, \ 1 \le x \le 3$$

The points (1, -1) and (3, 1) are included.

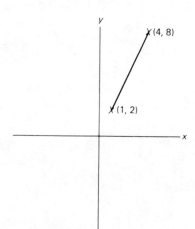

Figure 14A (c)

The function given by

$$y = 2x, \ 1 < x < 4$$

The points (1, 2) and (4, 8) are excluded.

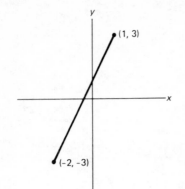

Figure 14A (d)

The function given by

$$y = 2x + 1, \quad -2 \le x \le 1$$

The points (-2, -3) and (1, 3) are included.

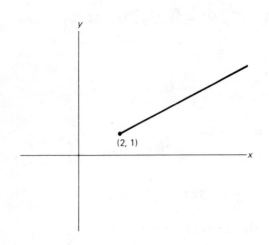

Figure 14A (e)

The function given by

$$y = \frac{x}{2}, \quad x \ge 1$$

The point (2, 1) is included.

Section 14.2 (page 125)

1. <   2. >   3. <   4. >   5. >   6. <

7. Suppose x < 2.   8. Suppose x ≤ 5.

   Then x + 2 < 2 + 2   Then 3x ≤ 3 · 5

9. Suppose x < -2.   10. Suppose x < 6.

   Then -2x > (-2)(-2)   Then $\frac{x}{3} < \frac{6}{3}$

Section 14.3 (page 126)

1. $(-\infty, 5)$ 2. $(14, \infty)$ 3. $(-\infty, 15]$

4. $(-\infty, -6]$ 5. $(-\infty, 2)$ 6. $(-\infty, 50]$

7. $(-\infty, -7)$ 8. $(-\infty, 2)$ 9. $(-2, 1)$

10. $(-1, 1)$ 11. $[10, 15]$ 12. $(-1, 0)$

Section 14.4 (page 127)

1. (a), (b), (d)   2. (a), (b), (c)

3. (a), (b)   4. (a), (b), (d)

5. (b), (d)   6. See Figure 14B (a).

7. See Figure 14B (b).   8. See Figure 14B (c).

9. See Figure 14B (d).   10. See Figure 14B (e).

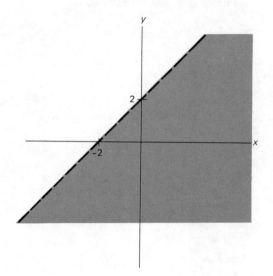

Figure 14B (a)

The graph of the inequality

$y < x + 2$

The line is excluded.

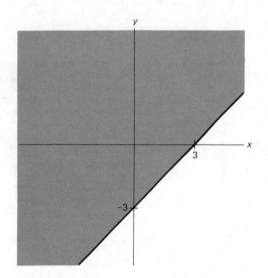

Figure 14B (b)

The graph of the inequality

$y \geq x - 3$

The line is included.

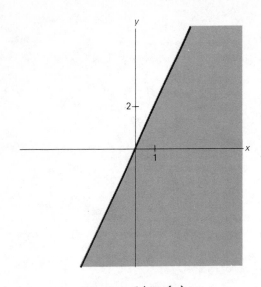

Figure 14B (c)

The graph of the inequality

$$y \le 2x$$

The line is included.

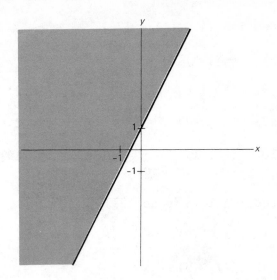

Figure 14B (d)

The graph of the inequality

$$y \ge 2x + 1$$

The line is included.

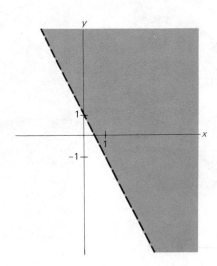

Figure 14B (e)

The graph of the inequality

$$y > 1 - 2x$$

The line is excluded.

Section 14.5 (page 128)

1. $(-2, 4)$ 2. $(-\infty, 0) \cup (3, \infty)$

3. $[1, 4]$ 4. $(-\infty, -4] \cup [2, \infty)$

5. All real numbers except -3

6. $[-3, 4]$ 7. $\left(\dfrac{-1}{4}, \dfrac{1}{4}\right)$

8. $(-\infty, -2] \cup [2, \infty)$ 9. $(0, 2)$

10. $\left(\dfrac{-3}{2}, 0\right)$ 11. $(-\infty, 2] \cup \left[\dfrac{5}{2}, \infty\right)$

12. $[-1, 1]$ 13. $(-2, \infty)$

14. $\left[\dfrac{1}{2}, 1\right]$ 15. $(-2, 0)$

16. All real numbers

Section 14.6 (page 129)

(The checks are given below.)

1. 4 and 8   2. -2 and 4   3. -12 and 8

4. $\dfrac{-11}{2}$ and $\dfrac{-9}{2}$ 5. $5, -5$ 6. no roots

7. $5, -1$ 8. $-4, -12$ 9. 18, 24

10. $\dfrac{9}{2}, \dfrac{-3}{2}$ 11. $\dfrac{2}{3}, -4$ 12. -3

13. no root   14. $\dfrac{2}{3}$ 15. no root

16. $\dfrac{1}{6}$

CHECKS.

7. $|5 - 2| \overset{?}{=} 3$ $|-1 - 2| \overset{?}{=} 3$

         $3 \overset{\checkmark}{=} 3$ $|-3| \overset{?}{=} 3$

                                        $3 \overset{\checkmark}{=} 3$

11. $\left|2\left(\frac{2}{3}\right)+1\right| \overset{?}{=} \left|3 - \frac{2}{3}\right|$ | $|2(-4)+1| \overset{?}{=} |3-(-4)|$

$\qquad \frac{7}{3} \overset{\checkmark}{=} \frac{7}{3}$ | $\qquad |-7| \overset{?}{=} |7|$

$\qquad\qquad\qquad\qquad 7 \overset{\checkmark}{=} 7$

13. no roots

$\left(\frac{-3}{2} \text{ is not a root.}\right)$

$\left|\frac{-3}{2} + 3\right| \overset{?}{=} \frac{-3}{2}$

Note that in the first equation, the left side is nonnegative. This, in itself, shows that $\frac{-3}{2}$ is not a root.

$\left|\frac{3}{2}\right| \overset{?}{=} \frac{-3}{2}$

$\frac{3}{2} \overset{\ne}{\ } \frac{-3}{2}$

14. $\frac{2}{3}$

$\left(\frac{2}{7} \text{ is not a root.}\right)$

$\left|5\left(\frac{2}{3}\right) - 2\right| \overset{?}{=} 2\left(\frac{2}{3}\right)$ | $\left|5\left(\frac{2}{7}\right) - 2\right| \overset{?}{=} -2\left(\frac{2}{7}\right)$

$\left|\frac{10}{3} - 2\right| \overset{?}{=} \frac{4}{3}$ | $\left|\frac{10}{7} - 2\right| \overset{?}{=} \frac{-4}{7}$

$\qquad \frac{4}{3} \overset{\checkmark}{=} \frac{4}{3}$ | $\qquad \frac{4}{7} \overset{\ne}{\ } \frac{-4}{7}$

15. (1 is not a root.)

$|1 - 2| \overset{?}{=} -1$

$\qquad 1 \overset{\ne}{\ } -1$

16. $\frac{1}{6}$

$\left(\frac{-1}{10} \text{ is not a root.}\right)$

$\left|\frac{1}{6} + \frac{1}{2}\right| \overset{?}{=} 4\left(\frac{1}{6}\right)$ | $\left|\frac{-1}{10} + \frac{1}{2}\right| \overset{?}{=} 4\left(\frac{-1}{10}\right)$

$\left|\frac{4}{6}\right| \overset{?}{=} \frac{4}{6}$ | $\left|\frac{4}{10}\right| \overset{?}{=} \frac{-4}{10}$

$\qquad \frac{2}{3} \overset{\checkmark}{=} \frac{2}{3}$ | $\qquad \frac{2}{5} \overset{\ne}{\ } \frac{-2}{5}$

Section 14.7 (page 131)

1. (-6, 6)   2. (-∞, -20) ∪ (20, ∞)

3. (0, 10)   4. (-∞, -12) ∪ (-4, ∞)

5. [-4, 5]   6. (-∞, -9] ∪ [3, ∞)

7. $\left(\frac{1}{5}, \frac{11}{5}\right)$ 8. All real numbers except $\frac{1}{4}$

9. 3   10. 6   11. 7   12. 5   13. 9   14. $\frac{1}{3}$

Section 14.8 (page 132)

1. (a) 1   (b) 0   (c) 3   (d) 6   (e) 12

2. (a) 3   (b) 0   (c) 1   (d) 9   (e) 10

3. (a) 9   (b) 3   (c) 2   (d) 0   (e) 3

4. (a) 0   (b) -1   (c) $\frac{-1}{2}$ (d) 0   (e) 9

5. See Figure 14C (a).   6. See Figure 14C (b).

7. See Figure 14C (c).   8. See Figure 14C (d).

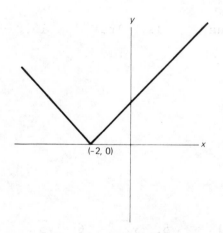

Figure 14C (a)

The graph of

$f(x) = |x + 2|$

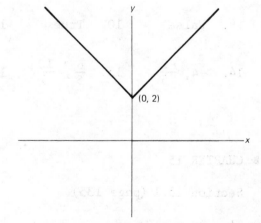

Figure 14C (b)

The graph of

$f(x) = |x| + 2$

A45

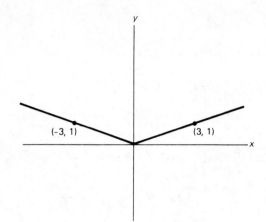

Figure 14C (c)

The graph of

$$f(x) = \frac{|x|}{3}$$

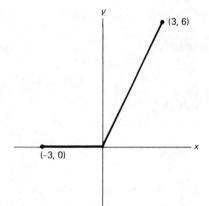

Figure 14C (d)

The graph of

$$f(x) = |x| + x, \ -3 \le x \le 3$$

The points (-3, 0) and (3, 6) are included.

9. False   10. True   11. True   12. True   13. $\frac{-5}{2}$

14. $-4, \frac{-2}{5}$ 15. $\frac{6}{5}, \frac{10}{3}$ 16. $\frac{7}{2}$

▶ CHAPTER 15

Section 15.1 (page 135)

1. 4   2. 8   3. 5   4. 13   5. $\sqrt{2}$ 6. $\sqrt{5}$

7. $4\sqrt{2}$ 8. $\frac{\sqrt{2}}{4}$ 9. 1   10. 3   11. $\frac{1}{2}$ 12. 5

13. 4   14. $\frac{15}{2}$

Section 15.2 (page 136)

1. (a) (0, 0)   (b) 10   2. (a) (4, 2)   (b) 5

3. (a) (-1, 6)   (b) 2   4. (a) $\left(\frac{1}{2}, \frac{-1}{4}\right)$ (b) $\frac{1}{2}$

5. (a) (8, -8)   (b) $2\sqrt{2}$ 6. (a) $(x - 1)^2 + (y - 2)^2 = 9$

7. $x^2 + (y + 7)^2 = 64$ 8. $(x - 2)^2 + (y + 1)^2 = 3$

9. $x^2 + (y + 4)^2 = 16$, center (0, -4), radius 4

10. $(x + 1)^2 + (y + 6)^2 = 37$, center (-1, -6), radius $\sqrt{37}$

11. $(x - 2)^2 + (y + 1)^2 = 9$, center (2, -1), radius 3

12. $\left(x + \frac{1}{2}\right)^2 + \left(y - \frac{3}{2}\right)^2 = \frac{5}{2}$, center $\left(\frac{-1}{2}, \frac{3}{2}\right)$, radius $\sqrt{\frac{5}{2}}$ or $\frac{\sqrt{10}}{2}$

Section 15.3 (page 138)

1. vertex (0, 0), axis: y-axis, focus (0, 1), directrix: y = -1
   [See Figure 15A (a).]

2. vertex (0, 0), axis: x-axis, focus (1, 0), directrix: x = -1

3. vertex (0, 0), axis: y-axis, focus (0, -3), directrix: y = 3

4. vertex (0, 0), axis: x-axis, focus (-2, 0), directrix: x = 2
   [See Figure 15A (b).]

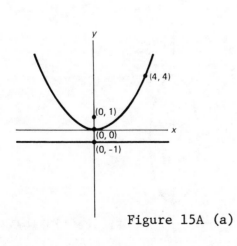

Figure 15A (a)

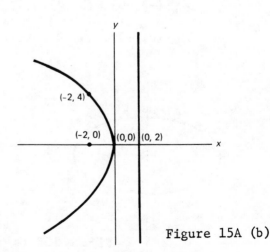

Figure 15A (b)

5. vertex $(0, 0)$, axis: y-axis, focus $\left(0, \frac{1}{2}\right)$, directrix: $y = \frac{-1}{2}$

6. vertex $(0, 0)$, axis: x-axis, focus $\left(\frac{1}{4}, 0\right)$, directrix: $x = \frac{-1}{4}$

7. vertex $(0, 0)$, axis: y-axis, focus $\left(0, \frac{-3}{4}\right)$, directrix: $y = \frac{3}{4}$

8. vertex $(0, 0)$, axis: x-axis, focus $\left(\frac{3}{8}, 0\right)$, directrix: $x = \frac{-3}{8}$

9. $y^2 = 8x$ 10. $x^2 = 20y$ 11. $y^2 = -20x$

12. $x^2 = -2y$ 13. $y^2 = 24x$ 14. $y^2 = -24x$

15. $x^2 = -8y$ 16. $x^2 = 8y$

Section 15.4 (page 139)

1. $(6, 0)$, $(-6, 0)$, $(0, 3)$, $(0, -3)$. [See Figure 15B (a).]

2. $(0, 5)$, $(0, -5)$, $(3, 0)$, $(-3, 0)$

3. $(4, 0)$, $(-4, 0)$, $(0, 3)$, $(0, -3)$

4. $(0, 5)$, $(0, -5)$, $(2, 0)$, $(-2, 0)$. [See Figure 15B (b).]

5. $(7, 0)$, $(-7, 0)$, $(0, 6)$, $(0, -6)$

6. $(0, 3)$, $(0, -3)$, $(1, 0)$, $(-1, 0)$

7. $(3, 0)$, $(-3, 0)$, $(0, 2)$, $(0, -2)$

8. $(0, 5)$, $(0, -5)$, $(4, 0)$, $(-4, 0)$

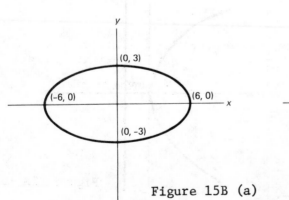

Figure 15B (a)

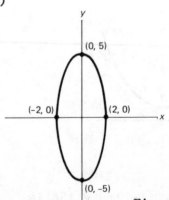

Figure 15B (b)

9. (a) $(0, 3)$, $(0, -3)$ (b) $y = \frac{3}{5}x$, $y = \frac{-3}{5}x$ (See Figure 15C.)

10. (a) $(1, 0)$, $(-1, 0)$ (b) $y = 4x$, $y = -4x$

11. (a) $(0, 6)$, $(0, -6)$ (b) $y = \frac{6}{5}x$, $y = \frac{-6}{5}x$

12. (a) $(2, 0)$, $(-2, 0)$ (b) $y = \frac{3}{2}x$, $y = \frac{-3}{2}x$

13. (a) $(5, 0)$, $(-5, 0)$ (b) $y = \frac{4}{5}x$, $y = \frac{-4}{5}x$

14. (a) $(0, 2)$, $(0, -2)$ (b) $y = \frac{2}{3}x$, $y = \frac{-2}{3}x$

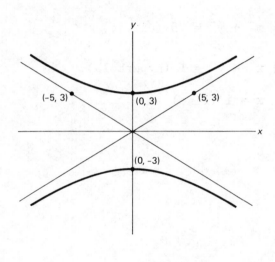

Figure 15C

The hyperbola given by

$$\frac{y^2}{9} - \frac{x^2}{25} = 1$$

Section 15.5 (page 140)

1. (a) $(3, 4)$, $(-3, 4)$ (b) $x^2 + y^2 = 25$ (circle), $y = 4$ (line)

   (c) [See Figure 15D (a).]

2. (a) $(0, 0)$, $(1, 1)$ (b) $y = x^2$ (parabola), $y = x$ (line)

   (c) [See Figure 15D (b).]

3. (a) $(0, -2)$, $(-2, 0)$ (b) $x^2 + y^2 = 4$ (circle),

                                   $x + y + 2 = 0$ (line)

A49

4. (a) $\left(\frac{3}{2}, \frac{3\sqrt{3}}{2}\right), \left(\frac{3}{2}, \frac{-3\sqrt{3}}{2}\right)$ (b) Both are circles.

   (c) [See Figure 15D (c).]

5. (a) no intersection   (b) Both are circles.

   (c) [See Figure 15D (d).]

6. (a) $\left(1, \frac{8\sqrt{2}}{3}\right), \left(1, \frac{-8\sqrt{2}}{3}\right)$ (b) $\frac{x^2}{9} + \frac{y^2}{16} = 1$ (ellipse),

   $x = 1$ (line), (c) [See Figure 15D (e).]

7. (a) (5, 0), (-5, 0)   (b) $\frac{x^2}{25} + y^2 = 1$ (ellipse),

   $x^2 + y^2 = 25$ (circle)

8. (a) (1, 0)   (b) $x^2 - y^2 = 1$ (hyperbola),

   $x = 1$ (line)

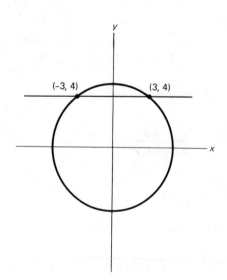

Figure 15D (a)

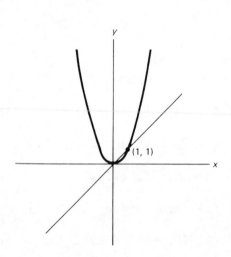

Figure 15D (b)

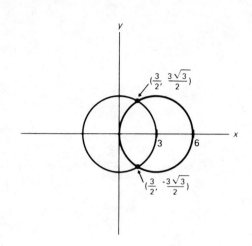

Figure 15D (c)

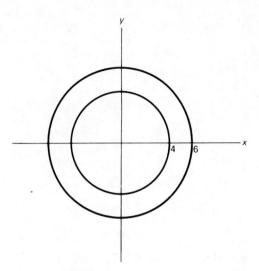

Figure 15D (d)

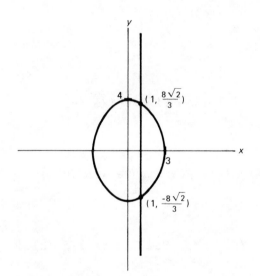

Figure 15D (e)

▶ CHAPTER 16 (page 142)

Section 16.1

1. 3   2. -2   3. 5   4. $\frac{1}{2}$ 5. -2   6. 40

7. -1   8. -24   9. $\frac{9}{5}$ 10. 4   11. 200   12. 81

Section 16.2 (page 143)

1. 10   2. 9   3. 4   4. 3   5. 2   6. 2

A51

7. -4 8. $\frac{1}{20}$ 9. 12   10. 1   11. $\frac{1}{8}$

Section 16.3 (page 144)

1. 2   2. $\frac{1}{2}$ 3. 32   4. -1

5. 54   6. -100 7. $\frac{-5}{2}$ 8. .008

9. 4   10. -16 11. 3   12. $\frac{-1}{6}$

13. 15   14. 64   15. -6 16. 9

▶ CHAPTER 17

Section 17.1 (page 147)

1. (a) 5, 6, 7, 8, 9, 10, 11, 12   (b) [See Figure 17A (a).]

   (c) increasing

2. (a) $\frac{1}{2}$, 1, $\frac{3}{2}$, 2, $\frac{5}{2}$, 3, $\frac{7}{2}$, 4   (b) [See Figure 17A (b).]

   (c) increasing

3. (a) 0, -1, -2, -3, -4, -5, -6, -7 (b) [See Figure 17A (c).]

   (c) decreasing

4. (a) 4, 4, 4, 4, 4, 4, 4, 4   (b) [See Figure 17A (d).]

   (c) neither of these

5. (a) -1, 1, 3, 5, 7, 9, 11, 13   (b) [See Figure 17A (e).]

   (c) increasing

6. (a) 6   (b) 14   (c) 20   (d) 40

7. (a) 3   (b) 0   (c) -4 (d) -20

8. (a) 1   (b) 3   (c) 1   (d) 3

A52

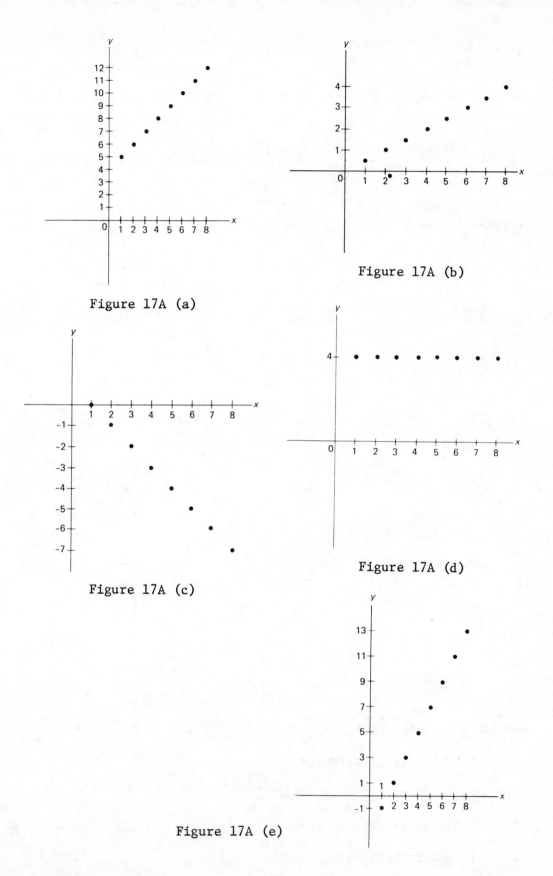

Figure 17A (a)

Figure 17A (b)

Figure 17A (c)

Figure 17A (d)

Figure 17A (e)

9. (a) $\frac{1}{3}$ (b) $\frac{3}{5}$ (c) $\frac{5}{6}$ (d) $\frac{9}{10}$

10. $a_i = i + 2$ 11. $a_i = -2i$ 12. $a_i = 2i + 1$

13. $a_i = 3(-1)^i$ 14. $a_i = 2^i$

Section 17.2 (page 148)

1. $\displaystyle\sum_{i=1}^{5} a_i$ 2. $\displaystyle\sum_{i=1}^{15} a_i$ 3. $\displaystyle\sum_{i=4}^{6} b_i$

4. $\displaystyle\sum_{i=101}^{150} c_i$ 5. 15   6. 22

7. $\frac{11}{12}$ 8. 30   9. $\displaystyle\sum_{i=5}^{10} i$ or $\displaystyle\sum_{i=1}^{6} (i+4)$

10. $\displaystyle\sum_{i=1}^{50} i^2$ 11. $\displaystyle\sum_{i=3}^{22} \frac{1}{i}$ or $\displaystyle\sum_{i=1}^{20} \frac{1}{i+2}$ 12. $\displaystyle\sum_{i=1}^{10} -3i$

13. 5   14. 20   15. 7

Section 17.3 (page 150)

1. arithmetic progression, 3

2. not an arithmetic progression

3. arithmetic progression, -2

4. not an arithmetic progression

A54

5. arithmetic progression, $\frac{1}{4}$

6. 32   7. 69   8. $3 + 38\pi$ 9. 58   10. 440

11. −400   12. 740   13. 690   14. 3740   15. 4960

16. −3260   17. 6020

Section 17.4 (page 152)

1. geometric progression, 2, not an arithmetic progression

2. not a geometric progression, arithmetic progression

3. geometric progression, −2, not an arithmetic progression

4. geometric progression, −1, not an arithmetic progression

5. geometric progression, $\frac{1}{3}$, not an arithmetic progression

6. 96   7. −13   8. $\frac{1}{25}$ 9. 126   10. 363

11. $\frac{255}{256}$ 12. −1

Section 17.5 (page 153)

1. 720   2. 144   3. 11 880   4. 1140   5. 576

6. 4   7. 1   8. 45   9. 21   10. 165

11. $x^4 + 4x^3 + 6x^2 + 4x + 1$

12. $x^4 - 4x^3a + 6x^2a^2 - 4xa^3 + a^4$

13. $x^5 + \frac{5x^4}{2} + \frac{5x^3}{2} + \frac{5x^2}{4} + \frac{5x}{16} + \frac{1}{32}$

14. $x^8y^4 - 4x^6y^3 + 6x^4y^2 - 4x^2y + 1$

15. (a) $\displaystyle\sum_{i=0}^{9} \binom{9}{i}x^{9-i}y^i$ (b) $x^9 + 9x^8y + 36x^7y^2 + 84x^6y^3$

16. (a) $\displaystyle\sum_{i=0}^{10} \binom{10}{i}x^{10-i}$ (b) $x^{10} + 10x^9 + 45x^8 + 120x^7$

17. (a) $\displaystyle\sum_{i=0}^{8} (-1)^i\binom{8}{i}x^{16-2i}$ (b) $x^{16} - 8x^{14} + 28x^{12} - 56x^{10}$

18. (a) $\displaystyle\sum_{i=0}^{8} \binom{8}{i}2^i x^{24-3i}\, y^{16-2i}$

(b) $x^{24}y^{16} + 16x^{21}y^{14} + 112x^{18}y^{12} + 448x^{15}y^{10}$

19. 2.1438 20. .3487 21. 1.0615

Common Logarithms

n	0	1	2	3	4	5	6	7	8	9
1.0	.0000	.0043	.0086	.0128	.0170	.0212	.0253	.0294	.0334	.0374
1.1	.0414	.0453	.0492	.0531	.0569	.0607	.0645	.0682	.0719	.0755
1.2	.0792	.0828	.0864	.0899	.0934	.0969	.1004	.1038	.1072	.1106
1.3	.1139	.1173	.1206	.1239	.1271	.1303	.1335	.1367	.1399	.1430
1.4	.1461	.1492	.1523	.1553	.1584	.1614	.1644	.1673	.1703	.1732
1.5	.1761	.1790	.1818	.1847	.1875	.1903	.1931	.1959	.1987	.2014
1.6	.2041	.2068	.2095	.2122	.2148	.2175	.2201	.2227	.2253	.2279
1.7	.2304	.2330	.2355	.2380	.2405	.2430	.2455	.2480	.2504	.2529
1.8	.2553	.2577	.2601	.2625	.2648	.2672	.2695	.2718	.2742	.2765
1.9	.2788	.2810	.2833	.2856	.2878	.2900	.2923	.2945	.2967	.2989
2.0	.3010	.3032	.3054	.3075	.3096	.3118	.3139	.3160	.3181	.3201
2.1	.3222	.3243	.3263	.3284	.3304	.3324	.3345	.3365	.3385	.3404
2.2	.3424	.3444	.3464	.3483	.3502	.3522	.3541	.3560	.3579	.3598
2.3	.3617	.3636	.3655	.3674	.3692	.3711	.3729	.3747	.3766	.3784
2.4	.3802	.3820	.3838	.3856	.3874	.3892	.3909	.3927	.3945	.3962
2.5	.3979	.3997	.4014	.4031	.4048	.4065	.4802	.4099	.4116	.4133
2.6	.4150	.4166	.4183	.4200	.4216	.4232	.4249	.4265	.4281	.4298
2.7	.4314	.4330	.4346	.4362	.4378	.4393	.4409	.4425	.4440	.4456
2.8	.4472	.4487	.4502	.4518	.4533	.4548	.4564	.4579	.4594	.4609
2.9	.4624	.4639	.4654	.4669	.4683	.4698	.4713	.4728	.4742	.4757
3.0	.4771	.4786	.4800	.4814	.4829	.4843	.4857	.4871	.4886	.4900
3.1	.4914	.4928	.4942	.4955	.4969	.4983	.4997	.5011	.5024	.5038
3.2	.5051	.5065	.5079	.5092	.5105	.5119	.5132	.5145	.5159	.5172
3.3	.5185	.5198	.5211	.5224	.5237	.5250	.5263	.5276	.5289	.5302
3.4	.5315	.5328	.5340	.5353	.5366	.5378	.5391	.5403	.5416	.5428
3.5	.5441	.5453	.5465	.5478	.5490	.5502	.5514	.5527	.5539	.5551
3.6	.5563	.5575	.5587	.5599	.5611	.5623	.5635	.5647	.5658	.5670
3.7	.5682	.5694	.5705	.5717	.5729	.5740	.5752	.5763	.5775	.5786
3.8	.5798	.5809	.5821	.5832	.5843	.5855	.5866	.5877	.5888	.5899
3.9	.5911	.5922	.5933	.5944	.5955	.5966	.5977	.5988	.5999	.6010
4.0	.6021	.6031	.6042	.6053	.6064	.6075	.6085	.6096	.6107	.6117
4.1	.6128	.6138	.6149	.6160	.6170	.6180	.6191	.6201	.6212	.6222
4.2	.6232	.6243	.6253	.6263	.6274	.6284	.6294	.6304	.6314	.6325
4.3	.6335	.6345	.6355	.6365	.6375	.6385	.6395	.6405	.6415	.6425
4.4	.6435	.6444	.6454	.6464	.6474	.6484	.6493	.6503	.6513	.6522
4.5	.6532	.6542	.6551	.6561	.6571	.6580	.6590	.6599	.6609	.6618
4.6	.6628	.6637	.6646	.6656	.6665	.6675	.6684	.6693	.6702	.6712
4.7	.6721	.6730	.6739	.6749	.6758	.6767	.6776	.6785	.6794	.6803
4.8	.6812	.6821	.6830	.6839	.6848	.6857	.6866	.6875	.6884	.6893
4.9	.6902	.6911	.6920	.6928	.6937	.6946	.6955	.6964	.6972	.6981
5.0	.6990	.6998	.7007	.7016	.7024	.7033	.7042	.7050	.7059	.7067
5.1	.7076	.7084	.7093	.7101	.7110	.7118	.7126	.7135	.7143	.7152
5.2	.7160	.7168	.7177	.7185	.7193	.7202	.7210	.7218	.7226	.7235
5.3	.7243	.7251	.7259	.7267	.7275	.7284	.7292	.7300	.7308	.7316
5.4	.7324	.7332	.7340	.7348	.7356	.7364	.7372	.7380	.7388	.7396
n	0	1	2	3	4	5	6	7	8	9

Common Logarithms (*Continued*)

n	0	1	2	3	4	5	6	7	8	9
5.5	.7404	.7412	.7419	.7427	.7435	.7443	.7451	.7459	.7466	.7474
5.6	.7482	.7490	.7497	.7505	.7513	.7520	.7528	.7536	.7543	.7551
5.7	.7559	.7566	.7574	.7582	.7589	.7597	.7604	.7612	.7619	.7627
5.8	.7634	.7642	.7649	.7657	.7664	.7672	.7679	.7686	.7694	.7701
5.9	.7709	.7716	.7723	.7731	.7738	.7745	.7752	.7760	.7767	.7774
6.0	.7782	.7789	.7796	.7803	.7810	.7818	.7825	.7832	.7839	.7846
6.1	.7853	.7860	.7868	.7875	.7882	.7889	.7896	.7903	.7910	.7917
6.2	.7924	.7931	.7938	.7945	.7952	.7959	.7966	.7973	.7980	.7987
6.3	.7993	.8000	.8007	.8014	.8021	.8028	.8035	.8041	.8048	.8055
6.4	.8062	.8069	.8075	.8082	.8089	.8096	.8102	.8109	.8116	.8122
6.5	.8129	.8136	.8142	.8149	.8156	.8162	.8169	.8176	.8182	.8189
6.6	.8195	.8202	.8209	.8215	.8222	.8228	.8235	.8241	.8248	.8254
6.7	.8261	.8267	.8274	.8280	.8287	.8293	.8299	.8306	.8312	.8319
6.8	.8325	.8331	.8338	.8344	.8351	.8357	.8363	.8370	.8376	.8382
6.9	.8388	.8395	.8401	.8407	.8414	.8420	.8426	.8432	.8439	.8445
7.0	.8451	.8457	.8463	.8470	.8476	.8482	.8488	.8494	.8500	.8506
7.1	.8513	.8519	.8525	.8531	.8537	.8543	.8549	.8555	.8561	.8567
7.2	.8573	.8579	.8585	.8591	.8597	.8603	.8609	.8615	.8621	.8627
7.3	.8633	.8639	.8645	.8651	.8657	.8663	.8669	.8675	.8681	.8686
7.4	.8692	.8698	.8704	.8710	.8716	.8722	.8727	.8733	.8739	.8745
7.5	.8751	.8756	.8762	.8768	.8774	.8779	.8785	.8791	.8797	.8802
7.6	.8808	.8814	.8820	.8825	.8831	.8837	.8842	.8848	.8854	.8859
7.7	.8865	.8871	.8876	.8882	.8887	.8893	.8899	.8904	.8910	.8915
7.8	.8921	.8927	.8932	.8938	.8943	.8949	.8954	.8960	.8965	.8971
7.9	.8976	.8982	.8987	.8993	.8998	.9004	.9009	.9015	.9020	.9025
8.0	.9031	.9036	.9042	.9047	.9053	.9058	.9063	.9069	.9074	.9079
8.1	.9085	.9090	.9096	.9101	.9106	.9112	.9117	.9122	.9128	.9133
8.2	.9138	.9143	.9149	.9154	.9159	.9165	.9170	.9175	.9180	.9186
8.3	.9191	.9196	.9201	.9206	.9212	.9217	.9222	.9227	.9232	.9238
8.4	.9243	.9248	.9253	.9258	.9263	.9269	.9274	.9279	.9284	.9289
8.5	.9294	.9299	.9304	.9309	.9315	.9320	.9325	.9330	.9335	.9340
8.6	.9345	.9350	.9355	.9360	.9365	.9370	.9375	.9380	.9385	.9390
8.7	.9395	.9400	.9405	.9410	.9415	.9420	.9425	.9430	.9435	.9440
8.8	.9445	.9450	.9455	.9460	.9465	.9469	.9474	.9479	.9484	.9489
8.9	.9494	.9499	.9504	.9509	.9513	.9518	.9523	.9528	.9533	.9538
9.0	.9542	.9547	.9552	.9557	.9562	.9566	.9571	.9576	.9581	.9586
9.1	.9590	.9595	.9600	.9605	.9609	.9614	.9619	.9624	.9628	.9633
9.2	.9638	.9643	.9647	.9652	.9657	.9661	.9666	.9671	.9675	.9680
9.3	.9685	.9689	.9694	.9699	.9703	.9708	.9713	.9717	.9722	.9727
9.4	.9731	.9736	.9741	.9745	.9750	.9754	.9759	.9763	.9768	.9773
9.5	.9777	.9782	.9786	.9791	.9795	.9800	.9805	.9809	.9814	.9818
9.6	.9823	.9827	.9832	.9836	.9841	.9845	.9850	.9854	.9859	.9863
9.7	.9868	.9872	.9877	.9881	.9886	.9890	.9894	.9899	.9903	.9908
9.8	.9912	.9917	.9921	.9926	.9930	.9934	.9939	.9943	.9948	.9952
9.9	.9956	.9961	.9965	.9969	.9974	.9978	.9983	.9987	.9991	.9996
n	0	1	2	3	4	5	6	7	8	9